GOVERNING AMERICAN CITIES

GOVERNING AMERICAN CITIES

Interethnic Coalitions,
Competition, and Conflict

Michael Jones-Correa
Editor

RUSSELL SAGE FOUNDATION
NEW YORK

The Russell Sage Foundation

The Russell Sage Foundation, one of the oldest of America's general purpose foundations, was established in 1907 by Mrs. Margaret Olivia Sage for "the improvement of social and living conditions in the United States." The Foundation seeks to fulfill this mandate by fostering the development and dissemination of knowledge about the country's political, social, and economic problems. While the Foundation endeavors to assure the accuracy and objectivity of each book it publishes, the conclusions and interpretations in Russell Sage Foundation publications are those of the authors and not of the Foundation, its Trustees, or its staff. Publication by Russell Sage, therefore, does not imply Foundation endorsement.

Library of Congress Cataloging-in-Publication Data

Governing American cities : interethnic coalitions, competitions, and conflict / Michael Jones-Correa, editor.
    p. cm.
    Includes bibliographical references and index.
    ISBN 0-87154-415-6
    1. Municipal government—United States.   2. Minorities—United States—Political activity.   I. Jones-Correa, Michael, 1965–
JS323 .G59 2001
320.8'5'0973—dc21   2001041782

Text design by Suzanne Nichols

RUSSELL SAGE FOUNDATION
112 East 64th Street, New York, New York 10021
10 9 8 7 6 5 4 3 2 1

Contents

Contributors

Michael Jones-Correa is associate professor of government at Cornell University.

Max Castro is senior research associate at the North-South Center at the University of Miami.

Guillermo J. Grenier is director of the Center for Labor Research and Studies and associate professor of sociology at Florida International University.

Patrick D. Joyce is lecturer in government at Harvard University.

Peter Kwong is director of the Asian American Studies Program at Hunter College and professor of sociology at the Graduate Center of City University of New York

Paula D. McClain is professor of political science and director of the Race, Ethnicity, and Politics Program in the Department of Political Science at Duke University.

Matthew McKeever is assistant professor of sociology at the University of Kentucky.

John Mollenkopf is professor of political science and director of the Center for Urban Research at the City University Graduate Center in New York.

David Olson is in the Planning and Analysis Unit of the Bronx District Attorney's office in New York City.

Edward J.W. Park is the director of the Asian Pacific American Studies program at the Loyola Marymount University in Los Angeles, California.

John S.W. Park is an assistant professor of American studies and Asian American studies at the University of Texas at Austin.

Timothy Ross is senior research associate at the Vera Institute of Justice in New York City.

Raphael J. Sonenshein is a political scientist at California State University, Fullerton, and a Fellow of the John Randolph Haynes and Dora Haynes Foundation.

Steven C. Tauber is assistant professor in the department of government and international affairs at the University of South Florida.

Acknowledgments

This volume would not have been possible, from at its earliest stages, without the support of the Russell Sage Foundation. The foundation funded the conference on Governing Cities from which this collection sprung, and the officers and staff of the foundation have provided encouragement at every stage of the process. Harvard's Center for American Political Studies gave additional logistical and moral support for the initial conference, and Harvard University and then Cornell have provided the academic shelter for the task of arranging and editing the work that follows. A great many people, in addition to the authors represented here, took the time to help make this project succeed. I want to thank Ted Brader, Regina Freer, Jacqueline Hagen, Bertram Johnson, Peggy Levitt, Don Nakanishi, Gary Orfield, Jenny Oser, Paul Peterson, Nestor Rodriguez, and Alvin Tillery for the insights they brought to bear during the conference and in the discussions that followed. Many thanks to Martin Shefter for telling me it could be done. Suzanne Nichols, the director of publications at Russell Sage, managed the initial publication process with a sure hand, and Emily Chang, the production editor, guided the project expertly to completion. Finally, I wanted to thank my wife, Ria, for her forbearance during the period this book took to come to light, and my daughter Miranda, for making me finish the manuscript by setting a concrete deadline—her birth.

Michael Jones-Correa
Ithaca, 2001

Introduction

Comparative Approaches to Changing Interethnic Relations in Cities

MICHAEL JONES-CORREA

I N 2000, the United States Census Bureau announced that first-generation immigrants—those born abroad—constituted 10.4 percent of the American population. This figure represents the highest proportion since the 1940s and is more than double the 1970s level of 4.7 percent. In the 1990s, 8.6 million immigrants came to America, adding to the 8.3 million who arrived in the 1980s and the 11.5 million who arrived before 1980 (Jaret 1991; Portes and Rumbaut 1990; Waldinger 1989). As the population grows, almost one out of every two new Americans is an immigrant. Yet even though the number of immigrants to the United States since 1965 is approaching—if it has not already surpassed—the levels of the last great wave of immigration between 1880 and 1920, few studies have undertaken to examine how contemporary immigrants are adapting to and becoming incorporated into the U.S. political system. Given such numbers, however, it is clear that an understanding of immigrants and their political incorporation is essential for an understanding of American politics.

This is particularly true when it comes to urban politics. Recent immigrants to the United States, like their predecessors around the turn of the twentieth century, have settled overwhelmingly in urban areas. Over a third, in fact, live in the New York and Los Angeles metropolitan areas alone (Waldinger 1996). Urban areas provide immigrants' first sustained experience of the American government and its institutions. In the cities where they settle, immigrants see the government at work in policing, housing, health care, education, and the job market, to name just a few areas. The impressions created are formative and lasting: immigrants' participation in a local context— forming advocacy groups, voting, and running for and holding office, among other things—provides them with the tools and skills of citizenship, leads to management of their relationships with their neighbors, and serves as a gateway into participation in the larger national polity.

Moreover, in addition to raising questions about when and how these new immigrants will be incorporated into American politics, the changing demographics of American metropolitan areas also raise questions about the shape of urban politics itself. How have these new urban residents affected existing urban political regimes? Are they entering the system as partners in existing governing coalitions, or are they forming new ones? Is the new urban ethnic mix characterized by cooperation or competition? If there is competition among new and old ethnic and racial groups, what are its characteristics? And how do the answers to these questions vary from city to city, region to region?

To some extent, these questions have been addressed with regard to particular cities and for particular ethnic groups. Mollenkopf (1988), for instance, has addressed some of these issues in the context of New York City, as has Sonenshein (1993) in Los Angeles, and Portes and Stepick have begun exploring these questions in Miami (Portes and Stepick 1993; see also Grenier and Stepick 1992). Jackson and Preston brought together a number of key articles in their volume on California politics (Jackson and Preston 1991). Nevertheless, there have been remarkably few comparative studies that bring this locally specific work together in one place. Peter Eisinger's work dwelt on the themes of ethnic succession and competition, but its focus was on the black-white racial struggles of the 1960s and 1970s (Eisinger 1976, 1980). Browning, Marshall, and Tabb's *Racial Politics in American Cities* began the task of assessing the dynamics of contemporary ethnic relations, but didn't address the role of new immigrants in American urban politics (Browning, Marshall, and Tabb 1990). Furthermore, although volumes edited by Rich (1996) and Jennings (1994) brought together new work on interethnic coalitions and conflict in U.S. cities, these collections address immigration only indirectly and make but rudimentary attempts at generating comparative urban theory. As it stands, Paula McClain's work is almost unique in its comparative overview of ethnic competition across major American metropolitan areas (McClain 1996; McClain and Karnig 1990) and in its effort to discern broader patterns among these individual cities.

This book seeks to contribute to this burgeoning literature on race and ethnic relations by focusing on recent immigration and its impact on urban politics in cities across the United States.

Immigrants in Cities

In 2000, the foreign-born population in the United States was estimated by the Census Bureau to be 28.4 million, the largest in American history and an increase of 43 percent over the 1990 census figure of 19.8 million. The foreign-born population is expected to keep growing by about a million people a year. In relative terms, the percentage of immigrants in the American population, at 10.4 percent, is not far below the peak of 14.7 percent, reached in 1910 (U.S. Bureau of the Census 2001).

The most recent wave of immigration is geographically concentrated. Six states had estimated foreign-born populations of 1 million or more in 2000, and together these states accounted for 71 percent of America's total foreign-born population. California led the nation in foreign-born inhabitants with 8.8 million, followed by New York (3.6 million), Florida (2.8 million), Texas (2.4 million), New Jersey (1.2 million), and Illinois (1.2 million). California's population is now about 26 percent second-generation immigrant, while New York's is 20 percent. Over 10 percent of the populations of Florida, Hawaii, New Jersey, Arizona, Massachusetts, and Texas are made up of immigrants. At the other extreme, twenty-six states had foreign-born populations under 5 percent in 2000; these included most of the states in the Midwest and South.

Yet whether large or small, immigrant populations in every state center on large metropolitan areas. Ninety-five percent of second-generation immigrants live in metropolitan areas, versus 79 percent for the native born population. Immigrants also compose an increasing percentage of the populations in these areas: first-generation immigrants and their children make up 56 percent of metropolitan Miami, 53 percent of metropolitan Los Angeles, and 41 percent of metropolitan New York and San Francisco. Differences in place of residence between foreign- and native-born are accounted for entirely by their differing proportions in central cities: 48 percent of the foreign-born population live in central cities, while only 29 percent of the native-born population does.

The figures in table I.1 indicate that immigrants are much more likely than the native born to live in central cities rather than suburbs or outlying municipalities. About 60 percent of immigrants are concentrated in eight major metropolitan areas: Los Angeles (4.8 million), New York (4.6 million), Miami (1.4 million), San Francisco (1.4 million), Chicago (1.1 million), Washington, D.C. (677,000), Boston (610,000), and Houston (539,000) (Schmidley and Gibson 1999, 16).

Figure I.1   Foreign-Born Population for States, 1997
(Civilian Noninstitutional Population Plus Armed Forces Living Off Post
or With Their Families on Post)

Percentage foreign born
(number of states in parentheses)

☐ Under 5.0 (31)
▨ 5.0 to 9.9 (10 plus D.C.)
▨ 10.0 to 14.9 (4)
▨ 15.0 to 19.9 (4)
■ 20.0 or more (1)

West 17.6%
Midwest 4.3%
Northeast 11.9%
South 6.9%

AK 3.8
WA 6.6
OR 9.2
ID 4.7
MT 1.0
ND 0.8
MN 4.6
VT 3.0
NH 3.4
ME 2.3
NV 11.1
WY 1.6
SD 1.0
WI 3.0
MI 4.5
NY 19.6
MA 8.0
UT 5.9
NE 3.5
IA 2.7
IL 9.3
IN 2.3
OH 2.3
PA 3.2
NJ 15.4
CT 7.5
RI 11.1
CA 24.9
CO 8.6
KS 4.1
MO 2.2
KY 1.2
WV 1.1
VA 6.6
MD 8.6
DE 4.9
AZ 14.4
NM 6.9
OK 2.0
AR 1.6
TN 1.2
NC 3.6
SC 1.2
DC 9.5
TX 11.3
LA 2.5
MS 2.0
AL 1.3
GA 3.0
FL 16.4
HI 18.1

United States
9.7%

Source: Schmidley and Campbell 1999.
Note: A metropolitan or "metro" area as defined by the Census Bureau is an urban
concentration containing a large population nucleus, together with adjacent
communities having a high degree of economic and social integration with that core.
A "central city" is the largest population nucleus in the metro area. For a further
discussion of definitions, see: *www.census.gov/population/www/estimates/aboutmetro.html*.

This book focuses on the central cities of these metro areas—the areas
which have received most of the new immigration into the United
States.[1]

Immigrants as Minorities

Most of America's most recent immigrants have come from either
Asia or Latin America. In 2000, 14.5 million, or 51 percent, of the

Table I.1   United States Population by Nativity and Metropolitan Residence, 1997

	Percentage Native-Born	Percentage Foreign-Born
Metro areas	78.9	94.4
Central cities	28.2	46.7
Outside central cities	50.7	47.7

Source: Schmidley and Gibson 1999, table 5-2, "Population by Nativity and Metropolitan-Nonmetropolitan Residence: 1997."

foreign-born population was from Latin America, and an additional 24 percent, or 6.8 million people, were from Asia (see figure I.2). The top ten countries of immigrants' origin in descending order (Mexico, China, Philippines, India, Vietnam, El Salvador, Korea, the Dominican Republic, Cuba, and Colombia) are all found in these two regions (Schmidley and Gibson 1999, 2). Immigrants from Mexico alone accounted for about 29 percent of the foreign-born population; first-generation Mexican Americans are about six times as numerous as the next highest foreign-born population.

The fact that these immigrants are people of color adds another factor to the patterns of interethnic relations in this country. Congress enacted the Civil Rights Act of 1964 and the Voting Rights Act of 1965 primarily in response to the long-term exclusion of African Americans from full participation in the political, economic, and social spheres of American life. However, the courts have ruled that immigrants arriving to the United States from Asia and Latin America following the opening created by the 1965 Immigration Act are covered by this civil rights legislation as well. This certainly benefits these immigrants—but it also indicates that immigrants of color were and are seen through the prism of black-white race relations in the United States (Jaynes 2000, 9).

Extending civil rights protections originally targeted at African Americans to immigrants has sparked a debate on the parameters and purpose of government programs intended to assist minorities. Should immigrants be included in programs for affirmative action in education and civil service hiring, minority-business set-asides, or electoral representation? The answers to these questions are not easily determined (Jaynes 2000). Clearly Latino and Asian immigrants are often discriminated against—but by whom and for what reasons? Are they discriminated against due to their race or for reasons of language? Is this discrimination at the hands of native-born whites, African Americans, or other ethnic minorities? In an era of limited commitment of public resources to social problems, how and to whom

Figure I.2   Foreign-Born Population by Region of Birth: Selected Years, 1850 to 1997

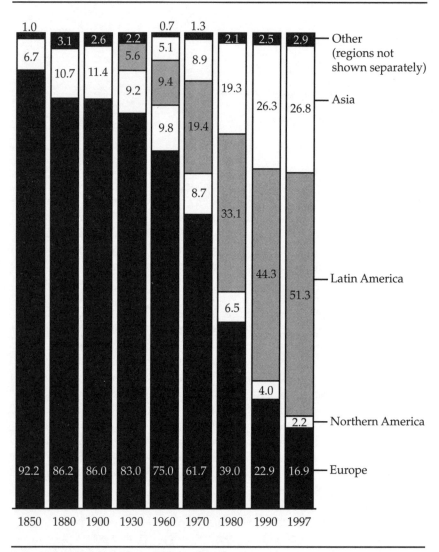

1850   1880   1900   1930   1960   1970   1980   1990   1997

Source: Schmidley and Gibson 1999.
Note: Percentage distribution excluding region not reported. For 1960 to 1990, U.S. resident population. For 1997, civilian noninstitutional population plus armed forces living off post or with their families on post.

should these resources be distributed? As the implementation of social policy is increasingly relegated from the federal to the state and local level, these questions have a direct bearing on discussions about urban policy, local immigrant politics, and competition and cooperation among ethnic groups in cities.

The Provenance of This Book

This volume presents the findings from "Governing American Cities: Inter-Ethnic Coalitions, Competition, and Conflict," a conference sponsored jointly by the Russell Sage Foundation and the Center for American Political Studies at Harvard University. Held on April 17 and 18, 1998, in Cambridge, Massachusetts, the conference sought to bring together scholars engaged in original research on immigration and urban interethnic relations and to have them address key questions raised by the changing demographics of American metropolitan areas.

The meeting amply demonstrated the tremendous intellectual energy and breadth of original scholarship dedicated to interethnic relations in American cities. The gathering of expertise from different cities also helped to emphasize the usefulness of conversations that cross boundaries—geographic as well as disciplinary—and address the issues of immigration, ethnic relations, and urban politics in the United States in a more systematically comparative fashion than any discussion limited to one region or discipline can on its own.

Each chapter in this volume results from this collaboration. The findings presented are comprehensive and address a number of critical areas: immigrant participation in the political process, the relationship between newcomers and established residents, the impact of immigrant enclaves on both immigrant organization and interethnic relations, competition between newer and established groups over jobs and elected positions, the possibilities of either ethnic conflict or cooperation, the ideological and generational differences facing coalition organizers and partners, and the role of interests and leadership in coalitional strategies. Together, these contributions furnish an overview of key issues surrounding and responses to what has emerged as the central dynamic in many American cities: the complex political negotiations between new immigrants and established residents as neighborhoods adjust to this most recent ethnic succession.

New Actors in Cities

Though immigrants today constitute a substantial portion of the American population and have made a particular impact on urban demographics, they have as yet to have a similar impact on politics. The most obvious reason for this is that recent immigrants have been slow to naturalize and, once naturalized, to exercise their rights as citizens. While the number of naturalized citizens increased by 46 percent (from 6.2 million to 9.0 million) between 1970 and 1990, the percentage increase in the total number of noncitizens living in the United States was markedly greater: 373 percent (from 3.5 million to 16.7 million) (Schmidley and Gibson 1999, 20). Even when naturalized, it appears that immigrants' political participation as voters is less than that of the native born (Ramakrishnan and Espenshade 2000; Bass and Casper 1999; DeSipio 1996). In chapter 1, "Immigrant Political Participation in New York and Los Angeles," John Mollenkopf, David Olson, and Tim Ross delineate participation patterns in these two cities that receive most of today's immigrants. Mollenkopf, Olson, and Ross break down voter turnout by neighborhood and nationality group to obtain a much more detailed, refined view of participation than that offered by previous studies. They find that there are important differences in participation among various immigrant groups as well as between the cities, findings that hold considerable portent for the future. Yet while immigrants may be lagging in their political activity now, their influence will only increase over time.

What are the mechanisms by which immigrant participation is constrained? In chapter 2, "Ethnic Subcontracting as an Impediment to Interethnic Coalitions: The Chinese Experience," Peter Kwong argues that for immigrant mobilization to occur, immigrants must surmount constraints from within their communities as well as from without. He points to New York's Chinatown as an example of an ethnic enclave where class divisions within immigrant communities often cripple immigrant political mobilization. In his rich case study of the difficulties of labor organizing among Chinese immigrants, Kwong finds that the enclave masks class cleavages and economic exploitation in the community. He finds Chinese entrepreneurs, for example, appealing to ethnic solidarity to dissuade their co-ethnic employees from organizing unions or bringing poor workplace conditions to the attention of city officials. Kwong's chapter highlights the importance of class in the analysis of ethnic-group dynamics and serves as a cautionary addendum to the generally positive view of the immigrant ethnic enclave as portrayed in the literature on the subject (Portes and Bach 1985).

Similar issues are addressed in chapter 3, "Korean Americans and the Crisis of the Liberal Coalition: Immigrants and Politics in Los Angeles," in which Edward J. W. Park and John S. W. Park examine internal differences in immigrant communities to explain trends in political participation and attitudes toward ethnic coalition building.

Where Kwong's analysis focuses on class, however, Park and Park emphasize generational divisions within immigrant groups. In the Parks' analysis, these divisions were brought into sharp relief for Los Angeles's Korean community by the 1992 civil unrest in the wake of the Rodney King verdict. These events had an enormous impact on Korean-American political involvement, spurring the mobilization of both conservative and liberal actors within the community. In addition to deepening ideological cleavages among Korean Americans, the events of 1992 accelerated generational change among the Korean-American leadership. The so-called 1.5 generation, born in Korea but raised in the U.S. since childhood, became more visible to the media and other actors outside their ethnic community, eclipsing other leaders of the community who had immigrated as adults. As the Parks trace generational and ideological divisions within the Korean community, they underscore the fact that no new immigrant population may properly be seen as homogeneous. Such communities contain complex internal politics that have implications for their willingness and ability to enter into partnerships with other ethnic and racial groups.

These two opening chapters, then, introduce immigrants as new actors in cities and highlight differences among and within nationality groups. As immigrants begin to make their way into the political arena, class and generational cleavages within their communities greatly influence the manner in which they are incorporated into the political process and the possibilities for coalition building.

Competition and Conflict

Given the changing composition of urban areas, one might expect to encounter tensions as new and old minority groups compete for public resources, jobs, and political positions. As Edward J. W. Park and John S. W. Park note in chapter 3, immigrants often emerge as new actors in political arenas where other minorities, notably African Americans, are already established players. What consequences do the political and economic resources held by one ethnic or racial group have on the outcomes for other communities? Do the successes of one group come at the expense of others, or can these successes be complementary? In chapter 4, "Racial Minority Group Relations in a Multiracial Society," Paula McClain and Steven Tauber provide an overview of the arenas of interethnic rivalry in cities across the United States. They find that while tensions are not present in every arena and among every set of actors, such tensions are particularly common in the electoral arena. The negative effects of competition is greatest in cities dominated by a single ethnic group.

These findings fit in with Guillermo Grenier's description of relations between blacks and Latinos in Miami in chapter 5, "Blacks and Cubans in Miami: The Negative Consequences of the Cuban Enclave on Ethnic Relations." Like Kwong in chapter 1, Grenier challenges the view that the ethnic enclave offers unmitigated benefits. Miami's Cuban-American population exerts considerable influence on virtually every aspect of life there, and while acknowledging that that community—centered around the enclaves of Little Havana and Hialeah—has accelerated the incorporation of Cubans and other Latin American immigrants into Miami's economic and political life, Grenier nevertheless points out that it has also created or at least reinforced structural barriers segregating the city's Latino community from African Americans. These two ethnic groups are thus now locked into hostile competition, in spite of sporadic attempts at cooperation. This hostility was not preordained: Grenier shows that black perceptions of Cuban Americans have worsened over time, while Cubans have largely ignored black points of view. The case of Miami is not a hopeful one, and while the conflict there might seem more intense and its sources more intractable than in other regions of the country, national trends identified by Grenier suggest that relations between African Americans and Latinos may well follow the Miami model. Growing Latino populations, combined with urban decay, could lead to increased tensions between Latinos and blacks, many cities' two largest ethnic minorities.

Sources of tension between groups are often easily determined; more difficult to pinpoint is what accounts for the forms by which such tension are expressed. When are tensions expressed as peaceful protest and when as outbursts of violence? In chapter 6, "Protest or Violence: Political Process and Patterns of Black-Korean Conflict," Patrick Joyce grapples with these questions by examining the tensions between African Americans and Korean Americans in cities across the United States. The 1980s and 1990s saw clashes between blacks and Koreans in a number of cities, with hostilities ranging from boycotts to outright violence. Joyce finds different causal processes shaping each of these expressions of tension. While the sociological dimensions of economic competition may account for violence, the emergence of boycotts is best explained by the character of local political systems. Overt, nonviolent conflicts, in the form of black-led boycotts of Korean stores, take place more often in cities where traditional political organizations have strong roots and where African Americans have greater political representation. Organization and representation lend structure to community political life and facilitate the grassroots organization that enables one group to engage others in protest. Although violence and boycotts are related to each other to a degree, these two forms of intergroup conflict follow different causal dynamics.

When conflicts do erupt, what happens in their aftermath? How are interethnic relations renegotiated, reestablished? In chapter 7, "Structural Shifts and Institutional Capacity Possibilities for Ethnic Cooperation and Conflict in Urban Settings," Michael Jones-Correa lays out four broad structural changes that took place in American cities in the 1980s and '90s: immigration transformed urban populations, significant portions of the middle class of all ethnic and racial groups left for the suburbs, urban economic bases shifted from manufacturing to service industries, and the federal government scaled back its financial support for urban areas. These structural shifts set the stage for a new round of interethnic tensions, culminating in serious civil disturbances in four cities. In the aftermath of these civil disturbances of the 1980s and '90s, urban institutional frameworks mediated and shaped the reconfiguration of interethnic relations. Jones-Correa argues that cities respond differently, and in fact, have different capacities to respond, depending on their institutional configurations. Some cities, such as Los Angeles, turned to the private sector to address interethnic relations, while others, among them New York, responded through political channels. In either case, the institutional framework present in these cities was key, as it set the parameters for policy responses. Jones-Correa discusses the implications that these institutional frameworks have for those seeking to ease the incorporation of new urban actors into the political process and encourage interethnic coalition building.

These middle chapters of the volume establish a theoretical groundwork for when we might expect conflict and competition to occur and for the forms that such conflicts might take. Competition in the political arena seems to be more intractable than that in the economic sphere, but on the other hand, political institutions can channel tensions into nonviolent, and perhaps more effective, forms of protest; in the absence of such institutional channeling, violence is more likely to erupt.

Cooperation and Coalition Building

While interethnic tensions exist and may be a fact of life, conflict and competition are not the only outcomes or expressions that they may take. The third section of *Governing Cities* focuses on avenues for cooperation and coalition building.

The difficulties confronting interethnic political coalitions are discussed by Raphael Sonenshein in chapter 8, "When Ideologies Agree and Interests Collide, What's a Leader to Do? The Prospects for Latino-Jewish Coalition in Los Angeles." What, he asks, would it take for a coalition to form between two actors in the urban polity who, on the one hand, share a surprising number of policy positions, but on the other, have little social overlap? Latinos and Jews have been seen by some as constituting a new moderate alliance in big-city politics; their common support for mayoral candidates opposed by African Americans in three cities has been cited as evidence to that effect. Other evidence, moreover, shows a broad compatibility in political beliefs and voting behavior between the two groups. In contemporary Los Angeles, however, there is but limited evidence of any emerging Latino-Jewish coalition. Despite an ideological basis for alliance, there are conflicts of interests that complicate political coalition. These obstacles to coalition building raise the question of how the goal of equity can be reached in big-city politics when the interests of immigrants conflict with those of "old" residents. The task for intergroup leadership in Los Angeles and elsewhere is to redirect urban issues away from zero-sum battles. Sonenshein's case study discusses the interplay between ideology and interest, mediated by leadership, in the formation of coalitions across racial and ethnic lines.

"Interethnic Politics in the Consensus City," Matthew McKeever's study of Houston, is the final chapter of *Governing Cities*. In his study, McKeever notes that in Houston, as in many cities in the West and Southwest, African Americans no longer compose the largest minority group, just as whites no longer are the majority of residents or voters. However, the ability to translate demographics into political power is variable, and greatly depends on the city's political traditions, the strength of its minority communities, and the strategies pursued by politicians. Blacks, Latinos, and whites are all significant players in Houston's complex local politics, and, McKeever points out, their interactions have rarely erupted into violent conflict. Houston, in fact, has a reputation as a "consensus city," or a city in which interethnic relations have historically been managed by elites who have kept the city relatively free of great tension or violence. Focusing his study on Houston's 1997 mayoral election, McKeever concludes that the key to a successful mayoral candidacy in a multi-ethnic city is a "multi-ethnic" rather than a "de-racialized" campaign. In multiethnic politics, race and ethnicity are acknowledged by all, but offer privilege for none.

Chapters 8 and 9, then, point to the possibilities of cooperation among urban ethnic and immigrant groups while at the same time recognizing the difficulties facing anyone attempting to forge genuine coalitions. There is a fine line between acknowledging ethnic differences and falling prey to ethnic chauvinism, but the balance can be reached, as the authors here argue, given the right combination of leadership and shared interests. And while this balance may be easier to find in the nitty-gritty of economic life or neighborhood concerns, it can also be achieved in politics on the larger metropolitan scale.

The influx of immigration into the United States, and particularly its metropolitan areas, has led to rapid demographic shifts in its urban areas. While the broad outlines of these changes in population are becoming ever more clearly defined, the corresponding political changes in governing regimes, ethnic alliances and competition, and urban politics remain understudied and little understood. These changes in the urban political context have important implications not just for the governability of American metropolitan areas, but ultimately for our understanding of American politics as a whole. The scholars represented in this volume together lay the foundation for a national, cross-city theoretical perspective on these significant long-term social and political changes in urban areas, which can serve as a springboard for more collaborative cross-city research in the area of ethnic and urban politics in the United States.

Note

1. Though the focus here is on these eight urban areas, this is not to imply that other urban areas are not also experiencing change. Indeed, cities in other parts of the country, such as Atlanta, Georgia, or Madison, Wisconsin, may be experiencing greater *relative* change. However, the focus of this book is on those cities experiencing the greatest *absolute* change: Los Angeles, New York, Miami, Houston, and the others listed.

References

Bass, Loretta E., and Lynne M. Casper. 1999. "Are There Differences in Registration and Voting Behavior Between Naturalized and Native-Born Americans?" Working paper. Washington, D.C.: Population Division, U.S. Bureau of the Census.

Browning, Rufus P., Dale Rogers Marshall, and David H. Tabb. 1990. *Racial Politics in American Cities*. New York: Longman.

DeSipio, Louis. 1996. "Making Citizens or Good Citizens? Naturalization as a Predictor of Organizational and Electoral Behavior Among Latino Immigrants." *Hispanic Journal of Behavioral Sciences* 18(2): 194–213.

Eisinger, Peter. 1976. *Patterns of Interracial Politics: Conflict and Cooperation in the City*. New York: Academic Press.

———. 1980. *The Politics of Displacement: Racial and Ethnic Transition in Three American Cities*. New York: Academic Press.

Frey, William. 1995. "Immigration and Internal 'White Flight' from U.S. Metro Areas: Toward a New Demographic Balkanization." *Urban Studies* 32: 733–57.

Grenier, Guillermo, and Alex Stepick, editors. 1992. *Miami Now! Immigration, Ethnicity, and Social Change*. Gainesville: University Press of Florida.

Jackson, Bryan, and Michael Preston, editors. 1991. *Racial and Ethnic Politics in California*. Berkeley: Institute of Governmental Studies, University of California at Berkeley.

Jaret, Charles. 1991. "Recent Structural Changes and U.S. Urban Ethnic Minorities." *Journal of Urban Affairs* 13(3): 307–36.

Jaynes, Gerald. 2000. "Immigration and the American Dream." In *Immigration and Race: New Challenges for American Democracy,* edited by Gerald Jaynes. New Haven: Yale University Press.

Jennings, James, editor. 1994. *Blacks, Latinos, and Asians in Urban America: Status and Prospects for Politics and Activism.* Westport, Conn.: Praeger.

McClain, Paula. 1996. "Coalition and Competition: Patterns of Black-Latino Relations in Urban Politics." In *From Polemics to Practice: Forging Coalitions Among Racial and Ethnic Minorities,* edited by Wilbur Rich. New York: Praeger.

McClain, Paula, and Albert K. Karnig. 1990. "Black and Hispanic Socioeconomic and Political Competition." *American Political Science Review* 84(2): 535–45.

Mollenkopf, John Hull, editor. 1988. *Power, Culture and Place: Essays on New York City.* New York: Russell Sage Foundation.

Portes, Alejandro, and Robert Bach. 1985. *Latin Journey: Cuban and Mexican Immigrants in the United States.* Berkeley: University of California Press.

Portes, Alejandro, and and Rubén Rumbaut. 1990. *Immigrant America: A Portrait.* Berkeley: University of California Press.

Portes, Alejandro, and Alex Stepick. 1993. *City on the Edge: The Transformation of Miami.* Berkeley: University of California Press.

Rich, Wilbur, editor. 1996. *From Polemics to Practice: Forging Coalitions Among Racial and Ethnic Minorities.* New York: Praeger.

Ramakrishnan, S. Karthick, and Thomas J. Espenshade. 2000. "Political Participation and Immigrant Behavior in U.S. Elections." Paper presented to the Conference of the Population Association of America. Los Angeles (March 23–25).

Schmidley, A. Dianne, and Campbell Gibson. 1999. *Profile of the Foreign Born Population in the United States, 1997.* United States Bureau of the Census Current Population Reports, Series P23–195. Washington: U.S. Government Printing Office.

Sonenshein, Raphael. 1993. *Politics in Black and White: Race and Power in Los Angeles.* Princeton, N.J.: Princeton University Press.

U.S. Bureau of the Census. 2001. *Current Population Reports: Foreign Born Population of the United States, March 2000.* Washington: U.S. Government Printing Office.

Waldinger, Roger. 1989. "Immigration and Urban Change." *Annual Review of Sociology* 15: 211–32.

———. 1996. "From Ellis Island to LAX: Immigrant Prospects in the American City." *International Migration Review* 30(4): 1078–86.

Winnick, Louis. 1990. *New People in Old Neighborhoods: The Role of New Immigrants in Rejuvenating New York's Communities.* New York: Russell Sage Foundation.

Winsburg, Morton. 1983. "Ethnic Competition for Residential Space in Miami, Florida, 1970–1980." *American Journal of Economics and Sociology* 42(3): 305–14.

PART I

NEW ACTORS IN CITIES

Chapter 1

Immigrant Political Participation in New York and Los Angeles

JOHN MOLLENKOPF, DAVID OLSON, AND TIMOTHY ROSS

ACCORDING to Current Population Survey data collected in March 2000, 28.4 million, or 10.4 percent, of the nation's 274.0 million residents were born abroad and migrated to the United States. Less noted, but of potentially even greater significance, is that these immigrants have 27.5 million American-born children, who themselves constitute another 10.0 percent of the national population. Putting these numbers together, then, reveals that immigrants and their American-born children today make up slightly more than one-fifth of the nation's total population (see table 1.1). Moreover, for-eign-born people represent 12.7 percent of the nation's voting age population and their children 7.9 percent—again, together roughly one-fifth of the national total.[1]

Because non-Hispanic blacks make up 12.6 percent of the national population and Latinos 12 percent, immigrants and their children, if regarded as a distinct group, would dwarf either of our nation's tradi-tional minority groups. (Of course, immigrants and their children have highly diverse backgrounds, as table 1.1 shows.) Because immi-gration will continue to drive demographic change in the United States for the foreseeable future and because the children of these immigrants will make up an increasing share of the nation's young people, the cultural and political influence of this most recent wave of immigrants will only grow. And because immigrants and their native

Table 1.1 Race by Immigrant Status: United States, March 2000

	Foreign Born	Second Generation	2.5 Generation	Native Stock	Total (Column Percentage)
Non-Hispanic white Row percentage	7,045,302 3.6%	5,681,841 2.9%	8,452,129 4.4%	172,454,008 89.1%	193,633,280 (70.6%)
Non-Hispanic black	1,789,890 5.2%	624,589 1.8%	479,083 1.4%	31,547,716 91.6%	34,441,278 (12.6%)
Non-Hispanic Native American	65,035 2.6%	35,118 1.4%	62,341 2.5%	2,309,972 93.4%	2,472,466 (0.9%)
Non-Hispanic Asian	6,637,546 61.8%	2,115,440 19.7%	725,715 6.8%	1,257,334 11.7%	10,736,035 (3.9)
Latino	12,841,461 39.1%	6,351,007 19.4%	2,983,702 9.1%	10,627,774 32.4%	32,803,944 (12.0%)
Total	28,379,234 10.4%	14,807,995 5.4%	12,702,970 4.6%	218,196,804 79.6%	274,087,003 100.0%

Source: U.S. Bureau of the Census 2000.

March 2000 Current Population Survey, March Final Weights. "Second generation" means both parents born abroad; "2.5 generation" means one parent born abroad; "native stock" means both parents born in the United States (including Puerto Rico).

children tend to live in large cities in California, New York, Florida, New Jersey, and Texas—key states in the electoral college—geography will magnify their potential political impact.

The metropolitan area with the greatest share of foreign-stock residents (that is, immigrants and their children) is Miami, where they make up almost two-thirds of the population. Immigrants and their children also contribute more than half of metropolitan Los Angeles's 15.9 million people, just under half of metro San Francisco's 7.1 million residents, and two-fifths of metropolitan New York's 20.5 million people. As we might expect, immigrants and their children constitute substantial majorities of the central-city populations within these metro areas, but table 1.2 illustrates that they also may be found in significant numbers among suburban populations (40.5 percent of metro L.A.'s suburban population, for example, and 32.8 percent of New York's). The ways in which immigrants and their children find a place in the political order of the nation's largest cities and suburbs thus has potentially enormous importance not only for political development of these regions, but for the nation as a whole.

To be sure, immigrants to the United States comprise an exceedingly diverse group. Their differences in race, ethnicity, education, culture, position in the labor force, and treatment by the white majority doubtless outweigh their shared experience as immigrants when it comes to the forms that their political mobilization will take. People with Latin American roots, mostly from Mexico, make up the largest portion of the foreign-born residents of the United States, but roughly a quarter are Asian, a quarter are white, and some are black (largely from the Anglophone Caribbean). These groups arrived in the United States at different times over the past decades, resulting in different median lengths of stay and different rates of naturalization. Only about one-third of all foreign-born residents of the United States have become citizens, though half of the whites have done so, as have two-fifths of Asians and one-third of blacks. Latinos have the lowest rate of naturalization; less than a quarter have chosen to become American citizens.

In 2001, thirty-five years old marks the maximum age of any child of parents who arrived in the United States following the 1965 Immigration Act. Hence, this cadre of second-generation immigrants is still rather young—and it continues to grow rapidly in size and share of the national population. At present, the naturalization of immigrants yields more new members of the nation's eligible electorate than the coming of age of the second generation. But as these new Americans' children pass their eighteenth birthday, they too will contribute an increasing number of potential voters. So, though most scholarly attention has focused on the first group, ultimately the latter, if mo-

Table 1.2 Metropolitan Region by Immigrant Status: United States, March 2000

	Foreign Born	Second Generation	2.5 Generation	Native Stock	Total (Column Percentage)
New York City Row percentage	2,665,799 34.8%	1,188,312 15.5%	462,837 6.0%	3,341,827 43.6%	7,658,775 (2.79%)
Rest of NY Consolidated Metropolitan Statistical Area	2, 022,531 15.8%	1,253,639 9.8%	855,881 6.7%	8,708,790 67.8%	12,840,841 (4.68%)
L.A. County	3,240,611 34.5%	1,769,129 18.8%	699,156 7.4%	3,681,387 39.2%	9,390,283 (3.43%)
Rest of L.A. CMSA	1,467,654 22.5%	724,403 11.1%	445,164 6.8%	3,873,191 59.5%	6,510,412 (2.38%)
Gateway Central Cities*	2,596,739 25.8%	1,036,612 10.3%	514,178 5.1%	5,899,114 58.7%	10,046,643 (3.67%)
Rest of Gateway Metropolitan Statistical Areas	3,383,832 18.7%	1,692,697 9.3%	1,230,445 6.8%	11,833,119 65.2%	18,140,093 (6.62%)
Other Central Cities	4,100,221 9.7%	1,906,420 4.5%	1,772,509 4.2%	34,295,065 81.5%	42,074,215 (15.35%)
Rest of Other Metropolitan Statistical Areas	5,347,394 6.7%	3,094,158 3.9%	3,603,991 4.5%	67,711,923 84.9%	79,757,466 (29.10%)
Elsewhere	3,554,451 4.1%	2,142,625 2.4%	3,118,808 3.6%	78,852,389 89.9%	87,668,273 (31.99%)
Total	28,379,232 10.4%	14,807,995 5.4%	12,702,969 4.6%	218,196,805 79.6%	274,087,001 100.0%

Source: U.S. Bureau of the Census 2000.
*Gateway cities are Boston, Chicago, Houston, Miami, and San Francisco.

bilized along distinct ethnic lines, will be the most important to politics. Still, these developments are not unprecedented: in places like New York City and Los Angeles County, which have experienced high levels of immigration over a long time, we can see the outlines of what this future might look like.

Despite their differences, immigrants share certain experiences: relocation to a new home; classification and processing by immigration authorities; treatment as outsiders by native Americans; and the struggle to find a place in environments that range from the grudgingly accepting to the downright hostile.[2] Most arrive without the ability to speak English well. They and their children face discrimination, the tendency of native whites to classify them alongside native-born minority groups, and limited opportunities (Waters 1999; Waters, Kasinitz, and Mollenkopf 1998).

Such circumstance engender conditions under which these immigrant groups are ripe for political mobilization in opposition to America's native white, typically Republican and Protestant, majority. At the same time, however, the white liberals, blacks, and Latinos who form the core of the Democratic vote may also be ambivalent about mobilizing immigrant groups. These core Democratic groups are traditionally strongest in many of the places where immigrant enclaves are growing most rapidly—alongside, in more than a few instances, declining native white, black, and Latino populations. Thus, when naturalized immigrants and their American-born children mobilize, those who occupy the offices they seek to gain, and who often block their way, are not white Republicans but native white liberals, blacks, and Latinos (Puerto Ricans in the East, third-or-later generation Chicanos in the West). How, then, will these newest Americans be mobilized? This chapter examines what New York and Los Angeles have to tell us about this question, with a focus on the 1996 presidential election.

In this study, four data sets are employed to analyze patterns of naturalization and political participation among post-1965 immigrants in New York City and Los Angeles County. (These two jurisdictions are home to almost one-fourth of all post-1965 immigrants.) The March 2000 Annual Demographic Supplement of the Current Population Survey (CPS) provides the latest figures on country of origin for U.S. residents (and their parents). The November 1996 CPS reports on voting in the 1996 presidential election and voter registration among citizens of voting age, while the November 1996 presidential election exit survey, which asked a national random sample of voters about whether they were foreign born, how they voted, and what issues they cared about.

Finally, 1990 Census demographic characteristics were matched to

5,500 election districts (EDs) in New York City and 1,647 Census tracts in Los Angeles County. (In New York, precincts are called election districts and contain on average about 800 eligible voters and 1,300 residents.) In New York City, we gathered election results for the 1996 presidential election (and many other local and state elections between 1989 and 1998), as well as voter registration statistics for 1990, 1994, and 1999. We allocated 1990 Census data to each ED based on 1990 block-level population information.

Similarly, for Los Angeles County, we utilize data from the Statewide Database of the Institute of Governmental Studies at the University of California at Berkeley. Assembled by Professor Bruce Cain and his colleagues, these data contain election results and voter-registration figures for statewide elections between 1992 and 1998, broken down by Census tract (which in Los Angeles County comprise, on average, 5,600 residents). We then matched additional tract-level information on race, income, nativity, and other demographic characteristics from the 1990 Census with these electoral results.[3]

These data sets have a variety of inherent strengths and weaknesses (well described by DeSipio 1997a) for the researcher. The CPS data, for instance, allow us to see the overall demographic context of citizenship, determine the broad contours of immigrant political participation, learn which groups, in which settings, tend to naturalize and vote, and ask how such factors as education or income may affect the distribution of these tendencies across groups. Ecological analysis of the small-area data sets provides a particularly clear picture of which groups mobilize and under what conditions they do so, and allows us to explore the effects of such important contextual factors as neighborhood concentration. The CPS and small-area data say nothing, however, about the motives and meanings that first- and second-generation immigrants attach to the political process.

Of all data sets, only the 1996 Voter News Service exit poll provides some initial information on these matters, for it was the first (and so far only) national exit poll to ask a subsample of voters whether they were born in the United States. Unfortunately, it did not ask immigrant voters where they were born or when they naturalized, thereby limiting the usefulness of this source. (Feeling that immigration was no longer a hot issue, the Voter News Service removed this question from its 2000 presidential-election exit poll.)[4]

This chapter thus sets the scene and raises questions, but only begins to posit causal relationships between immigration, immigrants, and political participation. Left to further research are some critical questions: Are new immigrants naturalizing mainly for prudential, strategic reasons (such as to protect access to benefits or rights) to the detriment of becoming engaged in the political fabric of their neighborhoods and cities? What features of the local political system and what characteristics of immigrant communities promote or retard political participation? How do new citizens and their children see themselves fitting into the racial and ethnic matrices of New York and Los Angeles? And if the future of the minority vote in these two cities lies in mobilizing the children of the new immigrants, how will native white, black, and Hispanic political elites respond? Will the dominant white political elites try to set "good" immigrants against "unworthy" native minority groups? How are the various native and immigrant minority groups relating to each other when their residential patterns overlap? Will political elites emerge from recent immigrant populations and form themselves into distinct "American" ethnic groups? Will the prejudices of the larger society force them into common cause with native minorities? These crucial questions remain to be addressed.

"Immigrant Political Participation in New York and Los Angeles" does describe the variation of naturalization and electoral participation rates across immigrant groups; examines how such individual and group factors as length of residence, education, income, and group concentration influence political participation; and looks at the specific experiences of the most important immigrant groups in national elections in these two cities. Through an ecological analysis of electoral outcomes in New York City and Los Angeles County, we compare voting rates as a function of the immigrant share of the neighborhood population. This analysis confirms results from the CPS indicating that eligible immigrants vote at low rates, especially in neighborhoods with the largest immigrant concentrations. But it also highlights the ways in which turnout varies across groups and points to the growth of voter registration among immigrants and their children and its decline among the native born.

The Demographic and Political Setting

Mirroring the pattern set in the nation's previous great wave of immigration (1880 to 1920), today's immigrants follow a few clear paths from their countries of origin to their destinations in the United States. These migration pathways are shaped by, among other factors, the sending country's proximity to the United States, the American presence in those countries' economies, and historical patterns of chain migration (Massey et al. 1993; Massey et al. 1994; Massey and Espinosa 1996; Massey 1999). As a result, the four main migration flows into the United States are as follows: from Mexico and Central America to Southern California and South Texas; from Cuba, the Dominican Republic, and elsewhere in the Caribbean to Southern Florida and New York City; from Asia to the West and East Coasts; and from Europe to the Northeast and north-central states.

The first flow, from Mexico and Central America, accounts for 43.3 percent of all noncitizen immigrants of the U.S., one-fifth of all naturalized immigrants, and one-third of second-generation immigrants (see table 3). The second flow, from Cuba, the Dominican Republic, Haiti, and the West Indies, accounts for another 9 percent of noncitizen U.S. immigrants, 12.8 percent of naturalized immigrants, and 7.1 percent of the second generation. Immigrants from the Caribbean basin are a smaller part of the total than those from Mexico and Central America, but they are nevertheless heavily concentrated in New York City, Miami, and Washington, D.C. Few have made their way west, and virtually none to Los Angeles.

Migration from East, Southeast, and South Asia constitutes the third large flow into the U.S. These regions account for 13.7 percent of noncitizen U.S. immigrants, 17.7 percent of naturalized immigrants, and 9.9 percent of the second-generation immigrants, while South Asians add 4.5 percent of noncitizens, 4.6 percent of the naturalized, and 2.6 percent of the second generation immigrants. Asian immigrants are mostly located on the major gateway cities of the two coasts: Los Angeles, San Francisco, New York, and, to lesser degrees, Boston, Washington, and Seattle.

Finally, we must remember that many foreign born residents of the U.S. arrived before the reform of the immigration law in 1965. Europe, including the former Soviet Union, thus still accounts for 10.1 percent of immigrants, 16.2 percent of naturalized immigrants, and 22.4 percent of the second generation (see table 1.3). Their comparatively large share of the second generation stems from the fact that, with the exception of the Russian Jewish émigrés of the 1990s, most of these European immigrants arrived quite some time ago. These "old" immigrants and ethnic groups live primarily in older northeastern cities.

These four streams of migration have had a tremendous impact on Los Angeles, San Diego, San Francisco, Houston, San Antonio, New York City, and Miami. With the exception of Cubans, many of whom arrived in the early 1960s, most of these immigrants have lived in the U.S. for less than twenty years—in fact, many have arrived just within the last decade. (By contrast, the median year of arrival for Italian and German immigrants is 1962.) The individuals who choose to immigrate generally have relatively low levels of educational attainment, take low-skilled jobs with low wages, and are relatively young. Partly because some think they may return to their country of origin, participants in these newer immigrant streams also have comparatively lower rates of naturalization than those who have been

Table 1.3   Immigrant First and Second Generation by Region of Origin: United States Population, 2000

	Foreign-Born Noncitizen	Foreign-Born Citizen	Second Generation	Total
Canada	274,143	178,077	286,470	738,690
Row percentage	37.1%	24.1%	38.8%	100.0%
Column percentage	1.5%	1.7%	1.9%	(1.7%)
Australia,	64,819	19,317	11,691	95,827
New Zealand,	67.6%	20.2%	12.2%	100.0%
Pacific Islands	.4%	.2%	.1%	(0.2%)
Italy	137,275	333,220	1,186,398	1,656,893
	8.3%	20.1%	71.6%	100.0%
	.8%	3.1%	8.0%	(3.8%)
Germany	239,848	335,451	256,272	831,571
	28.8%	40.3%	30.8%	100.0%
	1.4%	3.2%	1.7%	(1.9%)
United Kingdom	282,648	215,635	196,174	694,457
	40.7%	31.1%	28.2%	100.0%
	1.6%	2.0%	1.3%	(1.6%)
Ireland	91,735	127,668	256,238	475,641
	19.3%	26.8%	53.9%	100.0%
	.5%	1.2%	1.7%	(1.1%)
Other West	430,314	431,808	625,973	1,488,095
Europe	28.9%	29.0%	42.1%	100.0%
	2.4%	4.1%	4.2%	(3.4%)
Former Soviet Union	419,883	277,396	423,025	1,120,304
	37.5%	24.8%	37.8%	100.0%
	2.4%	2.6%	2.9%	(2.6%)
Other Eastern	185,991	192,025	380,620	758,636
Europe	24.5%	25.3%	50.2%	100.0%
	1.0%	1.8%	2.6%	(1.8%)
Mexico	6,201,951	1,572,912	4,448,792	12,223,655
	50.7%	12.9%	36.4%	100.0%
	34.9%	14.8%	30.0%	(28.3%)
Central America	1,455,331	453,756	565,144	2,474,231
	58.8%	18.3%	22.8%	100.0%
	8.2%	4.3%	3.8%	(5.7%)
West Indies	484,420	481,896	326,562	1,292,878
	37.5%	37.3%	25.3%	100.0%
	2.7%	4.5%	2.2%	(3.0%)
Cuba	385,133	502,397	229,910	1,117,440
	34.5%	45.0%	20.6%	100.0%
	2.2%	4.7%	1.6%	(2.6%)

(Table continues on p. 26.)

Table 1.3   (*Continued*)

	Foreign-Born Noncitizen	Foreign-Born Citizen	Second Generation	Total
Dominican	461,484	228,633	319,875	1,009,992
Republic	45.7%	22.6%	31.7%	100.0%
	2.6%	2.2%	2.2%	(2.3)%
Haiti	240,276	155,141	161,477	556,894
	43.1%	27.9%	29.0%	100.0%
	1.4%	1.5%	1.1%	(1.3%)
Colombia,	671,439	359,503	255,407	1,286,349
Ecuador, Peru	52.2%	27.9%	19.9%	100.0%
	3.8%	3.4%	1.7%	(3.0%)
Other South	325,447	168,750	83,415	577,612
America	56.3%	29.2%	14.4%	100.0%
	1.8%	1.6%	.6%	(1.3%)
Middle East	325,648	344,595	227,890	898,133
	36.3%	38.4%	25.4%	100.0%
	1.8%	3.2%	1.5%	(2.1%)
India	653,415	390,423	277,416	1,321,254
	49.5%	29.5%	21.0%	100.0%
	3.7%	3.7%	1.9%	(3.1%)
Pakistan and	143,949	91,697	102,003	337,649
Bangladesh	42.6%	27.2%	30.2%	100.0%
	.8%	.9%	.7%	(0.8%)
Southeast Asia	681,213	442,325	281,218	1,404,756
	48.5%	31.5%	20.0%	100.0%
	3.8%	4.2%	1.9%	(3.3%)
China, Hong	738,223	735,322	431,758	1,905,303
Kong, and	38.7%	38.6%	22.7%	100.0%
Taiwan	4.2%	6.9%	2.9%	(4.4%)
Philippines	446,557	752,702	477,471	1,676,730
	26.6%	44.9%	28.5%	100.0%
	2.5%	7.1%	3.2%	(3.9%)
Korea	363,681	343,550	172,346	879,577
	41.3%	39.1%	19.6%	100.0%
	2.0%	3.2%	1.2%	(2.0%)
Japan	208,162	55,575	98,031	361,768
	57.5%	15.4%	27.1%	100.0%
	1.2%	.5%	.7%	(0.8%)
Africa	426,819	242,509	153,316	822,644
	51.9%	29.5%	18.6%	100.0%
	2.4%	2.3%	1.0%	(1.9%)
Mixed or other	1,416,647	1,187,027	2,573,102	5,176,776
	27.4%	22.9%	49.7%	100.0%
	8.0%	11.2%	17.4%	(12.0%)

Table 1.3 *(Continued)*

	Foreign-Born Noncitizen	Foreign-Born Citizen	Second Generation	Total
Total	17,756,451	10,621,536	14,807,994	43,187,225
	41.1%	24.6%	34.3%	100.0%
	100.0%	100.0%	100.0%	100.0%

Source: U.S. Bureau of the Census 2000.
Note: Second generation includes only those with both parents born abroad.

here longer. For example, only a quarter of Mexicans, the nation's single largest immigrant group, have naturalized (see table 1.4). Caribbean immigrants have more nearly average rates, with Dominicans being on the low side and Cubans being on the high side. (Overall, an estimated 44.5 percent of all foreign-born individuals who had lived in the United States for five years or more had naturalized as of the March 2000 Current Population Survey.)

Immigrants from the Anglophone Caribbean tend to be better educated, occupy better jobs, and make more money than Hispanic immigrants, but they still have less education than many Asian immigrants. Racially, they tend to be classified as black and thus are faced with all that that entails in American urban life. (Indeed, many Dominicans, Cubans, Panamanians, and Nicaraguans also have varying degrees of African ancestry, and their home societies typically have words for many categories of racial shading.) Among all new immigrant groups, Afro-Caribbeans have been here the longest, and more than half have become American citizens.

The third stream of immigrants, from East, Southeast, and South Asia, is concentrated on the West Coast and in New York City. These groups traveled over longer distances, are less likely to return permanently to their native countries, and have more bimodal distributions of education and income than the Latin and Caribbean immigrants. Though many East Asian immigrants come from peasant or working-class urban origins, many others are well educated, often graduates of schools with English instruction, are highly skilled, and earn high incomes. (Among U.S. residents twenty-five years old and older, Indian and Filipino immigrants to the United States have higher rates of college education than native-born whites.) Because their home societies are distant and many are highly educated, Asian immigrants may be expected to naturalize at higher rates than other immigrants, and indeed, 58.2 percent of Chinese and 67.9 percent of Filipinos resident five years or more in the United States have become citizens. It remains to be seen, however, whether political participation will match the naturalization rate. Though we usually associate European immigration with the turn of the twentieth century, many Europeans arrived in the years around World War II, and substantial immigration still comes from Russia, nations of the former Soviet Union, and other Central European countries. Moreover, table 1.3 shows that 8.2 percent of foreign-born noncitizens, 15.3 percent of naturalized immigrants, and 20.8 percent of second-generation immigrants come from Western Europe and Canada. Table 1.4 clearly indicates that most Western Europeans have been in the United States for three decades or more, while Eastern Europeans are more recent arrivals. All other things being equal, these European groups should be the most economically and politically assimilated. As whites joining descendants of earlier immigrants from their home countries who had become well integrated by the 1950s, Europeans should face the least resistance and advance most quickly in terms of education, income, electoral participation, and diffusion away from the urban zones of immigrant settlement. Indeed, most recent white immigrants have become naturalized citizens.

These trends within and among the various immigrant groups are magnified in New York City and Los Angeles County. Less than half of the 7.6 million residents reported by the CPS for New York in 2000 are native born with native parents (table 1.2). And while its combined first- and second-generation immigrant population of 54 percent is well shy of the 78 percent reached in 1900, it is nevertheless a larger fraction than at any time since 1930. (Even if we reclassify the city's 750,000 second-generation whites as natives, the remaining foreign stock still makes up 44 percent of the total.)

As befits the city's role as ground zero for previous waves of immigration, table 1.5 shows that the city's immigrants are racially diverse: 28 percent of its foreign-born residents are white, 19 percent black, 20 percent Asian, and 32 percent Hispanic. Reflecting the city's role as a magnet for northward migration by blacks and Puerto Ricans in the 1950s and '60s, the native population is also racially diverse: 44 percent is white, 34 percent black, and 21 percent Hispanic, although there are virtually no native Asians with native parents. A powerful factor distinguishing New York from Los Angeles is that differences in immigrant heritage cut across racial and ethnic distinctions rather than reinforce them.

Immigration has had an even stronger impact on Los Angeles County in the last third of the twentieth century. Only 39 percent of its 9.4 million residents are natives born to native parents, while more than a third are foreign born (table 1.5). Another quarter of L.A. County's residents have at least one foreign-born parent. As we would expect from the area's proximity to Latin America and its

Table 1.4   Naturalization Status and Median Year of Arrival for Foreign-Born Residents by Region of Origin: United States, 2000

	Noncitizen	Naturalized	Total	Median Year of Arrival
Canada	193,008	175,062	368,070	1977
	52.4%	47.6%	100.0%	
	1.5%	1.7%	1.6%	
Australia, New	35,812	19,317	55,129	1992
Zealand, Pacific	65.0%	35.0%	100.0%	
Islands	.3%	.2%	.2%	
Germany	178,884	335,451	514,335	1962
	34.8%	65.2%	100.0%	
	1.4%	3.2%	2.2%	
Italy	116,502	331,476	447,978	1962
	26.0%	74.0%	100.0%	
	.9%	3.2%	1.9%	
United Kingdom	223,297	215,635	438,932	1972
	50.9%	49.1%	100.0%	
	1.7%	2.1%	1.9%	
Ireland	85,959	127,668	213,627	1972
	40.2%	59.8%	100.0%	
	.7%	1.2%	.9%	
Other West	311,768	431,808	743,576	1977
Europe	41.9%	58.1%	100.0%	
	2.4%	4.2%	3.2%	
Former Soviet	199,935	277,396	477,331	1992
Union	41.9%	58.1%	100.0%	
	1.5%	2.7%	2.0%	
East Europe	125,965	192,025	317,990	1986
	39.6%	60.4%	100.0%	
	1.0%	1.9%	1.4%	
Mexico	4,729,859	1,525,265	6,255,124	1988
	75.6%	24.4%	100.0%	
	36.6%	14.7%	26.8%	
Central America	1,116,346	442,217	1,558,563	1988
	71.6%	28.4%	100.0%	
	8.6%	4.3%	6.7%	
West Indies	413,032	447,526	860,558	1984
	48.0%	52.0%	100.0%	
	3.2%	4.3%	3.7%	
Cuba	274,955	492,350	767,305	1977
	35.8%	64.2%	100.0%	
	2.1%	4.7%	3.3%	
Dominican	388,898	216,346	605,244	1988
Republic	64.3%	35.7%	100.0%	
	3.0%	2.1%	2.6%	

(Table continues on p. 30.)

Table 1.4   (*Continued*)

	Noncitizen	Naturalized	Total	Median Year of Arrival
Haiti	160,079	155,141	315,220	1988
	50.8%	49.2%	100.0%	
	1.2%	1.5%	1.4%	
Columbia, Ecuador, Peru	508,726	347,413	856,139	1988
	59.4%	40.6%	100.0%	
	3.9%	3.3%	3.7%	
Other South America	181,084	166,791	347,875	1990
	52.1%	47.9%	100.0%	
	1.4%	1.6%	1.5%	
Middle East	245,388	338,275	583,663	1984
	42.0%	58.0%	100.0%	
	1.9%	3.3%	2.5%	
India	344,128	376,760	720,888	1990
	47.7%	52.3%	100.0%	
	2.7%	3.6%	3.1%	
Pakistan-Bangladesh	114,211	78,818	193,029	1990
	59.2%	40.8%	100.0%	
	.9%	.8%	.8%	
Southeast Asia	501,651	430,216	931,867	1990
	53.8%	46.2%	100.0%	
	3.9%	4.1%	4.0%	
China, Hong Kong, Taiwan	518,959	722,797	1,241,756	1986
	41.8%	58.2%	100.0%	
	4.0%	7.0%	5.3%	
Philippines	350,722	741,576	1,092,298	1982
	32.1%	67.9%	100.0%	
	2.7%	7.1%	4.7%	
Korea	275,377	342,504	617,881	1984
	44.6%	55.4%	100.0%	
	2.1%	3.3%	2.7%	
Japan	96,097	55,575	151,672	1990
	63.4%	36.6%	100.0%	
	.7%	.5%	.7%	
Africa	249,805	226,106	475,911	1990
	52.5%	47.5%	100.0%	
	1.9%	2.2%	2.0%	
Mixed-other	979,745	1,163,880	2,143,625	1984
	45.7%	54.3%	100.0%	
	7.6%	11.2%	9.2%	
Total	12,921,436	10,377,620	23,299,056	
	55.5%	44.5%	100.0%	
	100.0%	100.0%	100.0%	

Source: U.S. Bureau of the Census 2000.
Note: Naturalization rates are for those who have lived in the U.S. for five or more years. Median arrival date is for all foreign-born.

orientation to the Pacific, its first- and second-generation population is predominantly Latino (62.4 percent) and Asian (22.5 percent).

Los Angeles County's native population is dominated by whites who migrated there between 1910 and 1950 and their descendants, who together constitute 63 percent of the native population. (L.A. County's foreign-born population is but one-seventh white.) Because L.A. was also a magnet for African American migration during and shortly after World War II, blacks make up a substantial proportion (19 percent) of the native stock, but almost none of its foreign stock. Finally, as Latino residents pass into the third and later generations, the Latino share of the native stock has climbed to 16 percent, even as Latinos continue to represent the lion's share of the foreign born (62 percent). (For further elaboration of these trends, see Waldinger and Bozorgmehr 1996.)

The contrasts between the Los Angeles and New York stand out in table 1.5. Los Angeles's native stock, for example, is far more white and its immigrant stock far less white than in New York. In Los Angeles County, therefore, the natives are largely white and whites—as well as blacks—are predominantly native, while Latinos and Asians are predominantly foreign stock and the foreign stock is predominantly Latino and Asian. L.A.'s whites and blacks thus both lack the immigrant heritage that each group has in New York. This may affect white and black attitudes toward immigrants in the respective cities. And because the black population of Los Angeles County has not been fed in recent decades by newcomers from other parts of the country or abroad and is not expanding rapidly, it poses less of a demographic and political challenge to the county's native whites than the black population of New York City might to whites there. Indeed, while Tom Bradley, an African American, reigned as L.A.'s mayor from 1973 to 1993, native whites and blacks participated in a coalition in which Latinos were, if not excluded, certainly underrepresented considering their numbers in the city's population (Sonenshein 1993). This same cleavage appeared in the 2001 mayoral election in L.A., in which a white was elected with black support against a Latino candidate. In L.A. County, Latinos make up 45.4 percent of the population, while blacks are only 8.1 percent (table 1.5). And although Latino immigration has also had a major impact on New York City, Latinos still make up only 26.8 percent of the city's population, with blacks standing at 25.7 percent.

A similar scenario exists when considering naturalization. Overall, fewer of Los Angeles County's immigrants have become citizens than New York's, and this holds true even despite L.A.'s white, black, and Asian immigrants naturalizing at higher rates than their counterparts in New York (table 1.6). The reason? L.A.'s far more numerous Latino immigrants have naturalized at lower rates than Latinos in New York. The "sleeping giant" of L.A. County's potential electorate is thus to be

Table 1.5 Immigrant Generation by Race, New York City and Los Angeles County, 2000

	Non-Hispanic White	Non-Hispanic Black	Non-Hispanic Asian	Latino	Total
New York City					
Foreign-born	752,929	513,593	539,308	851,534	2,657,364
Row percentage	28.3%	19.3%	20.3%	32.0%	100.0%
Column percentage	26.1%	26.1%	72.3%	41.5%	34.8%
Second generation	428,595	246,467	156,469	356,782	1,188,313
	36.1%	20.7%	13.2%	30.0%	100.0%
	14.9%	12.5%	21.0%	17.4%	15.5%
2.5 generation	224,847	70,566	30,340	137,085	462,838
	48.6%	15.2%	6.6%	29.6%	100.0%
	7.8%	3.6%	4.1%	6.7%	6.1%
Native stock	1,474,155	1,134,590	19,302	706,445	3,334,492
	44.2%	34.0%	.6%	21.2%	100.0%
	51.2%	57.7%	2.6%	34.4%	43.6%
Total	2,880,526	1,965,216	745,419	2,051,846	7,643,007
	37.7%	25.7%	9.8%	26.8%	100.0%
	100.0%	100.0%	100.0%	100.0%	100.0%

Los Angeles County					Total
Foreign-born	451,574	39,329	727,631	2,020,212	3,238,746
Row percentage	13.9%	1.2%	22.5%	62.4%	100.0%
Column percentage	13.8%	5.2%	67.2%	47.5%	34.6%
Second generation	199,638	19,189	231,649	1,317,707	1,768,183
	11.3%	1.1%	13.1%	74.5%	100.0%
	6.1%	2.5%	21.4%	31.0%	18.9%
2.5 generation	310,231	27,588	35,904	325,434	699,157
	44.4%	3.9%	5.1%	46.5%	100.0%
	9.5%	3.6%	3.3%	7.7%	7.5%
Native stock	2,301,820	672,323	87,832	587,649	3,649,624
	63.1%	18.4%	2.4%	16.1%	100.0%
	70.5%	88.6%	8.1%	13.8%	39.0%
Total	3,263,263	758,429	1,083,016	4,251,002	9,355,710
	34.9%	8.1%	11.6%	45.4%	100.0%
	100.0%	100.0%	100.0%	100.0%	100.0%

Source: U.S. Bureau of the Census 2000.

Table 1.6   Naturalization by Race for Immigrants to New York City and Los Angeles County in United States for Five or More Years, 2000

Urban Region	Race	Foreign-Born Noncitizen	Foreign-Born Citizen	Total
New York City	Non-Hispanic white	335,224	303,135	638,359
		52.5%	47.5%	100.0%
	Non-Hispanic black	247,271	233,335	480,606
		51.4%	48.6%	100.0%
	Non-Hispanic Asian	241,663	180,794	422,457
		57.2%	42.8%	100.0%
	Latino	502,910	238,432	741,342
		67.8%	32.2%	100.0%
	Total	1,327,068	955,696	2,282,764
		58.1%	41.9%	100.0%
Los Angeles County	Non-Hispanic white	155,705	224,650	380,355
		40.9%	59.1%	100.0%
	Non-Hispanic black	10,733	28,596	39,329
		27.3%	72.7%	100.0%
	Non-Hispanic Asian	292,503	384,906	677,409
		43.2%	56.8%	100.0%
	Latino	1,348,944	436,238	1,785,182
		75.6%	24.4%	100.0%
	Total	1,807,885	1,074,390	2,882,275
		62.7%	37.3%	100.0%

Source: U.S. Bureau of the Census 2000.

found among its nonnaturalized Latino immigrants, mostly Mexicans but also Salvadorans and other Central American groups.

Shifting focus, table 1.7 breaks down the two cities' voting-age citizens along racial and nativity lines. Quite extraordinarily, the eligible electorates of the two jurisdictions reveal almost identical breakdowns by immigrant status: each city's voting population is just over half native stock, with the remainder divided slightly in favor of naturalized immigrants over second- and 2.5-generation people. Whites also make up half the *potential* electorates—all voting age citizens—in each place. The remainders, however, are divided differently: blacks make up twice as much of the potential electorate in New York as they do in L.A. County, while Latinos and Asians are more important in L.A. than they are in New York City. In New York, 40 percent of the white and 30 percent of the black eligible electorate are first or second generation, but in Los Angeles County, three-quarters of the eligible whites and nine-tenths of eligible blacks are native stock. Owing to a considerable Puerto Rican population, more than half New York's eligible Latinos are native stock, while only a quarter of

Table 1.7 Eligible Electorate by Race and Immigration Status, Voting-Age Citizens, New York City and Los Angeles County, 2000

Urban Region	Race	Foreign-Born	Second or 2.5 Generation	Native Stock	Total (Column Percentage)
New York City	Non-Hispanic white	300,755	509,845	1,189,465	2,000,065
	Row percentage	15.0%	25.5%	59.5%	(47.2%)
	Non-Hispanic black	235,915	96,547	804,942	1,137,404
		20.7%	8.5%	70.8%	(26.8%)
	Non-Hispanic Asian	178,323	34,414	15,671	228,408
		78.1%	15.1%	6.9%	(5.4%)
	Latino	237,351	147,227	490,053	874,631
		27.1%	16.8%	56.0%	(20.6%)
	Total	952,344	788,033	2,500,131	4,240,508
		22.5%	18.6%	59.0%	100.0%
Los Angeles County	Non-Hispanic white	222,246	344,959	1,837,394	2,404,599
		9.2%	14.3%	76.4%	(50.6%)
	Non-Hispanic black	28,596	33,972	473,942	536,510
		5.3%	6.3%	88.3%	(11.3%)
	Non-Hispanic Asian	381,706	83,469	67,723	532,898
		71.6%	15.7%	12.7%	(11.2%)
	Latino	428,643	528,385	321,549	1,278,577
		33.5%	41.3%	25.1%	(26.9%)
	Total	1,061,191	990,785	2,700,608	4,752,584
		22.3%	20.8%	56.8%	100.0%

Source: U.S. Bureau of the Census 2000.

L.A. County's Latinos are native stock. In short, native whites make up only a quarter of New York City's eligible electorate, but more than a third of Los Angeles County's. In New York, native blacks form the second-largest electoral bloc, while first-generation Latinos occupy the same position in Los Angeles. If we think of electoral competition as being most likely between the first- and second-largest groups, each of which recruits other groups to bolster their majority, then New York's native whites might seek support from immigrant-stock whites, Latinos, and even immigrant blacks in competition with native blacks. In Los Angeles County, by contrast, native whites might seek support from native blacks in order to fend off competition from immigrant-stock Latinos.

In New York City, 1.5 million nonnaturalized immigrants of voting age have been United States residents for five or more years and stand just outside this eligible electorate. About one-third of them are Latino, one-quarter white, and one-fifth each black and Asian. In the wake of adverse changes in national legislation in 1996, these groups become increasingly inclined to apply for citizenship in recent years. Similarly, 1.9 million nonnaturalized immigrants of voting age live in L.A. County. Almost three-quarters of them are Latino. And though they have naturalized at a lower rate than have New York's Latinos, Los Angeles County's Latino citizenship rate has been climbing in recent years.

Finally, the political contexts in which immigrants and first- and second-generation immigrants live may shape their propensity to become citizens and vote. As DeSipio (1997a, 23) says, "The political incorporation of contemporary immigrants cannot be separated from the political environments of the areas in which they reside, primarily urban areas and primarily on the coasts." (See also DeSipio 1997b.) In this regard, Shefter (1984), for example, has noted that established political elites play a significant role in ushering immigrant groups into the electorate, particularly through their determination of whether or not reaching out and mobilizing new groups will gain them political advantage.

The political configurations of Los Angeles County and New York City's jurisdictions could hardly be more different, as table 1.8 indicates. New York City's immigrants live inside one overall political jurisdiction, whereas L.A. County's immigrants are spread across eighty-eight separately incorporated jurisdictions as well as unincorporated areas. The City of Los Angeles contains less than a third of the county's population; the remainder lives in such L.A. County communities as Glendale, Pasadena, Compton, Downey, and Torrance. And whereas New York City is a highly partisan, highly organized political environment, Los Angeles County is nonpartisan and weakly organized. Illustrative of the Los Angeles environment is the open primary system that California adopted in 1996. Under this arrangement, primary voters are allowed to cast a ballot for a candidate from any party, not just their own, with the highest vote-getters from each party on the general election ballot. This weakens party members' control over their own party's nominations. By contrast, New York Republicans sought to restrict access to the primary ballot to the party establishment's choice in the 2000 presidential primary.

As table 1.8 shows, New York City is three times as densely populated as the City of Los Angeles and five times as dense as L.A. County. In all three jurisdictions, whites and blacks are overrepresented among legislative officeholders relative to their shares of the population, Latinos are underrepresented, and Asians are virtually excluded. In New York City, the municipal government spends about twice as much per capita as the City of Los Angeles and Los Angeles County combined. While the New York City Council has three foreign-born members, the L.A. city and county councils have none.

Newcomers to each place have quite different access to elected office, as is reflected in the representation ratios given in table 1.8. New York City's entry-level political offices include membership on the community school boards (all thirty-five have fifteen seats), the state assembly (sixty seats in the city), and the city council (each of its fifty-one members represents about 140,000 people). In Los Angeles County, five county supervisors represent almost 2 million constituents apiece. In the state assembly, the County controls, proportionally, only about a third as many seats as New York City does in New York State's assembly. (The California State Assembly has fewer seats in relationship to its population than does New York.)

Campaign contributions, media exposure, and elite support therefore play a much larger role in determining who can gain access to the lowest level of elected office in Los Angeles than in New York, where friends, neighbors, and grassroots organizational networks can often determine the outcome in local elections. Indeed, a few thousand votes may determine a contested primary race for the New York State Assembly. It is true, however, that Los Angeles County comprises many other jurisdictions, ranging from the City of Los Angeles to smaller cities like Monterey Park, where immigrants can hope to gain access to local office. Statewide propositions directed against services to (undocumented) immigrants (Proposition 187 in 1994, for example), affirmative action (Proposition 209, 1996), and bilingual education have repeatedly convulsed California politics. While the changes in national welfare and immigration legislation in 1996 undoubtedly galvanized immigrant voters nationwide, polarization around the immigration issue has probably affected potential immi-

Table 1.8 The Political Systems of New York City, the City of Los Angeles, and Los Angeles County

	New York City		City of Los Angeles		Los Angeles County	
Population (1997)	7,644,371		3,615,498		9,324,811	
Non-Hispanic white (percentage)	35.9		31.3		35.4	
Non-Hispanic black (percentage)	29.4		10.1		8.2	
Non-Hispanic Asian (percentage)	8.4		8.6		11.5	
Hispanic (percentage)	26.2		49.9		44.7	
Habitable land area (mi^2)	322		466		1,989	
Population density (persons per mi^2)	23,740		7,759		4,688	
Voting-age population (1997)	5,590,119		2,510,985		6,483,004	
Foreign-born	2,284,518	(40.9%)	1,306,900	(52.0%)	2,847,425	(43.9%)
Foreign-born naturalized	857,731	(37.5%)	298,278	(22.8%)	780,220	(27.4%)
Eligible electorate (1997)	4,163,332		1,502,363		4,415,799	
Registered voters (1997)	3,532,348		1,401,336		3,759,498	
Registration rate	84.8%		93.3%		85.1%	
Votes cast, 1996 presidential election	1,796,533		750,102		2,410,976	
Turnout (votes cast–eligible electorate)	43.2%		49.9%		54.6%	

Votes cast, 1997 mayoral election	1,319,795	378,965	n.a.
Turnout (votes cast–eligible electorate)	31.7	25.2	n.a.
Non-Hispanic white voters (percentage)	53 (1997)	65 (1997)	62 (1996)
Jewish voters (percentage)	23	15	14
Non-Hispanic Black voters (percentage)	21	13	8
Non-Hispanic Asian voters (percentage)	4	4	3
Hispanic voters (percentage)	20	15	26
Jurisdictions	1	1	88
Total seats on local legislature	51	15	5
White representation ratio	1.47	2.12	1.69
Black representation ratio	1.00	1.32	2.44
Asian representation ratio	0.00	0.00	0.00
Hispanic representation ratio	0.67	0.40	0.45
Adopted budget, 1996 to 1997 (billions)	$34,946	$4,063	$12,143

Sources: 1997 population figures from the U.S. Bureau of the Census 1997; registration and votes from New York City and Los Angeles County Boards of Elections; 1997 voter composition from *New York Times* and *Los Angeles Times* exit polls; 1996 Los Angeles County voter composition from Voter News Service 1996, L.A. sample.

Note: The representation ratio is percentage of legislators of given background to percentage of population from that background.

grant voters in Southern California more than any other part of the country.

Naturalization: Overcoming the First Barrier to Participation

The shift toward citizenship among immigrants in New York and Los Angeles County is at present slow but will ultimately have an enormous impact on each area's electorate. Drawing on a 1988 national survey of Latino immigrants who were legal residents eligible to become citizens, DeSipio found that one-third had naturalized and one-third were in the process, but one-third remained uninterested in doing so (Pachon and DeSipio 1994). (Similar data do not appear to exist for any other group.) Scholars have identified a variety of individual, group, contextual, and historic factors that influence the rate at which immigrants become naturalized (DeSipio 1996, 1997a; Jones-Correa 1998). Length of residence, arrival in the United States early in life, education, income, professional employment, and English-language ability are all associated with naturalization. Participation in organizations outside of one's own ethnic group and an "ideology of return" are also influential characteristics.

Even after controlling for these individual characteristics, however, differences among immigrant groups remain. Some concern matters external to life in the United States, such as ease of return to the home country, whether or not the home country recognizes or encourages dual citizenship, and uneven denial rates and processing times across Immigration and Naturalization Service (INS) district offices. Changing U.S. policy regarding the rights and entitlements of foreign-born permanent residents, together with such legislation as Propositions 187 and 209 in California, certainly enhanced the incentive to become naturalized and, in fact, prompted a fivefold increase in applications for citizenship. Nevertheless, many aspects of a group's internal dynamics may also affect the inclination to naturalize. (For insight into the dynamics of naturalization within one family group of Dominicans in New York City, see Singer and Gilbertson 2000.) Certainly, a group's average levels of education, income, and property ownership are all likely to affect individual decisions to naturalize.

Neighborhood context also exerts an influence. Although New York City has a substantially larger black population than does Los Angeles County, blacks are segregated from whites in both places. In New York, Afro-Caribbean immigrants have settled in a pattern that overlaps with but also differentiates itself from the centers of native black residence, particularly in central Brooklyn. Black immigrants constitute the expanding, middle-class edge of the black communities of central Brooklyn and southeast Queens (Mollenkopf 1993a). Roughly speaking, Asian and Latino immigrants to New York tend to live spatially, as well as racially, "in between" whites and blacks, with Asians toward the white sides of these intermediate zones and Latinos on the black side, particularly in cases where the Latino group has substantial African ancestry. Where possible, Asian and nonblack Latino immigrants have sought to distance themselves from the native poor, whether black or Puerto Rican. This has given rise to large swaths of territory in which Asians and Hispanics—Chinese, Koreans, South Americans, and Dominicans—live intermingled or in close proximity to one another. The Jackson Heights, Elmhurst, and Corona neighborhoods of Queens offer models of this new pattern of settlement.

Roughly comparable settlement patterns can be found in Los Angeles County, though Latino immigrants are a far more dominant group there than they are in New York. Between the former and now-disappearing black ghetto of South-Central, the middle-class black neighborhoods to the west, and the white enclaves along the coast and in the San Fernando Valley may be found large zones of Asian and Hispanic immigration (Clark 1996). As the County's black population has matured, and even begun to decline, Mexican and Central American immigrants have entered black neighborhoods, resulting in growing black-Latino conflict (Johnson, Farrell, and Guinn 1999; Fletcher 1998).

If 2000 Current Population Survey data is any indication, length of residence is clearly the single strongest determinant of naturalization among immigrants not only in New York City and Los Angeles County, but in the rest of the country as well. Individual income and education levels are also positively associated with naturalization. Even after controlling for these three factors, however, immigrants living in New York City are still significantly more likely to have naturalized than those in L.A. County. In both cities, too, different groups naturalize at different rates.[5] In particular, Latinos in Los Angeles are less likely than Latinos in New York to have naturalized, even after controlling for age, length of residence in the U.S, and level of education. It may be that the constant arrival of large numbers of new immigrants retards the process of political assimilation among those who arrived previously (DeSipio 1997a, 15, 20).

Even though most immigrants have not naturalized, demand for naturalization has surged and new Americans are swelling the potentially eligible electorate in both cities. New York's 1.5 million foreign-born adult noncitizens may be compared to its 3.3 million registered voters, less than 2 million of whom actually voted in 1996. Similarly,

L.A. County's 3.8 million registered voters cast 2.1 million ballots in the 1996 presidential election, but 1.9 million potential new American voters might ultimately emerge from among its foreign born noncitizen residents. The Immigration and Naturalization Service district offices in both places had substantial backlogs of citizenship applications in the latter 1990s.[6]

The contemporary politics of naturalization in these two cities as well as in America at large deserves much more detailed study. In addition to the changing legislative incentives regarding naturalization, bureaucratic discretion exercised by local INS offices has generated national political controversy. Democrats have complained about the slow pace of naturalization and large backlogs of applicants, while Republicans have expressed outrage over faulty grants of citizenship and the possibility of noncitizens voting, which may have happened in the 1996 Dornan-Sanchez congressional race in Orange County, California.[7] When combined with the potentially divided loyalties resulting from dual citizenship, notably evidenced by the Mexican government's attempt to organize the Mexican diaspora within the United States to influence American politics, this topic is destined to remain controversial.[8]

In New York City, Mayor Rudolph Giuliani strongly favors immigrant rights and has established a program to assist people in becoming citizens (though its neighborhood offices do tend to be found in areas that voted for the mayor). In addition, a consortium of foundations in the City funds a variety of immigrant services that include citizenship advocacy, and the New York Immigration Coalition undertook drives to promote naturalization, register new citizens to vote, and get out the immigrant vote in the 2000 presidential elections. The Immigration Coalition also assists local organizations in running federally funded citizenship-training programs.

In New York, many Jewish, white Catholic, native black, and Puerto Rican officeholders represent districts with substantial immigrant populations; thus, a wide spectrum of elected officials supports immigrant rights and naturalization, at least as a rhetorical goal. But like all local elected officials, these incumbents and their county party organizations like the electorate that put them in office and are skeptical about enlarging—and perhaps destabilizing—said electorate or introducing immigrant competitors for political office. Michael Jones-Correa (1998, 67–90), in one instance, details how the Queens County Democratic organization resisted recognizing the borough's rapidly developing Latino community. This resistance from established officeholders has been fed by competition between Puerto Rican and Dominican politicians, for example, or between native-born and West

Indian black politicians (Falcon 1988). Meanwhile, emerging Asian politicians complain about lack of access or representation.

Los Angeles, the classic "fragmented metropolis," exhibits the same barriers to citizenship while offering fewer overt supports. A key aspect of the politics of immigrant incorporation in Los Angeles has been the struggle by Mexican Americans to achieve political representation on the city council, on the Los Angeles County Board of Supervisors, and in the region's congressional delegation, a struggle that has been complicated by a Democratic establishment dominated by the fraying, and now broken, coalition between blacks and white liberals, especially Jewish voters (Regalado 1988; Sonenshein 1993, 1997). Though Latino voters supported former mayor Tom Bradley, his coalition did not actively promote the careers of Latino politicians. Twelve years elapsed between Mayor Bradley's first election in 1973 and the seating of the first Mexican American, Richard Alatorre, on the city council. It took a voting-rights lawsuit to create a second Latino city council district after 1990; in 1993, a third Mexican American was elected in the San Fernando Valley. Bradley did form a close relationship with the first Asian councilman, Michael Woo, and protected him from the redistricting process in 1992—but Woo lost badly to the Republican candidate, Richard Riordan, in the 1993 mayoral election, winning only a slim majority of Latino votes in the process. By 1997, Latinos swung firmly behind Riordan in his race against a white-liberal challenger, Tom Hayden. In 2001, whites and blacks supported the winner, James Hahn, against Antonio Villaraigosa, the Latino candidate. Only one Latina, Gloria Molina, has been elected to the powerful Los Angeles County Board of Supervisors.

Just as Mexican American elected officials are wary of the black-white liberal coalition—even in its decline—they view the growth of the Salvadoran and Guatemalan communities as spawning grounds for potential competitors in the contest for Latino political leadership. Accordingly, Mexican American political elites are divided over their long-term strategy and often distance themselves from immigrant concerns (Gutierrez 1997). Because their "safe" seats are also undergoing demographic change, Mexican American incumbents have little incentive to promote naturalization among the polyglot Latino immigrants of their districts. Moreover, the weak linkage between grassroots and political elites and the relative paucity of community organization in Los Angeles hampers a bottom-up galvanization of a Latino panethnic identity, notwithstanding the spur of Proposition 187 (Skerry 1993).

Outside the City of Los Angeles, the established political elites of smaller jurisdictions have also impeded political mobilization and the emergence of political leadership among new immigrants. For example, the black political establishment in Compton has resisted Latino demands for more representation and employment within that city's government (Johnson, Farrell, and Guinn 1999). The decision in a 1990 voting-rights case, *Garza v. Los Angeles County*, ordered the creation of a new Latino seat for the county board of supervisors after finding that those responsible for redistricting had fragmented the Latino vote.

Meanwhile, the emergence of immigrant majorities in many of Los Angeles County's smaller jurisdictions has in a few cases facilitated the election of immigrant municipal officials. In the well-documented case of Monterey Park, the advent of an Asian population majority, the shared "newcomer" status among the various Asian groups, and instances of native prejudice led to increased Asian voter registration and cooperation among Chinese, Japanese, and other Asian voters to support Asian (in this case Chinese) elected officials (Saito and Horton 1994; Saito 1998). To extrapolate from this example, the relatively small size of the Asian immigrant stream relative to those from Mexico or El Salvador may possibly lead, in an environment of ethnically polarized electoral competition, to the formation of an Asian panethnic political identity more durable than that of Latinos (Espiritu 1992).

Mexican Americans currently hold many of the Los Angeles–area county, state, and congressional seats where Asian populations are growing, creating the potential for conflict. The two groups succeeded in working together on the 1992 county redistricting process (Saito and Horton 1994, 256–57), but, given the level of Latino-Asian conflict in the 1992 Los Angeles riots and the underlying differences in socioeconomic status between the two groups, it is unclear whether this cooperation can endure.

In short, the experiences of New York City and Los Angeles County suggest that established native minority politicians are quite unlikely to promote political mobilization of immigrant groups. Nor are they likely to support bids for elective office by emerging leaders from those groups, even those from racially or ethnically related immigrant groups, let alone any from racially different and potentially competitive groups. While California's Propositions 187 and 209 and the changes in national welfare and immigration legislation in 1996 did create widespread concern among immigrant groups and spurred applications for citizenship, they did not stimulate new broad-based, grassroots movements or propel new leaders to prominence. To the contrary, the heterogeneity of the immigrant population and the hostility of political incumbents to demographic trends they cannot control, not to mention overt Republican opposition, mean that naturalization will continue to be a relatively slow process.

Electoral Participation by New Citizens

Table 1.9 shows national voting rates for the 1996 presidential election, sorted by race and immigrant status as reported in the November 1996 Current Population Survey. Remarkably, black and Latino naturalized citizens were significantly more likely to have voted than their native counterparts. Naturalized and native whites voted at similar rates, as did Asian new citizens in comparison to native Asians (of whom there are relatively few). This may be due to the fact that naturalized white and Asian immigrants are more likely than other immigrants to have lived in the United States for a long time and to be in circumstances similar to those of native whites. Overall, whites had the highest voting rate (almost 61 percent), blacks stood about 7 percentage points behind, and Asians and Latinos lagged another 10 points behind blacks.

Equally interesting are the distinctions between the naturalized first-generation immigrants and their children, the second generation. Voting among white second-generation individuals was significantly more common than among the naturalized whites. Among minority groups, rates were the same between second- and naturalized first-generation Asians, but they decreased significantly for blacks and Latinos. This raises the troubling possibility that the children of black and Latino immigrants are experiencing a downward political mobility akin to that which some identify in these groups' educational and employment outcomes (Waters, Kasinitz, and Mollenkopf 1998). However, it may also represent the relative youthfulness of the second generation compared to their immigrant parents: among all groups, the young are far less likely to vote than are the old.

The comparable voting rates for racial groups and immigrant generations in New York City and Los Angeles County are given in table 1.10. (Due to small sample size, table 1.10 omits some of the national categories.) Contrary to the national pattern, naturalized white immigrants in New York and Los Angeles were five to seven percentage points less likely to vote than their native-stock counterparts. And as in the national sample, black and Latino naturalized immigrants were ten points more likely than natives to vote in New York while Latinos in Los Angeles were sixteen points more likely to do so (L.A. had too few immigrant blacks for comparison). Again as in the national sample, whites voted at the highest rates overall, followed by blacks and then Latinos and Asians at considerable distances behind.

The national pattern showing second-generation American Latinos to be less likely to vote than immigrant Latino citizens holds true for both New York City and Los Angeles County. The national gap of 6.6

Table 1.9   Voting in 1996 Presidential Election by Race and Immigrant Status, United States Voting-Age Citizens

		No/NA/DK	Voted
Non-Hispanic white	Foreign-born citizen	1,359,473	1,866,637
		42.1%	57.9%
	Second generation	3,903,023	9,099,864
		30.0%	70.0%
	Native stock	50,729,775	75,637,744
		40.1%	59.9%
	Total	55,992,271	86,604,245
		39.3%	60.7%
Non-Hispanic black	Foreign-born citizen	225,358	284,024
		44.2%	55.8%
	Second generation	182,022	180,298
		50.2%	49.8%
	Native stock	9,476,399	10,692,116
		47.0%	53.0%
	Total	9,883,779	11,156,438
		47.0%	53.0%
Non-Hispanic	Foreign-born citizen	1,180,355	995,008
		54.3%	45.7%
	Second generation	499,027	420,105
		54.3%	45.7%
	Native stock	339,995	289,305
		54.0%	46.0%
	Total	2,019,377	1,704,418
		54.2%	45.8%
Latino	Foreign-born citizen	1,108,437	1,185,601
		48.3%	51.7%
	Second generation	1,726,403	1,417,381
		54.9%	45.1%
	Native stock	3,446,146	2,325,226
		59.7%	40.3%
	Total	6,280,986	4,928,208
		56.0%	44.0%

Source: U.S. Bureau of the Census 1996.
Notes: No/NA/DK means the respondent said no, gave no answer, or did not know whether they voted. Yes means they said they voted.
Native stock people are native-born with two native-born parents.

Table 1.10   Voting in 1996 Presidential Election by Race, Immigrant Status, and Location, Voting-Age Citizens in New York City and Los Angeles County (Categories with Fewer Than Thirty Cases Suppressed)

Region	Race	Immigrant Status	No/NA/DK	Yes
New York City	Non-Hispanic White	Foreign-born	138,714 (44.8%)	170,886 (55.2%)
		2 or 2.5	204,250 (35.7)	368,088 (64.3)
		Native stock	404,544 (38.8)	638,481 (61.2)
		Total	747,508 (38.8)	1,177,455 (61.2)
	Non-Hispanic Black	Foreign-born	71,358 (39.8)	107,917 (60.2)
		2 or 2.5	34,617 (40.6)	50,648 (59.4)
		Native stock	426,443 (49.8)	430,158 (50.2)
		Total	532,418 (47.5)	588,723 (52.5)
	Non-Hispanic Asian	Foreign-born	121,489 (69.6)	53,167 (30.4)
		Total	149,413 (68.4)	68,913 (31.6)
	Latino	Foreign-born	88,652 (45.7)	105,547 (54.3)
		2 or 2.5	60,742 (64.9)	32,852 (35.1)
		Native stock	332,446 (55.0)	271,554 (45.0)
		Total	481,840 (54.0)	409,953 (46.0)
Los Angeles County	Non-Hispanic White	Foreign-born	74,092 (39.0)	115,972 (61.0)
		2 or 2.5	87,968 (26.0)	250,982 (74.0)
		Native stock	601,776 (31.8)	1,290,173 (68.2)
		Total	763,836 (31.6)	1,657,127 (68.4)
	Non-Hispanic Black	Native stock	167,966 (34.5)	318,192 (65.5)
		Total	179,184 (35.3)	328,229 (64.7)
	Non-Hispanic Asian	Foreign-born	165,025 (53.2)	145,430 (46.8)
		2 or 2.5	42,657 (43.0)	56,636 (57.0)
		Native stock	33,696 (52.1)	31,009 (47.9)
		Total	241,378 (50.9)	233,075 (49.1)
	Latino	Foreign-born	123,892 (45.0)	151,389 (55.0)
		2 or 2.5	213,008 (48.6)	224,853 (51.4)
		Native stock	173,083 (61.0)	110,744 (39.0)
		Total	509,983 (51.2)	486,986 (48.8)

Source: U.S. Bureau of the Census 1996.
Notes: No/NA/DK means the respondent said no, gave no answer, or did not know whether they voted. Yes means they said they voted.
Native stock people are native-born with two native-born parents.

points between the first-generation and second-generation Latino immigrants may be compared to the 19.2-point gap in New York and a 3.6-point gap in Los Angeles. In the national sample, native Latinos (second generation and beyond) voted even less often than the first generation. Los Angeles did not deviate from this trend, but in New York, however, native Latinos (mostly Puerto Ricans) were more likely to vote than second-generation Latinos (mostly Dominicans). Los Angeles County had too few immigrant black citizens for comparison, but New York's West Indian second generation was no less likely to vote than naturalized West Indian immigrants, and indeed were apparently more likely than native blacks to vote.

As the general literature on political participation has robustly established, older, better educated, higher-income, home-owning, and female people are all more likely to vote than others. This is evident for 1996 CPS respondents as well: logistic regression shows that in order of significance, home ownership and education followed by family income and age and finally gender, have the strongest impact on voter participation. The same factors are less useful in explaining voting among naturalized citizens, but they do seem accurate for the second-generation.[9]

The strong impact of age, education, and income on increasing the voting rate suggests that as immigrant citizens and their native children age, attain higher levels of education, and earn more income, their political participation rates will rise. Because immigrants start out in relatively low positions in all of these dimensions, we can expect substantial future growth in the immigrant electorate, especially where immigrant locales succeed in providing access to the American dream.

For now, though, some questions: For whom do these immigrant citizens vote? And how do their preferences compare to those of native-born voters of similar racial and ethnic backgrounds? To answer these questions, we must turn to the exit poll conducted by the Voter News Service during the 1996 presidential election.[10] As portrayed in table 1.11, white immigrants were less likely than white natives to vote for the Democratic candidate, Bill Clinton, but black, Latino, and Asian immigrants were all more likely to vote for Clinton than their native counterparts. Immigrant blacks voted for Clinton 3.1 percentage points more often than native blacks, immigrant Hispanics 8.5 percentage points more than native Hispanics, and Asian immigrants 10.0 percentage points more than native Asians. (These shifts must be read in the context of the fact that blacks were already most likely to vote Democratic, followed by Hispanics, with Asians evenly split.)

Between California's Proposition 187 and the Republican Party's association with anti-immigrant positions on national legislation, it

Table 1.11 Presidential Vote by Race and Nativity, 1996 (Row Percentages Except for Column Percentages for Total)

		Clinton	Dole	Perot	Other	N	Percentage of Total
Native-born voters	Non-Hispanic white	43.2%	46.3%	8.5%	2.1%	2,933	79.0
	Non-Hispanic black	82.6	12.6	3.8	.9	340	9.2
	Latino	68.1	19.0	9.5	3.4	116	3.1
	Non-Hispanic Asian	42.9	57.1	—	—	14	0.4
	Non-Hispanic other	62.8	27.9	9.3	—	43	1.2
	Total	48.1	41.8	8.0	2.0	3,446	92.8
Foreign-born voters	Non-Hispanic white	32.6	61.0	6.4	—	172	4.6
	Non-Hispanic black	85.7	9.5	4.8	—	21	0.6
	Latino	76.6	23.4	—	—	47	1.3
	Non-Hispanic Asian	52.9	41.2	—	5.9	17	0.5
	Non-Hispanic other	90.0	—	10.0	—	10	0.3
	Total	47.9	46.8	4.9	.4	267	7.2

Source: Voter News Service 1996, unweighted nativity subsample (N = 3,713).
Note: N is number of respondents.

seems that national debate on immigration-related issues pushed significant numbers of nonwhite immigrants toward the Democrats in 1996. While Republicans enjoyed an advantage among white immigrants (of whom residents of the former Soviet Union form the most numerous group), this support did not come close to offsetting their disadvantage among black, Latino, and Asian immigrant voters. Although small sample sizes do not permit us to look at the 1996 exit poll for the cities of New York and Los Angeles, urban residents of the states of New York and California evidence the same patterns as the national sample.

Immigrant Voting in New York and Los Angeles

What was voter turnout from immigrant neighborhoods in New York City and Los Angeles County in 1996? For whom did the immigrants vote? What is the relationship between the various neighborhoods' immigrant concentrations and the turnout rates among eligible voters? We can address these questions through ecological analysis of voting results and demographic variables from the U.S. Census.[11] While ecological inference has certain well-known problems, most notably what Robinson (1950) called the "ecological fallacy" of mistaking which component of an area's population is actually producing the outcomes being examined, ecological analysis can nevertheless provide insights that elude sample surveys because it analyzes the entire universe of activity, allows consideration of the role of place and context, and does not rely on self-reported behavior.[12]

Though necessarily preliminary, our results suggest a marked contrast between New York and Los Angeles. The immigrant neighborhoods of Los Angeles County exhibited significantly lower registered-voter turnout rates in 1996 than did New York's, and while immigrant voters in each area generally favored the Democrats, Los Angeles showed much more uniformity in that regard. New York's immigrant voters also evidently favored Bill Clinton, but the relationship of immigrant status, neighborhood, and voting behavior was much less clear-cut. These relationships held even after controlling for such important factors as age, education, homeownership, and gender. By itself, the foreign-born percentage of a neighborhood explained more than a quarter of the variance in turnout and almost a fifth of the variance in the Democratic vote in Los Angeles County, but none of the turnout or Democratic vote in New York City.

Research by Peter Tuckel and Richard Maisel (1994) has revealed that at the turn of the last century, immigrant neighborhoods in New York City turned out to vote at high rates as a share of voting age citizens. During the 1908 election, for example, wards with the highest proportion of the white immigrants voted at higher rates than the rest of the city. (Though note, however, that Tucker and Maisel found the reverse to be true elsewhere in New York State.) Tuckel and Maisel attributed these higher rates of participation to an emerging sense of ethnic identity within immigrant communities and to the appeals made by candidates to these identities. They rejected the "immigrant apathy hypothesis," according to which immigrant areas will have low turnout because people of low socioeconomic status and recently enfranchised voters are less likely to vote.

Our small-area data suggest that while in Los Angeles living amidst large numbers of immigrants clearly dampened the turnout rate among registered voters in the 1996 presidential election, the same was not true of New York. (If anything, turnout rates among registered voters in immigrant areas were somewhat higher, all other things being equal.) Of course immigrant areas still cast fewer votes because fewer people are eligible to vote.

New York City

As the earlier discussion and data attest, New York City is home to a highly heterogeneous immigrant population. According to the 1990 Census, the countries of origin for the largest numbers of foreign-born New York residents included the Dominican Republic, Ecuador, Colombia, Peru, Jamaica and the other Afro-Caribbean nations, and the former Soviet Union, with significant populations also born in Italy and Poland, sources of the previous century's immigrants. In this section, we particularly focus on immigrant enclaves of Dominicans, Chinese, West Indians, South Americans (specifically Colombians, Ecuadorans, and Peruvians), and people from areas in the former Soviet Union in comparison to native whites, native blacks, and Puerto Ricans. These groups constitute New York's major established as well as emerging racial and ethnic groups. Their population sizes and distributions across election districts (EDs) are given in table 1.12.

In general, as table 1.13 shows, median turnout among registered voters in the most heavily immigrant election districts in New York City tends to fall below the median district for the entire city. That is to say, context counts. Eligible voters living in majority immigrant areas are evidently less likely to vote than eligible voters living in areas with fewer than 10 percent immigrants. Note, however, that the median turnout in these latter areas is also well below the citywide median. Indeed, for the presidential elections for which data was collected, the median turnout in the most native EDs was below that for the most heavily immigrant EDs.

Table 1.12   Size and Distribution of Selected Ethnic Groups, New York City, 1990

Group	Population	Minimum Percentage	Maximum Percentage	Mean Percentage
Native Black	1,702,146	0	96.7	21.7
Puerto Rican	886,817	0	100.0	12.0
West Indian	384,124	0	57.8	4.7
Haitian	78,500	0	34.7	0.9
Dominican	216,497	0	47.9	2.4
Colombian- Ecuadoran-Peruvian	129,262	0	41.4	1.7
Former Soviet Union	74,503	0	75.7	1.6
Chinese	238,268	0	98.2	3.3

Source: New York City election-district database.

New York's 1989 and 1993 mayoral races pitted David Dinkins, the city's first African American mayor, against Republican Rudolph Giuliani, and these highly racially polarized elections drew relatively high percentages of voters to the polls. By 1997, though, Giuliani, who narrowly won the 1993 election, had developed broad and solid support compared to his challenger, Manhattan borough president Ruth Messinger, whom he decisively defeated. Voters were evidently far less interested in this lopsided contest. Similarly, the 1992 contest between incumbent President George H. W. Bush and Democratic challenger Bill Clinton (and Reform Party candidate H. Ross Perot) elicited a substantial turnout in New York City, but turnout was considerably lower (as it was in the nation as a whole) for the 1996 race between Clinton and Robert Dole.

Contrary to these numbers, however, voters in the immigrant neighborhoods of New York City had differentially greater involvement in the 1996 presidential election than the 1992 election. In EDs where immigrants constituted a majority, registered voters turned out at *higher* rates than voters in any of the other categories of EDs, indeed at higher rates than in the most native areas. We may speculate that this was at least partly due to the 1996 welfare-reform act and changes in immigration legislation that New York's immigrant communities perceived to be significantly adverse to their interests. The decline in political interest from the levels shown in the 1992 presidential and 1993 mayoral elections, then, was least in immigrant districts: there was in fact hardly any falloff at all, even though median turnout dropped ten points overall.

Closer analysis shows that this sustained participation in the political process was particularly strong in nonwhite election districts. Fig-

Table 1.13   Median Turnout Among New York City Election Districts
(EDs) Classified by Foreign-Born Percentage

	EDs	1989	1993	1997	1992	1996
Under 10 percent	530	63.3	63.3	39.3	59.2	54.2
10 to 23 percent	1,855	64.5	64.5	43.8	71.6	58.2
24 to 49 percent	2,020	64.5	63.0	41.0	68.6	58.1
50 percent and over	420	61.3	57.7	36.6	64.5	63.9
Total	4,825	64.0	63.3	41.4	68.8	58.3

Source: New York City election-district database. The 1989, 1993, and 1997 elections
were for mayor, the 1992 and 1996 elections for president. Only EDs with complete
data were included.

ure 1.1, for instance, shows a clear linear relationship between rising
turnout among registered voters in 1996 and the foreign-born percentage of each ED's population in 1990. (This factor alone explains
13 percent of the variation in turnout in nonwhite EDs; every additional 10 points of immigrant population adds 2.65 points to the turnout rate.) There are two ways to think about the information presented in this figure. On the one hand, issues in the 1996 presidential
election may have motivated voters in immigrant neighborhoods
more than those in non-immigrant neighborhoods. On the other,
lower interest or other factors may have dampened turnout among
voters in native-born black and Puerto Rican neighborhoods.

Multivariate analysis sheds further light on the relatively high
turnout in immigrant election districts. Two models are presented in
table 1.14: the first includes the basic demographic characteristics
known to affect turnout: education, income, home ownership, mobility, and immigrant status. This model explains a moderate portion
of the variation in voter turnout across EDs in ways that are consistent with the general model, except for immigrant status. Education,
income, and home ownership are associated with higher levels of
turnout, population turnover with lower levels. The largest coefficient, however, applies to the percentage of foreign born.

Contrary to what might be anticipated, but consistent with Tuckel
and Maisel's (1994) analysis of the last century, districts with more
foreign-born people exhibited higher voter turnout in 1996. Model
two unpacks this coefficient: the addition of specific ethnicities (with
the excluded group that provides the implicit reference standard being native whites) takes away most of the explanatory power of the
foreign-born percentage. This model shows that voters who live
among higher concentrations of New York's largest immigrant ethnic
groups, West Indians and Dominicans, have a higher propensity to

Figure 1.1   1996 Voter Turnout for New York City Election Districts with Consistent Data in Which Whites Were Not a Majority, by 1990 Percentage of Foreign-Born Residents

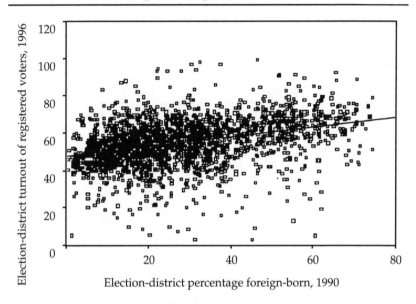

Source: New York City election-district database.

turn out than do those who live among their native counterparts, native blacks and (especially) Puerto Ricans. Those who live among immigrants from Colombia, Ecuador, and Peru have particularly high turnout rates, while those who live among the Chinese and immigrants from the former Soviet Union have lower turnout rates. In short, the immigrant-mobilization dimension of the 1996 presidential election in New York City appears to have been concentrated in black and Latino immigrant areas against a backdrop of relative demobilization among native blacks and Puerto Ricans.

When used to explain the vote for Bill Clinton in 1996, the same two models do a much better job in accounting for the variation in outcomes across election districts (table 1.15). In the first model, factors that favored turnout in table 1.14 tend to work against Clinton. In general, higher incomes and rates of home ownership are associated with lower levels of support for Clinton, while, perhaps paradoxically, higher education is positively, but not significantly, associated with the Clinton vote. In this model, the ED's percentage of foreign-born residents works against Clinton. We know, however, that ethnicity is strongly associated with partisan choice, and when we intro-

Table 1.14   Regression Models of Presidential-Election Voter Turnout, New York City, 1996 (Expressed as Percentage of Registered Voters)

	Model 1			Model 2		
	B	Sig.	Beta	B	Sig.	Beta
(Constant)	51.405	.000		56.098	.000	
Foreign born	.214	.000	.280	.094	.002	.082
College (25+ years old)	.157	.000	.240	.138	.000	.200
Income over $60K	.091	.000	.130	.061	.001	.092
Owner-occupied home	.066	.000	.151	.050	.000	.121
Not same house >85	−.182	.000	−.146	−.166	.000	−.114
Non-Hispanic native black				−.034	.000	−.110
Puerto Rican				−.130	.000	−.197
West Indian				.184	.000	.162
Haitian				.059	.445	.018
Dominican				.181	.000	.114
Colombian-Ecuadoran-Peruvian				.366	.000	.138
Chinese				−.117	.000	−.075
Former USSR				−.063	.559	.007
Adjusted R^2	.207, sig. = .000			.243, sig. = .000		

Source: New York City election-district database, N = 4,825 EDs with consistent data.

duce it in model two, the amount of variance explained leaps to .745 and the signs on various coefficients change.

In this second, more robust racial and ethnic model (where native-white residents again serve as the implicit reference group), higher levels of income still favor Republican voting, while higher levels of college education become even more strongly favorable to the Democrat. Mobility remains a relatively unimportant factor, but the level of immigrant population becomes more important and now favors Democratic voting rather than Republican voting. Race is the single most powerful factor, with voters in native-black election districts heavily favoring Clinton.

Voters in predominantly Puerto Rican, Dominican, and Haitian EDs also strongly supported Clinton. Voters in West Indian districts were not more statistically significant more favorable toward him than were native blacks, while voters in Chinese and Russian immigrant districts only slightly favored Clinton more than voters in native areas, all other things being equal.

These findings are given specific texture in Table 1.16, which presents mean turnouts and voting for Clinton by election districts that

Table 1.15   Regression Models of Presidential Vote for Bill Clinton, New York City, 1996 (Expressed as Percentage of Votes Cast for President)

	Model 1			Model 2		
	B	Sig.	Beta	B	Sig.	Beta
(Constant)	90.160	.000		59.314	.000	
Foreign born	−.101	.000	−.087	.116	.000	.101
College (25+ years old)	.092	.629	.009	.452	.000	.461
Income over $60K	−.345	.000	−.326	−.297	.000	−.283
Owner-occupied home	−.198	.000	−.297	−.026	.002	−.038
Not same house	.117	.000	.062	−.023	.156	−.012
Non-Hispanic native black				.404	.000	.693
Puerto Rican				.411	.000	.372
West Indian				.052	.171	.026
Haitian				.417	.000	.062
Dominican				.453	.000	.145
Colombian-Ecuadoran-Peruvian				.142	.005	.028
Chinese				.016	.500	.006
Former USSR				.057	.025	.017
Adjusted R^2	.324, sig. = .000			.749, sig. = .000		

Source: New York City election-district database. N = 4,825 EDs with consistent data.

Table 1.16   Mean Turnouts and Clinton 1996 Vote, by Election Districts One Standard Deviation or More Above Mean for Group Distribution

	1989	1993	1997	1992	1996	Clinton 1996	EDs
West Indian	64.9	65.1	36.3	60.5	60.3	93.4	531
Haitian	64.7	66.9	37.1	61.5	61.1	91.9	383
Native black	62.6	61.8	35.5	55.9	55.0	96.2	928
Dominican	53.0	50.3	35.9	55.6	56.1	91.4	390
Colombian-Ecuadoran-Peruvian	59.6	57.4	38.3	65.3	60.3	76.4	398
Puerto Rican	51.9	49.7	32.8	53.4	49.3	91.8	756
Chinese	63.0	61.1	41.9	68.3	57.6	70.2	451
Former Soviet Union	65.5	64.5	45.1	68.1	57.4	74.5	230
Jewish ancestries	67.2	67.3	49.5	77.1	60.5	74.1	858
Irish ancestry	68.9	70.7	50.9	75.6	60.6	57.4	605
Citywide	62.7	62.5	42.0	66.6	57.2	78.7	4825

Source: New York City election-district database. N = 4,825 EDs with consistent data.

exceed one standard deviation above the mean for the groups included in the table. In general, turnout rates were significantly lower than city average in EDs where Latino groups were concentrated and highest in EDs where the native Jewish and Irish population was concentrated, with black areas below the native whites but above the citywide mean and substantially above the Latino areas. Across the board, turnout was slightly higher in the West Indian and Haitian EDs than in the native black EDs, and higher in the Colombian-Ecuadoran-Peruvian and Dominican EDs compared to the Puerto Rican EDs. Turnout of registered voters in EDs where immigrants from the former Soviet Union and China settled were about on a par with the city-wide average. In short, voters living in the ethnic neighborhoods with growing (or "emerging") immigrant presences appear to be turning out at higher rates than voters living in comparable native-born minority concentrations. (Further analysis is needed to be certain about whether the voters actually come from immigrant ethnic backgrounds, and to take into account underlying demographic change across the 1990s, a period in which the eligible native population declined and the eligible immigrant population rose.)

Los Angeles

Table 1.17 shows the size and distribution of different immigrant and native minority groups for Los Angeles County. (As does table 1.12 for New York City, this table draws on the Census's race, Hispanic origin, and ancestry, but not country of birth, tables, except in the case of persons from the former Soviet Union.) Like New York City, Los Angeles County has a significant native black population and growing numbers of Chinese, Korean, and former Soviet immigrants. Both places have large Latino populations, but those populations are quite different: Los Angeles's Latinos are predominantly of Mexican ancestry, with growing Salvadoran and Guatemalan communities; L.A. has few of New York's Puerto Ricans, Dominicans, or West Indians. And as befits its Pacific Rim situation, Los Angeles County also has large numbers of Filipino and Vietnamese residents.

In sharp contrast to New York City, the registered voters who live in L.A. County's immigrant neighborhoods are considerably less likely to vote than those who do not live among immigrants. This is quite clear both in figure 1.2, which shows the clear linear relationship between rising rates of foreign-born population and falling turnout rates among eligible voters, and in table 1.18 (the counterpart of table 1.13 for New York), which gives turnout in the median tract stratified by the percentage of foreign born. Not only are overall median turnout rates for Los Angeles County below those for compara-

Table 1.17   Size and Distribution of Selected Ethnic Groups, Los Angeles County, 1990

		Minimum Percentage	Maximum Percentage	Mean
Chinese	232,582	0	49.8	1.5
Filipino	223,276	0	33.4	1.7
Korean	143,672	0	40.0	1.6
Vietnamese	61,391	0	12.7	0.6
Mexican	2,519,383	0	100.0	25.8
Salvadoran	253,076	0	30.2	2.2
Guatemalan	125,087	0	24.0	1.1
Iranian	51,764	0	21.4	0.8
Former Soviet Union	51,971	0	25.0	0.6
Black	946,842	0	95.0	11.1

Source: Los Angeles County tract database (N = 1,647).

Figure 1.2   1996 Voter Turnout for Los Angeles County Census Tracts, by 1990 Percentage of Foreign-Born Residents

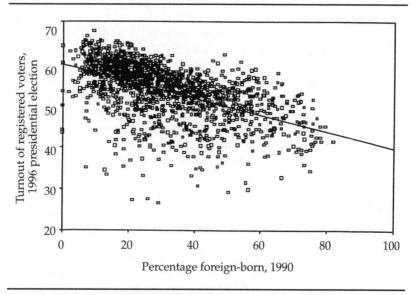

Source: Los Angeles County tract database.

Table 1.18   Median Tract Turnout by Foreign-Born Population, Los Angeles County

	1992	1994	1996
Under 13.8 percent	61.3	45.9	58.9
13.9 to 27.6 percent	56.9	42.0	57.1
27.7 to 47.5 percent	45.9	33.3	53.3
Over 47.5 percent	35.0	26.0	49.3
Total	49.7	36.5	54.6

Source: Los Angeles County tract database.

ble elections in New York City, but turnout falls sharply as the tracts become predominantly immigrant. In New York, the turnout difference between the election districts with the largest immigrant populations and the citywide median was only 4.3 points; the same figure for Los Angeles County is 14.7 points.

When multivariate regression models similar to those used for New York City are applied to the L.A. County data (see tables 1.19 and 1.20), some important differences between the two areas emerge. In particular, the percentage foreign born per Census tract in Los Angeles now appears to have a powerfully negative impact on the turnout rate among registered voters, as opposed to the positive impact shown in New York City. Moreover, model 1 in table 1.19 explains much more of the variation in L.A.'s turnout than table 1.13's model 1 did for New York. Indeed, percentage foreign-born voters in a neighborhood alone can explain more than a quarter of the variance in Los Angeles County's turnout in the 1996 presidential election. For every ten-point increase in the percentage foreign born, turnout dropped two points. Eligible voters in immigrant areas of Los Angeles County clearly vote at far lower rates than the countywide norm or in New York City.

With this exception, however, the factors in the basic model for Los Angeles County have coefficients that are similar in direction and magnitude to those in New York City: income, education, and home ownership promote turnout; population turnover tends to depress it. When the racial and ethnic categories are added (model 2 in table 1.19), these factors remain robust, though the sign changes on median household income. Indeed, percent of foreign-born tract residents becomes even more important—the overall explanatory power of this factor is increased. After controlling for all of the basic factors (income, education, home ownership, and mobility), comparison of immigrant areas to areas where the omitted group, native whites, predominate, minority tracts tend to have lower turnout rates, though

Table 1.19   Regression Models of Voter Turnout, Los Angeles County, 1996

	Model 1			Model 2		
	B	Sig.	Beta	B	Sig.	Beta
(Constant)	51.311	.000		60.025	.000	
Percentage foreign-born	−.0845	.000	−.223	−.198	.000	−.521
Percentage college	.122	.000	.310	.103	.000	.263
Median household income	.000112	.405	.033	−.000322	.025	−.064
Percentage homeowner	.0759	.000	.318	.0625	.000	.262
Percentage not same house > 85	−.0464	.000	−.080	−.0934	.000	−.161
Percentage black				−.121	.000	−.373
Percentage Mexican				−.0208	.002	−.078
Percentage Salvadoran				.103	.000	.074
Percentage Chinese				−.0375	.260	−.036
Percentage Filipino				.0210	.844	.009
Percentage Iranian				.0985	.131	.032
Percentage former Soviet Union				.225	.000	.064
	Adjusted R^2 = .498, sig. = .000			Adjusted R^2 = .609, sig. = .000		

Source: Los Angeles County tract database.

this is apparently far stronger among blacks than the Latino-immigrant areas. Indeed, controlling for all other factors, tracts with more Salvadorans have somewhat higher turnout rates. So, too, do tracts with more immigrants from the former Soviet Union.

As they do for New York City, the basic and extended regression models do a good job of explaining the variance in support for Bill Clinton across L.A. County in 1996. Also as in New York, the basic model reveals that education, income, and home ownership worked against support for the Democratic candidate. Unlike in New York, though, the foreign-born percentage in L.A. works against Clinton in the basic model—but once the other factors are entered, it turns substantially positive. In the extended model, as expected, the black percentage of a tract has a powerful relationship to that tract's tendency to support Clinton. Every additional ten percentage points of black population boosts tract support for Clinton by almost six points. Voters in Mexican American areas also gave the president strong support. Interestingly, it is possible that, controlling for the other factors,

Table 1.20 Regression Models of Democratic Vote, Los Angeles County, 1996

	Model 1			Model 2		
	B	Sig.	Beta	B	Sig.	Beta
(Constant)	101.214	.000		46.473	.000	
Percentage foreign-born	−.0177	.488	.019	.284	.000	.299
Percentage college	−.132	.000	−.134	.318	.000	.322
Median household Income	−.00230	.000	−.268	−.000109	.000	−.127
Percentage homeowner	−.198	.000	−.331	−.086	.000	−.144
Percentage not same house > 85	−.412	.000	−.282	−.137	.000	−.094
Percentage black				.583	.000	.717
Percentage Mexican				.317	.000	.476
Percentage Salvadoran				−.0052	.453	−.015
Percentage Chinese				−.187	.000	−.071
Percentage Filipino				−.136	.061	−.024
Percentage Iranian				.240	.026	.031
Percentage former Soviet Union				.212	.070	.024
	Adjusted R² = .421, sig. = .000			Adjusted R² = .794, sig. = .000		

Source: Los Angeles County tract database.

voters living among Salvadorans can be seen as less likely to support Clinton (the coefficient is not significant, but the sign was negative). Finally, whereas the predominantly Chinese election districts in New York did not lean one direction or the other, voters in the Chinese tracts in Los Angeles County leaned away from Clinton.

The trends in turnout can be observed in the concentrated cases. Los Angeles County tracts with a concentration of Mexican residents had a mean turnout of just 38.3 percent in the 1992 presidential election, eleven percentage points below the countywide average. Turnout rates among registered voters in Salvadoran and Guatemalan neighborhoods were even lower for that election. Rates in Chinese, Korean, Filipino, and Vietnamese tracts were somewhat higher, but still below the countywide average. Only in the neighborhoods where white immigrants from the former Soviet Union and Iran have chosen to settle (many of whom are Jewish) are 1992 turnout rates at or above the countywide average. Only in the neighborhoods where

Table 1.21   Mean Turnouts and Clinton 1996 Vote, by Los Angeles County Tracts One Standard Deviation Above Mean or More for Group Distribution

	1992	1994	1996	Clinton 1996	Tracts
Native black	47.2	33.4	48.1	85.6	209
Mexican	38.3	31.7	50.8	74.3	301
Salvadoran	35.8	25.4	47.0	73.5	166
Guatemalan	35.6	25.0	47.2	73.6	152
Chinese	48.1	39.2	52.8	56.5	122
Korean	46.7	36.3	52.0	55.6	120
Filipino	44.8	35.3	52.5	61.0	153
Vietnamese	43.6	34.2	51.4	61.2	150
Iranian	59.1	43.3	57.0	57.3	218
Former Soviet Union	50.5	34.1	53.8	65.7	95
Jewish ancestries	63.3	46.6	57.7	62.4	185
Irish ancestry	58.6	46.5	58.7	46.9	289
Citywide	49.5	38.2	53.7	61.7	1,643

Source: Los Angeles County tract database.

older white Jewish and Irish ancestry groups live are voter-turnout rates are well above the Los Angeles County average.

Table 1.21 suggests that just as it was for New York City, the 1996 presidential election marked something of a departure from past trends for Los Angeles County. Although 1996 turnout rates were still comparatively low in Mexican American and other Latino neighborhoods, they were much closer to the countywide average than they had been in 1992 or the 1994 gubernatorial election. Indeed, while overall average turnout rose 4.2 points between 1992 and 1994, it rose 10.0 points or more in all the Latino neighborhoods. This may likely be attributed to the dismay caused by the passage of Proposition 187 in 1994.

Conclusion

While much more work remains to be done, two conclusions may nevertheless be drawn from this analysis of immigrant voting behavior in Los Angeles County and New York City. First, immigrants face many barriers on the road to political incorporation. The process by which immigrants first become citizens and then achieve parity in the voting booth and in elected offices will be slow and uneven. Ever more immigrants are seeking to overcome the hurdle of naturalization, but there is a fair amount of evidence to show that naturalization does not lead in any simple and direct way to political mobilization. Both national and local data suggest that context counts a great deal in this regard: eligible and registered voters in immigrant neighborhoods often vote at lower rates than voters who live among citizens of older vintage, though this was not the case in New York in 1996.

Naturalization is a selective process: those who undertake it have generally lived in the United States longer, are more educated, and earn more than those who do not. These same factors are associated with the likelihood of voting. Thus, although the Current Population Survey data show that naturalized immigrants have higher raw voting rates than do their native-born racial and ethnic counterparts, they are less likely to vote once age, education, and income are also taken into account. Moreover, the case of Los Angeles County suggests that at least in some circumstances, immigrant concentration deters mobilization among eligible voters.

In the long, slow process of creating "new Americans," the second generation, not the immigrants themselves, will ultimately be decisive. Just as it was the children of turn-of-the-century immigrants, not the first generation, who made an enormous impact as they came of age during the New Deal elections of the 1930s, the children of today's immigrants will have a significant impact on political trends in New York City and Los Angeles County, not to mention many other regions, in coming decades. The preliminary predictors of what they will do offer mixed prognoses: among more advantaged white and Asian immigrants, the second-generation is voting at a higher rate than their naturalized parents; among less advantaged blacks and Hispanics, the second generation is apparently voting at lower rates, though, in the case of Latinos, at rates still above those of native-stock voters. Because the second generation is still young and relatively poor, we can expect that, all other things being equal, their rate of political participation will rise as they age and advance on the income scale. Whether this trend will actually play out as anticipated deserves, and is gradually receiving, more serious analysis.[13]

Our second conclusion is that change is under way and that the political context of New York City evidently promotes immigrant political participation—indeed, *overall* political participation—to a far greater degree than does Los Angeles County. (For additional thoughts on this comparison, see Mollenkopf 1999.) New York offers an instructive contrast to Los Angeles in this respect. It is centralized, politicized, and organized, while L.A. is decentralized, depoliticized, and fragmented, if not disorganized. New York's political system offers a framework through which different groups are forced to bargain with one another, at least when they put sufficient votes, sufficiently cohesively cast, on the table. That system has taken strong rhetorical steps to incorporate new immigrants and has provided Dominicans and West Indians with access to elected office in the city council and state legislature. With the departure of thirty-five of the city council's fifty-one members due to term limits in 2001 and the redistricting of the council in 2002, there is a substantial window of opportunity for previously excluded groups to gain political footholds.

Despite the inclination of incumbents to yield nothing without a fight, one can expect that New York City's emerging immigrant groups will struggle mightily to inscribe their pattern on the city's "gorgeous mosaic." Certainly, as the native-born black and Puerto Rican populations mature and gravitate toward the suburbs, black and Latino political leaders must look to immigrant populations to bolster their vote. To the extent that white liberals depend on an alliance with minorities, they, too, must promote naturalization, voter registration, and mobilization among the new immigrants and their children (Mollenkopf 1993b). And while the advantage is modest, the figures offered here suggest that New York's black and Latino immigrant citizens are already more likely to vote than their counterparts nationwide.

Los Angeles County offers a more troubling picture. Mexican immigrants and Mexican Americans dominate the fate of the county's immigrant world. At the moment, Mexican immigrants are less likely to become citizens than immigrants from other racial and ethnic backgrounds and less likely to vote if and when they do naturalize. Moreover, second-generation Latinos show signs of political downward mobility in Los Angeles. Mexican Americans, for instance, were the odd group out in the biracial liberal coalition that held sway under Mayor Tom Bradley in the City of Los Angeles. For while Bradley appointed many Latino commissioners, his coalition did not embrace Latinos as equal partners to blacks and liberal whites; nor did it promote Mexican American or Salvadoran representation on the city council or county board of supervisors. This pattern may continue under incoming Mayor Hahn.

With the defeat of Antonio Villaraigosa, it is not clear where Mexican American political leaders think their future lies, or what alliances they will form. It is possible that Mexican Americans will adopt a go-it-alone approach in jurisdictions where they approach a majority of voters. Should such a scenario come into being, the potential for conflict between racial and ethnic groups, and indeed among Mexican Americans, Mexican immigrants, and Salvadoran immigrants, seems quite real. Meanwhile, the far smaller Asian immigrant populations of Los Angeles County seem further behind on the road to political incorporation either as allies to the white Democratic establishment in the City of Los Angeles or as elected officials in small jurisdictions outside the city.

All of this must tempt native white politicians to try to maintain their political dominance by playing these groups off against each other. Certainly, neither the city council nor the county board of supervisors—both dominated by native whites—appears to provide a venue through which different groups can strike bargains in pursuit of their mutual gain. Particularly important, then, are the relationships that Latinos and Asians forge with each other, since they often live in overlapping patterns and thus must develop a community of interest. This poses considerable challenges to the immigrant communities of Los Angeles County. And although the same process is not going to be easy in New York City either, at least discussions about redistricting within and between new immigrant groups is taking place there.

Outside of immigrant communities proper, the polarization between Democrats and Republicans over immigration and multiculturalism may shape immigrant first- and second-generation political activity as well. Already, the Republican stand on these topics seems to have pushed many new immigrants, especially those from Latino and Afro-Caribbean backgrounds, toward the Democrats. To the extent that the Democratic Party embraces the new immigrants as a way to broaden its racial profile beyond its close association with African Americans, its national and statewide political appeals and policy stances may help to surmount local ethnic divisions. Whether it can bring itself to play the same role for the immigrant vote that it did for the civil rights movement remains to be seen, however.

Finally, if the glass of immigrant political participation is half full in New York City and somewhere shy of that in Los Angeles County, it is nonetheless inexorably filling up. In both places, there is a strong correlation between the percentage of foreign-born residents in an election district or tract in 1990 and the increase in voter registration that occurred over the decade of the 1990s.[14] Given that certain political contexts do clearly cause immigrant voters to mobilize, that the arrival of the 2000 Census results herald advent of widespread redistricting, and that first generation levels of income and education have gradually but steadily increased during the 1990s, political destiny is bound to become more closely related to immigrant demography in the decade ahead.

Research for and writing of the original version of this paper was supported by the International Center for Ethnicity, Migration, and Citizenship of the New School University in New York City. We thank Aristide Zolberg and Peter Benda for their support and criticism. Additional helpful comments were contributed by Hector Cordero-Guzman, Louis DeSipio, Peter Dreier, David Halle, Leland Saito, Rogers Smith, and Raphael Sonenshein.

Notes

1. These figures come from the March 2000 Annual Demographic Supplement of the Current Population Survey using the March final weight (which includes a Hispanic supplemental sample). Other data presented here are drawn from the November 1996 Current Population Survey, which gathered data on voter registration and voting rates among all citizens for the 1996 presidential election as well as on the racial, immigrant or native-born status, and other characteristics of the entire population. The foreign-born figure excludes a small number of people born abroad to American parents; sampling error may also occur.

2. Readers are undoubtedly familiar with the 1990s shift toward more restrictive legislation concerning immigrants, which included denial of benefits to illegal immigrants through the adoption of Proposition 209 in California in 1994, and the removal of immigrants' eligibility for federal welfare, food stamps, and disability in 1996. These measures enjoyed substantial popular support. In the exit poll for the 1996 presidential election, for instance, 49 percent of California voters wanted legal immigration decreased, 42 percent wanted to keep it the same, and 9 percent wanted an increase. In New York, 53 percent of the voters favored a decrease in immigration (authors' calculations).

3. Specifically, we drew on Summary Tape File 3 of the 1990 Census for a wide range of information including education, home ownership, median household income, type of household, racial and ethnic compositions, the foreign born by country of birth, and citizenship among the foreign born. We also used detailed ancestry data from Summary Tape File 4.

4. The state exit poll samples for 1996 did not ask about immigrant or native status, so even though the samples shed some light on the motivations of voters in New York and Los Angeles, they provide no help on the question of immigrant voters.

5. Results are derived from binary logistic regression of these factors on naturalization among voting-age foreign-born residents of New York City and Los Angeles who have lived in the U.S. for five years or longer.

6. The Immigration and Naturalization Service's Southern California office is responsible for seven counties and accounted for one-fourth the national backlog of 1.7 million citizenship applications. Staffing is being doubled in response to complaints from the area's elected officials and citizenship advocates, according to Jodi Wilgoren (Jodi Wilgoren, "INS to Add Staff for Citizenship," Los Angeles Times, March 19, 1998).

7. At the January 1998 meeting of the Republican National Committee, Southern California Republican Party officials proposed that the party send poll-watchers to check for immigrant voting and that it support legislation tightening voting procedures. (See Peter M. Warren, "GOP Leaders Present Plan to Tighten Voter Scrutiny," Los Angeles Times, Janu-

ary 18, 1998.) The House Oversight Committee considered a "Ballot Integrity Plan" that would require voters to show photo identification at the polling place. In the contested Dornan–Sanchez race, Congress upheld the Sanchez victory even though it found that 624 non-citizens had illegally cast ballots in that race, which Sanchez won by 984 votes. (See Mark A. Warren, "Republicans Want to Require Voters to Show Identification," *Los Angeles Times*, March 16, 1998; see also Jodi Wilgoren, "House Dismisses Dornan Challenge of Sanchez's Win," *Los Angeles Times*, February 13, 1998.)

8. In 1998, Mark Fritz of the *Los Angeles Times* reported that Colombia, Ecuador, the Dominican Republic, and Mexico "have allowed nationals to become citizens elsewhere without losing their original nationality" and that South Korea and India may follow suit. (See Mark Fritz, "Pledging Multiple Allegiances," *Los Angeles Times*, April 6, 1998; see also Fritz, "Dual Citizenships Create Dueling Family Allegiances," *Los Angeles Times*, January 18, 1998.)

9. Determined through binary logistic regression with voting as the dependent variable, and family income, age, and education as cardinal independent variables, and homeownership and gender as categorical independent variables.

10. These data were secured from the Voter News Service, which conducted a national poll and polls for each state. The national sample contains 16,637 respondents, but only one-fourth, or 3,828, were asked about their immigrant or native status. The table presents the weighted results of these cases.

11. A large and growing literature in political geography, and to a lesser extent political science, undertakes the ecological regression analysis of voting results. Ecological data typically violates the assumptions required for regression analysis, since conditions are rarely distributed across space in a normal fashion. Because conditions in one unit are often influenced by those in adjacent units, spatial autocorrelation is also an issue. Other methological concerns include the "modified areal unit problem," the nonsensical assumption in standard linear regression that a given population acts the same way in each unit (which is what a single regression coefficient implies), and the difficulties in drawing inferences about individual behavior from aggregate data. (For an excellent overview of the current state of this literature, go to *www.colorado.edu/IBS/PEC/spatialconf.html* to see the papers presented at "New Methodologies for the Social Sciences: The Development and Application of Spatial Analysis for Political Methodology," a conference organized by John O'Laughlin and Michael Ward and held at the University of Colorado at Boulder, March 10–12, 2000.) Despite these concerns, most studies still rely on multivariate linear regression, and we adopt this approach knowing that it has shortcomings and more refined analysis is needed. Because our data sets contain large numbers of small units not drawn with the dependent variable in mind, which also vary

widely on almost all the dimensions being examined, these methodological problems should be minimized.

12. King (1997) recently proposed a method for overcoming some of the technical problems in ecological analysis, which suggests possibilities for future analysis. The major drawback to using his method for the purposes of this chapter is that it does not easily allow for multivariate analysis.

13. Political participation among immigrants' children is a focal topic for the Immigrant Second Generation Study being undertaken by Mollenkopf and his colleagues Philip Kasinitz and Mary Waters.

14. The regression coefficient of tract percentage foreign-born residents on percent change in registration between 1992 and 1998 is .544 with an adjusted R^2 of .188 in Los Angeles County, meaning that every 10-percentage-point increase in foreign born is associated with a 5.44 percent growth in registration over this period. In New York, the foreign-born percentage explains less of the variance of overall change, with an adjusted R^2 of only .042, but the coefficient is .414, suggesting that every 10-percentage-point increase in the foreign born is associated with a 4.14 percent growth in registration between 1990 and 1999.

References

Clark, William A.V. 1996. "Residential Patterns: Avoidance, Assimilation, and Succession." In *Ethnic Los Angeles*, edited by Roger Waldinger and Mehdi Bozorgmehr. New York: Russell Sage Foundation.

DeSipio, Louis. 1996. *Counting the Latino Vote: Latinos as a New Electorate*. Charlottesville: University of Virginia Press.

———. 1997a. "Building America, One Person at a Time: Naturalization and Political Behavior of the Naturalized in Contemporary U.S. Politics." Paper presented to the Social Science Research Council, Conference on Immigrants, Civic Culture, and Modes of Political Incorporation. Santa Fe, N.M. (May 16 and 17, 1997).

———. 1997b. "The Dynamo of Urban Growth: Immigration, Naturalization, and the Reshaping of Urban Politics." Paper presented at the Annual Meeting of the American Political Science Association. Washington (August 28, 1997).

Espiritu, Yen Le. 1992. *Asian American Panethnicity*. Philadelphia: Temple University Press.

Falcon, Angelo. 1988. "Black and Latino Politics in New York City: Race and Ethnicity in a Changing Context." In *Latinos and the Political System*, edited by F. C. Garcia. South Bend, Ind.: University of Notre Dame Press.

Fletcher, Michael A. 1998. "In Rapidly Changing L.A., a Sense of Future Conflicts." *Washington Post*, April 7, 1998, p. A1.

Gutierrez, David. 1997. *Walls and Mirrors: Mexican Americans, Mexican Immigrants, and the Politics of Ethnicity*. Berkeley: University of California Press.

Johnson, James H., Jr., Walter C. Farrell Jr., and Chandra Guinn. 1999. "Immigration Reform and the Browning of America: Tensions, Conflicts, and Community Instability in Metropolitan Los Angeles." In *The Handbook of International Migration: The American Experience*, edited by Charles Hirschman, Philip Kasinitz, and Josh DeWind. New York: Russell Sage Foundation.

Jones-Correa, Michael. 1998. *Between Two Nations: Immigrants, Citizenship, and Politics in New York City*. Ithaca, N.Y.: Cornell University Press.

King, Gary. 1997. *A Solution to the Ecological Inference Problem*. Princeton, N.J.: Princeton University Press.

Los Angeles County Database. File of Census and Voting Characteristics. Compiled by authors.

Massey, Douglas. 1999. "Why Does Immigration Occur? A Theoretical Synthesis." In *The Handbook of International Migration: The American Experience*, edited by Charles Hirschman, Philip Kasinitz, and Josh DeWind. New York: Russell Sage Foundation.

Massey, Douglas, Joaquin Arango, Graeme Hugo, Ali Kouaouci, Adela Pellegrino, and J. Edward Taylor. 1993. "Theories of International Migration: A Review and Appraisal." *Population and Development Review* 19: 431–66.

———. 1994. "An Evaluation of International Migration Theory: The North American Case." *Population and Development Review* 20: 699–752.

Massey, Douglas, and Kristin Espinosa. 1996. "What's Driving Mexico–U.S. Migration? A Theoretical, Empirical, and Policy Analysis." Paper presented to the Social Science Research Council, Conference on "Becoming American/America Becoming." Sanibel Island, Fla. (January 18–21, 1996).

Mollenkopf, John. 1993a. *New York in the 1980s: A Social, Economic, and Political Atlas*. New York: Simon & Schuster Academic Reference.

———. 1993b. *A Phoenix in the Ashes: The Rise and Fall of the Koch Coalition in New York City Politics*. Princeton, N.J.: Princeton University Press.

———. 1999. "Urban Political Conflicts and Alliances: New York and Los Angeles Compared." In *The Handbook of International Migration: The American Experience*, edited by Charles Hirschman, Philip Kasinitz, and Josh DeWind. New York: Russell Sage Foundation.

New York City Election District Database. File of Census and Voting Characteristics. Compiled by authors.

Olson, David, and Melissa Levitt. 1996. "Immigration and Political Incorporation: But Do They Vote?" Paper presented at the Annual Meeting of the Northeast Political Science Association. Boston, Mass. (November 14–16, 1996).

Pachon, Harry, and Louis DeSipio. 1994. *New Americans by Choice: Political Perspectives on Latino Immigrants*. Boulder, Colo.: Westview Press.

Ramakrishnan, S. Karthick. 2000. "Generation Gaps: Race, Immigrant Incorporation, and Voting Participation." Paper presented at the Annual Meeting of the American Political Science Association, Washington, D.C.

Regalado, James. 1988. "Latino Representation in Los Angeles." In *Latino Empowerment: Progress, Problems, and Prospects*, edited by Roberto E. Villareal, Norma G. Hernandez, and Howard D. Neighbor. New York: Greenwood Press.

Robinson, William S. 1950. "Ecological Correlation and the Behavior of Individuals." *American Sociological Review* 15: 351–57.

Saito, Leland T. 1998. *Race and Politics: Asian Americans, Latinos, and Whites in a Los Angeles Suburb.* Champaign-Urbana: University of Illinois Press.

Saito, Leland T., and John Horton. 1994. "The New Chinese Immigration and the Rise of Asian American Politics in Monterey Park." In *The New Asian Immigration in Los Angeles and Global Restructuring,* edited by Paul Ong, Edna Bonacich, and Lucie Cheng. Philadelphia: Temple University Press.

Shefter, Martin. 1984. "Political Parties, Political Mobilization, and Political Demobilization." In *The Political Economy,* edited by Thomas Ferguson and Joel Rogers. Armonk, N.Y.: M. E. Sharpe.

Singer, Audrey, and Greta Gilbertson. 2000. "Naturalization in the Wake of Anti-Immigrant Legislation: Dominicans in New York City." International Migration Policy Program working paper 10. Washington, D.C.: Carnegie Endowment for International Relations.

Skerry, Peter. 1993. *Mexican Americans: The Ambivalent Minority.* New York: Free Press.

Sonenshein, Raphael. 1993. *Politics in Black and White: Race and Power in Los Angeles.* Princeton, N.J.: Princeton University Press.

———. 1997. "Post-Incorporation Politics in Los Angeles." In *Racial Politics in American Cities,* edited by Rufus Browning, Dale Marshall, and David Tabb. New York: Longman.

Tuckel, Peter, and Richard Maisel. 1994. "Voter Turnout Among European Immigrants to the United States." *Journal of Interdisciplinary History* 24(3): 3407–30.

U.S. Bureau of the Census. 1996. *November 1996 Current Population Survey.* Public Use Microdata File. Washington: U.S. Government Printing Office.

———. 1997. *March 1997 Current Population Survey.* Public Use Microdata File. Washington: U.S. Government Printing Office.

———. 2000. *March 2000 Current Population Survey.* Public Use Microdata File. Washington: U.S. Government Printing Office.

Verba, Sidney. 1995. "The Citizen as Respondent: Sample Surveys and American Democracy." *American Political Science Review* 90(1): 1–7.

Voter News Service. 1996. National Presidential Election Exit Survey.

Waldinger, Roger, and Mehdi Bozorgmehr, editors. 1996. *Ethnic Los Angeles.* New York: Russell Sage Foundation.

Waters, Mary. 1999. *Black Identities: West Indian Immigrant Dreams and American Realities.* Cambridge, Mass.: Harvard University Press.

Waters, Mary, Philip Kasinitz, and John Mollenkopf. 1998. "Transnationalism and the Children of Immigrants in the Contemporary United States: What Are the Issues?" Paper presented to the Rockefeller Center for Latin American Studies, Conference on Transnationalism and the Second Generation. Cambridge, Mass. (April 3, 1998).

Chapter 2

Ethnic Subcontracting as an Impediment to Interethnic Coalitions: The Chinese Experience

PETER KWONG

THROUGHOUT American history, American businesses have recruited wave after wave of immigrants during times of economic expansion, both to address perceived labor shortages and to undermine upward pressures on wages. Immigrants generally encountered low wages, poor working conditions, and hostility from other workers, who saw them as economic competitors. In the case of the Chinese, this hostility from Americans assumed a racial dimension as well, and was therefore much more intense than that encountered by most other immigrants. Chinese immigrants were perceived as unassimilable "aliens." In the late nineteenth century, this perception prompted white workers not only to call for the permanent exclusion of the Chinese from the American labor market but to prohibit them from immigrating to America altogether. Even today, contemporary images of Chinese immigrant workers are still negative: they are seen as passive, cliquish, and unwilling to work with others. Their isolation from other workers, and their absence from multi-ethnic coalitions, however, may stem not from their own desires. Rather, the very manner in which the group is being incorporated into the American labor market—namely, as a separate entity—creates structural impediments to crossethnic alliances. In this chapter, I discuss the problems Chinese immigrants have confronted in becoming part of the American working class and in their attempts to form interethnic coalitions with other groups.

Historical Background

Chinese first came to this country during the middle of the nineteenth century, just about the same time as did the so-called old immigrants such as the Irish and Germans. Unlike the cases of the Irish and Germans, however, the structured segregation of the Chinese under the subcontracting system—in which employers contracted a middleman to handle the problems of recruitment, management, and payment of the workers—was so powerful that even though the Chinese too fought for better working conditions and tried to reach out to establish class alliances, they were unable to gain the sympathy of white workers. Unlike European immigrants, the Chinese never had the chance to be assimilated. For one thing, they could not become U.S. citizens according to the Nationality Act of 1790 because they were not "free white persons." And when the 1882 Chinese Exclusion Act was passed, it specifically barred Chinese from becoming naturalized.

American labor was among the most forceful lobbies for the legal prohibition of Chinese immigration. Then, after the 1882 Exclusion Act took effect, anti-Chinese forces turned their attention to those Chinese still in the country and unleashed an "abatement" campaign to drive them from the mines, ships, and lumber camps by force. Already in the 1870s, western miners had been rioting and striking, ostensibly for higher wages and shorter hours, but more specifically for the discharge of the Chinese, who generally received half the pay of white workers and often accepted more arduous work.

Chinese immigrants, then, were muscled out of the American labor market because white workers objected to working alongside them, could not get working-class jobs and were forced into self-employment, mainly in the restaurant and laundry trades. They were also driven into isolated ghettos, where they fell under the control of Chinese contractors and merchants. Thus, the Chinese were neither part of the American working class nor part of the American workers' struggle—and therefore in no position to benefit from the gains made by the American labor movement of the 1930s.

The conditions of Chinese in the United States did not improve until the 1960s. First, there was the civil rights movement, which outlawed overt racial discrimination and significantly increased their chances of upward mobility. Then, the 1965 Immigration Act set equal legal immigration quotas for all countries and thus opened the door for a rapid increase in Asian immigration. After its passage, many relatives of Chinese Americans arrived to join their families in the U.S. The population of Chinatowns across the nation surged, and more concentrations of Chinese developed in other areas as well.

Before the 1960s, Chinatowns were home to no industry, and Chinese immigrants were barred from seeking industrial jobs outside the enclave. Since then, due to the decentralization of American industry, the situation has been reversed—manufacturing and service jobs have entered ethnic communities as employers seek to tap their cheap labor potential. In New York City, for instance, the majority of the Chinese in Chinatown today are no longer self-employed small-business owners. They are instead truly working class, employed by others. Chinatown has, in effect, been transformed from a small-business ghetto into a working-class neighborhood and manufacturing center.

Yet while the new Chinese immigrants often work in manufacturing and are therefore ostensibly part of the American working class, they are still isolated. Many Chinese are laboring under Chinese contractors within Chinese enclaves dominated economically and politically by Chinese labor contractors. Within their isolated enclaves, Chinese immigrants typically work under conditions well below minimum American labor standards. And unlike other immigrant workers, few Chinese are employed in open and competitive labor markets. Chinese as well as other immigrants generally have to cope with low wages, long hours, undesirable and dangerous jobs, and contend with employers who try to use the fear of deportation to make them work harder (Mahler 1995), but other immigrants' predicaments rarely match that of Chinese due to the degree of control that Chinese employers exercise over Chinese workers within Chinese enclaves, beyond the scrutiny of American society.

The Ethnic Enclave

Urban ethnic neighborhoods are not new. At the turn of the last century, they served as transitional communities where newly arrived European immigrants adjusted to their new environment. Once these immigrants learned English and found jobs in the general labor market, they moved on, eventually integrating into American society. From the beginning, however, Chinatowns were different. Housing restrictions required the Chinese to live in segregated neighborhoods; this segregation was further maintained by the exclusion of Chinese workers from jobs in the larger American labor market, because for almost a century, whites refused to work alongside the Chinese. When the new wave of immigrants from Asia and Latin America began to arrive after the passage of the new immigration law in 1965, ethnic immigrant concentrations began to emerge again and old ones expanded. However, because the Civil Rights Act of 1965 outlawed racial exclusion in housing, the Chinatowns across the nation no longer owed their existence to legal sanctions. One could therefore expect that Chinatowns would finally play the role of transitional neighborhoods, like the old European-immigrant ghettos had.

However, many of these new non-white ethnic immigrant districts, like the Cuban community in Miami and Chinatowns across the country, have developed viable economic structures that can provide new immigrants with jobs within the community and relieve them of the need to ever learn English or move into the larger society in search of livelihood. These new ethnic communities, then, have become much more enduring and stable than the European immigrant ghettos of the past.

These "ethnic enclaves" (as they are referred to by sociologists) and their emergence has coincided with the restructuring of the American economy. Previously, large corporations had located their production in large urban manufacturing centers; in recent decades they have moved to decentralized operation sites where labor costs are low and the labor force unorganized. American garment manufacturers in New York City, for instance, have sent most of their work to Third World countries—though an important part of their operations is farmed out domestically to immigrants living in communities like Chinatown.

Until 1965, New York City's Chinatown was largely a bachelor society whose residents engaged in meager self-employed trades. Then, the families and wives of residents, taking advantage of liberalized immigration policies, began to arrive under the "family unification" provision of the new law. This influx added a substantial number of ready and willing women to the labor force, which the garment industry quickly took advantage of by subcontracting work to Chinatown garment-factory operators. For the garment industry, the Chinese situation was ideal: not only had the industry solved the problem of low-wage labor, but garment manufacturers could also leave factory management to Chinese contractors, who handled language differences, worked out wage scales, and even dealt with union issues. By the early 1980s, there were already four hundred garment factories in Chinatown employing roughly twenty thousand workers.

The rise of the garment industry in New York's immigrant-Chinese community stimulated the growth of Chinese restaurants and other services, leading to a local economic boom and providing new job opportunities, which in turn attracted more Chinese immigrant workers and more Hong Kong investment. Chinatown's economy, with the additional labor and capital, expanded both vertically and horizontally, adding more restaurants and service businesses while also diversifying into wholesale food distribution, restaurant equipment, and the construction trades. This rapid growth also spawned new satellite Chinese communities in the city's other boroughs and lured bilingual professionals to service the new immigrant residents. By the early 1980s, Chinese ethnic enclaves in New York and elsewhere had become thriving, predominantly working-class economic entities inhabited primarily by non-English-speaking immigrants.

The original Chinatown in Lower Manhattan and the newer enclave in Brooklyn's Sunset Park (established since the late 1980s) have proven to be very attractive destinations for arriving immigrants. Immigrants arriving in the United States are able to find plenty of jobs in these ethnic enclaves without ever having to learn English. Chinese employers, for their part, can count on the services of this cheap labor supply, because these immigrant workers without English and professional skills have problems finding jobs in the broader low-wage labor markets outside of Chinatown. This is all good for employment in these areas; indeed, one study has shown that immigrants in Chinatown-type enclaves like those in New York, San Francisco, and Los Angeles have significantly lower unemployment rates than immigrants participating in the low-end, competitive, unskilled labor pool usually referred to as in the "secondary labor market" (Ong 1984). In this respect, the new immigrant ethnic enclaves differ from present-day African American ghettos, which are characterized by their lack of capital resources and a high degree of unemployment. African American ghetto residents usually have no choice but to find jobs outside their communities in the low-wage secondary labor market.

The new immigrant ethnic enclaves comprise both ethnic entrepreneurs and ethnic immigrant workers, which perhaps benefits both parties. Alejandro Portes and Robert Bach, authors of *Latin Journey: Cuban and Mexican Immigrants in the United States*, argue that the ethnic-enclave economy established by Cuban refugees in Miami allows a significant portion of Cubans to escape the "dead-end jobs" of the secondary labor market. Furthermore, these two authors assert that working in the enclave offers better pay, more promotional opportunities for promotion, and a greater possibility of self-employment than working in the secondary labor market (Portes and Bach 1985, 351). In the same vein, University of California at Los Angeles sociologist Min Zhou has come to believe that the Chinese ethnic networks within New York's Chinatown facilitate new immigrants' social mobility and eventually lead immigrants into the American mainstream without forcing them to lose their ethnic identity and solidarity (Zhou 1992). To these scholars, ethnic enclaves represent a real alternative to traditional American social mobility, which nearly always ends in complete assimilation.

However, in his study of Chinatowns in San Francisco, New York and Los Angeles, Paul Ong of UCLA (1984) points out that focusing only on the lower unemployment rates in these enclaves, which many want to use to symbolize the Chinese system of mutual-help and ethnic solidarity, ignores the fact that these workers' chances of being laid off in Chinatown are much higher than those of workers in the secondary labor market. Restaurant, garment, or construction jobs within the enclaves are subject to cyclical and seasonal fluctuations. Moreover, there is no indication that Chinese employers, because of ethnic sentiment, retain workers when there is a slowdown. And yet, according to Ong, despite the low wages, job instability, and limited returns, Chinese workers do not become "discouraged workers" who drop out of the labor market entirely. Because of the lack of English skills, to survive, they have no choice but to stay in the labor market until other jobs become available—and staying in the labor market usually means having to accept ever-lower wages.

While it is initially easy for a new Chinese immigrant to settle into a Chinatown enclave, it may not be the best option in the long run. This is so because once settled there, new immigrants are not likely to learn English, there being no need for it in their daily activities and social interactions in the enclave. This is not to say that immigrants lack desire to learn the language: several different versions of "English made easy" audiocassette tapes and bilingual microcomputers are available in Chinese bookstores, and thousands of Chinese immigrants attend dozens of weekly English-language classes offered by nonprofit groups such as unions, churches, and social-service organizations. But spending two hours in a language class on Sunday, without a chance to converse and practice until class a week later, or sitting alone with a tape, produces meager results.

Thus it is common to meet Chinatown residents who, despite having lived in the United States for upwards of twenty-five years, are unable to communicate in simple English. Because there are few jobs for non-English-speakers outside the enclave, breaking out of the ethnic immigrant community is usually not an option. So, immigrants remain trapped and vulnerable to the power of Chinese employers. The very existence of ethnic enclaves like Chinatown actually inhibits new immigrants' attempts to seek other options. Additionally, the choices for illegal immigrants from Fuzhou, say—where most illegal Chinese immigrants are from—outside of the Chinese environment is even more limited. This, however, accords with employers' interests by keeping new immigrants' employment opportunities tied to the

Chinese enclave. Chinese employers, in fact, promote an ideology of ethnic solidarity to reinforce immigrants' dependency on the ethnic enclave.

We Are All Chinese

From the moment of their arrival, Chinese immigrants, legal and otherwise, rely on ethnic networks to survive. The newcomers turn to their relatives or friends to get them jobs; on the job, they depend on their contacts to teach them how to do the work. With most immigrants working twelve or so hours a day, no one else *but* a close friend or relative would take the time to teach a newcomer how to sew, set tables, or drive nails. And though at times mistake prone and time consuming, this process also benefits employers, who use informal ethnic and kinship networks to screen out undesirable applicants and to train their workers at no cost to themselves.

Finding jobs through their friends' recommendations immediately forces newcomers into a system of social obligations. The friend performs a ren-qing (personal favor) by means of guanxi (connections) to get the newcomer a job. The newcomer, especially if he or she is illegal, then owes a ren-qing to the employer for giving him a job that could have gone to any one of a number of applicants. Moreover, the employer is credited for his good-heartedness in wanting to help a fellow Chinese and a fellow villager, and, as the case may be, by taking the risk of hiring an illegal. The newcomer is expected to return these favors when he is in the position to do so—to begin with, by being a compliant, diligent worker. Respectful and loyal behavior also ensures special consideration when it comes to individual job assignment, workload, wages, and benefits. Thus, traditional Chinese regard for ren-qing transforms a typical labor-capital class relationship into an association based on personal favor and obligation.

Employers in the garment industry certainly play up the ethnic factor to inspire worker loyalty. One tactic is to try to create a work environment that is culturally familiar by disregarding rigid American rules. Mothers, for instance, are allowed to leave work at four in the afternoon to pick up their children at school and bring them back to the factory. Then, if the family is in financial distress—which all debt-paying illegals are, usually owing a huge amount to the smugglers—the owners "help out" by hiring their children or allowing them to take consignments home, even though such practices violate U.S. labor laws. Furthermore, lonely old ladies with nothing to do are allowed to work as thread cutters on completed garments, and older men are paid a few dollars to wash dishes so they feel useful and have others to gossip with during the day.

The rules on the shop floor are also casual. Working on a per-piece rate, seamstresses are paid by the work completed. In order to make money, they must act as their own disciplinarians. If workers do not want to have the legally mandated half-hour lunch break, they can eat right at the machines. To encourage this, factory owners usually set up a makeshift kitchen on the shop floor where the workers can heat their lunch boxes, and they also provide a pot of hot rice for everyone, free. In addition, almost all work places, including restaurants, reserve a small corner for a shrine and make sure that it is regularly attended with fresh fruit and burning incense. On the Chinese Lunar New Year, workers get two days off—their longest holiday of the year. But even then they are expected to show up on the second day of the New Year at least for part of the day, to wish the employers happy New Year and to receive a red envelope with a small bonus—five dollars, usually. Then the workers set off firecrackers and place tangerines on the sewing machines and at all strategic locations to ward off bad spirits and thereby ensure that will always have work and not get injured on the job. During the Moon Festival, every employee is given a couple of moon cakes to take home.

Employees in the garment trade and others like it consider cash payment a major benefit. It saves them from paying taxes and the impossible task of filing for returns if they are legal; illegals, of course, try to avoid all government scrutiny. Here again, employers are quite flexible. They are willing to "cook the books" for those who work in union shops and need to show a minimum income of $7,000 a year to be eligible for a union's Blue Cross Blue Shield health insurance benefits, or for those interested in receiving public assistance, such as food stamps, Medicaid, public housing, or even welfare, which requires them to have a total family income below the poverty line. Factory owners can even be accommodating enough to "sell" signed checks (at a percentage cost) for that purpose. In this manner both labor and capital cooperate to participate in Chinatown's underground economy.

Cash payments, however, also increase the leverage that employers wield over their employees. If a legal immigrant wants to apply for a family member to come to this country, he or she has to show that employment is available upon the relative's arrival and that the person applying has a certain stable and dependable annual income. In order to fulfill both requirements, the applicant must turn to his or her employer to notarize a document stating that he or she, the employer, will provide the newcomer with a job, and another stating that the applicant's annual income is above the minimum required. Then the sponsor must work out a tax arrangement with the employer to avoid problems with the IRS. Illegals who want to help relatives come to the United States legally are even more dependent on the good graces of their employers.

Why would an employer provide such services? First, because paying employees in cash means a lower tax liability for the employer. Second, by reporting such low wages for his employees, the employer can claim that most of his workers are part-time, thus relieving him of his responsibility to make workers' compensation and other insurance payments that are the normal obligations of American employers. And above all, employers who pay workers in cash also get a 5 to 7 percent kickback from the employees' total gross income, and even more from the illegals, ostensibly for the purpose of paying taxes. If these illegal immigrants are not satisfied, they can always look for another job—although wherever they turn in Chinatown, they would most likely be confronted with the same practice.

To preempt hostility over such practices, employers appeal to the new immigrants' aspirations to ownership. They portray themselves as new immigrants as well—they too were workers once, and they had to work hard to arrive where they are now. They stress that "we are all Chinese," desiring the same goals of ownership and prosperity. Meanwhile, immigrant employees are lectured regularly to save every cent they make and avoid wasting money on smoking, drinking, gambling, and philandering.

Through this indoctrination, newcomers are made to think that working hard for someone else is just the starting point: being a good worker teaches them the discipline and endurance that are necessary for entrepreneurship. Immigrant workers are told they should focus solely on their work and not be distracted, for America is a very different country from China—there are a lot of bad people here. If one is du-si (nosy), one gets into trouble. Moreover, newcomers are warned not to trust anyone—even when someone offers you a bundle of money, don't accept it, because it may be drug money being offered to get you arrested. If someone falls on the street, keep walking, for if you help and things take a bad turn, the Americans will turn around and sue you. Most of all, do not get involved in any form of politics, for the consequences could be worse than they would be in China. As these examples show, the advice handed out by employers does nothing to encourage immigrant contact with the broader society around them.

You Can't Trust the "Foreigners"

Even immigrants who are unhappy working for Chinese employers in Chinatown have a difficult time imagining working for "Americans," with whom they are unable to communicate on even the most basic matters. The language problem breeds an overwhelming sense of isolation and vulnerability. New York's garment workers, for example, resign themselves to working for a few pennies less per hour in Chinatown just so that they do not have to contemplate the scary prospect of traveling on subways to "strange places" and working for "strange people." For this very reason, the Chinese enclave along Eighth Avenue in Sunset Park, Brooklyn, boomed only after regular privately run Chinese minibus service to and from Manhattan's Chinatown became available. For $1.25, one can be picked up anywhere between Fortieth and Seventieth Streets along Brooklyn's Eighth Avenue and be dropped off on virtually any street corner in Manhattan's Chinatown. Consequently, many Chinese immigrants in New York don't even have basic public contact with "Americans"—let alone any clear understanding of American society. Ah Chong, an illegal alien from Fuzhou who had been in New York more than three years, confided that she had yet to befriend an "American," to visit a movie theater, or to travel anywhere outside of Brooklyn, where she lives and works—not even to the Empire State Building, Rockefeller Center, or the Statue of Liberty. Her isolation is such that in conversations she refers to native-born Americans as lao wai—"foreigners."

Because of this isolation, Chinese employers are able to impart to their workers the image of a hostile and racist American society, which further enhances a sense of ethnic solidarity. New immigrants are told that Americans are prejudiced and look down on the Chinese, an idea that is not too difficult for them to accept, considering the long history of Western imperialism in China. Chinese employers explain that lo fan (barbarian) manufacturers offer the Chinese contractors such low prices for their contracts that nobody can make a living from them. Again, considering the way that many American manufacturers have been squeezing small suppliers, this putative discrimination seems credible. Thus, Chinese contractors blame "American" manufacturers as the source of all their problems, including why they cannot pay the workers decent wages, why they operate in dilapidated buildings, why they don't have the money to replace the old and dangerous machines, and why there is no proper ventilation or fire protection in the factories.

Chinese workers are instructed not to fight Chinese owners, but instead to appreciate that they are all victims of an unjust, racist system. Yet while they depict themselves as the victims, the contractors don't propose fighting the manufacturers: the racist system is stacked against them anyway. Their solution for their employees is to work harder to overcome all obstacles and show that Chinese immigrants can make it no matter what, consciously promoting and exploiting the racial stereotype that Chinese, and particularly the Fuzhounese, are capable of unremitting toil, unlike blacks or even whites, who are soft and enjoy too much of the good life.

This sense of a hostile external environment is further strengthened by employers' efforts to portray all outside intervening forces as harmful to Chinese interests. They depict trade unions, for example, as alien organizations interested only in collecting dues and indifferently protecting workers' rights. Unfortunately, this cynical view of union efforts often seems to be confirmed by workers' experiences. For example, almost 90 percent of the seamstresses working in lower Manhattan's Chinatown are members of Local 23-25 of the Union of Needletrades, Industrial and Textile Employees (UNITE), previously the International Ladies' Garment Workers Union (ILGWU). As union members, their negotiated legal union minimum wage is supposed to be between $6.00 and $9.45 per hour, depending on job title. However, despite their employees' union membership, contractors take advantage of variations in clothing design to quote piece rates arbitrarily, so that they can vary even from one person to another working on the same consignment. Thanks to such sleight of hand, average hourly rates for Chinese garment workers rarely approach the federal minimum wage, let alone the union minimum.

Chinese workers' opinions of unions are colored by a legacy of the early 1980s as well. At that time, Chinese workers were regularly challenging management and succeeding in forcing employers to honor their piece rates according to the actual work involved. The workers even staged sit-down strikes until prices and wages were adjusted. Since the mid-1980s, however, the fear of driving subcontractors into closing their shops—and thereby eliminating jobs— has made the garment workers' union reluctant to side with labor in further similar disputes. Hence, workers have given up on such challenges, resigning themselves to the fact that a union contract is one thing, union wages another. In fact, a 1992 internal survey conducted by the ILGWU's Sunset Park Garment Worker's Center revealed that nonunion workers were better paid in some cases than ILGWU members. The average gross nonunion hourly wage in 1992 was $4.97, while the average union hourly wage was $3.73—at a time when the federal minimum was $4.25 (Weisman 1997, 52–53). Both illegal and legal workers who are interested in making more money and are not afraid of health problems simply work in nonunion shops.

When addressing the subject of the government with their workers, factory management seldom hesitates to play up race. They make the argument to their workers that Chinese, being a minority group in the United States, have great disadvantages in competing with mainstream American businesses. That's why, they say, Chinese subcontractors have to ignore American laws: if they followed all of the rules, they would not survive. Chinese workers are told that American labor enforcement is nothing but a white racist plot to destroy Chinese small businesses and to take jobs away from Chinese workers.

A highly publicized incident from 1996 illustrates just how convincing these arguments can be to isolated immigrant workers—even when the government's intention is quite the opposite. In August 1996, soon after the intense media coverage of the scandal surrounding television personality Kathie Lee Gifford's (unknowing) endorsement of a line of sweatshop-produced Wal-Mart clothing, Brooklyn district attorney Charles Hynes, in coordination with the New York State Departments of Labor and Finance and the New York City Fire Department, conducted raids on Chinese sweatshops in Sunset Park. Dozens of officers, wearing bulletproof vests and armed with semi-automatic weapons, smashed into the sweatshops, ordering everyone to freeze, place their hands on the table, and keep silent. Meanwhile, government agents broke into employers' offices, turning over files and searching for incriminating documents. Several owners were arrested and handcuffed on charges of violating minimum-wage laws, flouting the tax code, and breaking factory-safety and fire regulations. Workers were permitted to leave the factories only after they were questioned, photographed, and had their files reviewed.

The Hynes action was meant to enforce labor standards, but the high-handedness of the operation terrorized and baffled Chinese workers. One illegal worker stated in written testimony that the police never explained that the raids were meant to protect the workers' interests by arresting employers who were violating the law. None of the workers saw the raid in that light. The D.A.'s sudden interest in sweatshops, which had existed for years in Brooklyn, gave credence to accusations that the raids were politically motivated—and exacerbated the mistrust that the employers had labored to instill in their workers.

The Chinese factory owners responded to the raids with defiance. While none contested government charges that they had violated the minimum-wage standards and had operated their businesses under sweatshop conditions, they accused the D.A.'s office of racism for targeting only Chinese establishments. After the raids, several employers claimed that they were on the verge of closing down and could no longer pay their workers on time. They also spread the rumor that the real reason for the raids was to obtain information that would help them arrest illegals. A week after the raids, factory owners organized their own offensive in the form of a demonstration by 1,500 Chinese workers who marched down Eighth Avenue, in the heart of Brooklyn's Chinatown, in order "to keep their jobs." The aim was to show the D.A.'s office that all Chinese, regardless of class, objected to police raids. The workers had banners at the rally that read "GARMENT FACTORY IS THE HEART OF CHINATOWN'S ECONOMY," "CLOSING OF FACTORIES WILL LEAD TO WORKERS' UNEMPLOYMENT," "AGAINST ARBITRARY ARREST," and "WE NEED OUR JOBS."

With these tactics, the owners seemed to cleverly turn the clumsy handling of the raids into an opportunity to rally workers to their side. They closed their factories for a couple of hours that day and paid the workers three dollars each to show up at the march. They orchestrated the whole event and even led the chants. The workers, for their part, had no choice—many were afraid of being fired if they did not participate. Unfortunately, uninformed outsiders, unaware of such details, were led to believe that Chinese workers really did not mind working under sweatshop conditions and that the rally was a manifestation of Chinese ethnic solidarity.

The Employers' Organizational Power

In addition to successfully drawing a veritable color line that keeps their workers from all external contacts, Chinatown employers also dominate all social organizations within the Chinese community. When Chinese in the United States were forced into segregated communities in the 1880s, the political structure that emerged as the self-policing force of these communities was transplanted from the rural regions of China, where most of the immigrants hailed from. In fact, it closely followed the pattern of unofficial local civic organization that developed during the Q'ing dynasty (1644 to 1912). Because American Chinese communities remained in relative isolation until the 1960s, this imported structure had a long time to evolve and establish itself. It is still operative today, despite the profound external changes of recent years.

The basic unit of this traditional rural structure was the clan. Early Chinese immigrants, the majority of whom were male, tended to live communally, sharing apartments to save money. This arrangement evolved into a formal collective called a fong, which literally means a "room." Members of a fong developed close relationships and great loyalty to one another. Several fongs made up of people from the same village formed a "village association"; several fongs composed of people of the same surname formed family or surname associations. A village association might raise funds for famine relief or for the building of schools and hospitals in the home village. But the associations also carried out joint functions and lent support to each other. They could accomplish more through collective action, they found, so then even larger organizations were created—the huiguan ("meeting hall") brought together several family and village associations. The huiguan continued to carry out mutual-aid and charity functions, but at the same time, they were also more commercially oriented than the family or village associations that they contained. They arbitrated disputes among members and served as credit and employment agencies. They ensured that members met their obligations in business transactions with others.

The huiguan were originally formed to defend their members against a hostile larger society and to provide order within the community. But an internal hierarchy soon developed: the members who owned shops and restaurants commanded the respect of other members, who depended on them for jobs. Those who received jobs and favors willingly became followers, forming patron-client relationships. The patrons thus, in addition to being business owners, became association leaders too. These association big shots, or kiu ling, were the leaders of Chinese overseas communities, because as the most active and generous members of their associations, they pledged the most during community fund-raising drives, making them de facto leaders of the associations. The resulting hierarchy that developed within the Chinese community was based entirely on wealth. Wealthy Chinatown shop owners and merchants used the associations to maintain social and political control of the community.

Each association was, in principle, independent, and serious disputes, particularly among the large associations, could result in continuous, unresolved fights. In order to avoid such conflicts, most Chinatowns in the United States established umbrella organizations like New York's Chinese Consolidated Benevolent Association (CCBA). The elite was also able to enforce compliance by purchasing the services of the tongs, secret fraternal organizations known for their criminal ties and affinity for violence.

Today, the social-class basis of Chinatown's political structure remains basically unchanged. Local power is still concentrated in the hands of factory owners, merchants, and landlords, who are able to impose their personal interests through their official positions in the associations. When association leaders gather in the CCBA, they constitute an informal government that represents the interests of the Chinatown elite. The community may be divided vertically along lines of kinship, village ties, trade, and fraternities, but the political structure does not cut across class lines—power is concentrated exclusively in the hands of the wealthy.

Of the two hundred or so listed family, clan, surname, village, county, tong, and social-welfare organizations in Chinatown, practically none represent the interests of the working people. Without an effective challenge from other forms of local association, the owners are able to set rules, define "acceptable behavior," and impose sanctions against violators, using tactics such as blacklisting, public humiliation, ostracism, and the threat of physical violence. By monopolizing the political, economic, and social structures of Chinatown, the manufacturing elite are recognized as the "community leaders" by outsiders as well. Hence, whenever the mayor's office, a federal official, or law-enforcement authorities want to reach out to the Chinese community, they do so through the Chinatown elite.

The Uniqueness of the Chinatown Enclave

Ethnic-immigrant concentrations have always been an American phenomenon. As noted earlier, the current revival of this type of immigrant community reflects in part the restructuring of the American economy, particularly the decentralization of American manufacturing as it seeks cheaper labor. Today, there are Cuban enclaves in Miami, Dominican enclaves in New York, Mexican and Central American enclaves in Los Angeles, and many other smaller ethnic-immigrant concentrations scattered in various locales across the country. None of them, though, is as intensely compact as Chinese immigrant enclaves, particularly the ones in New York City. Chinatowns are communities of new immigrants with limited English and professional skills, residing in geographically specific areas where they also work and socialize. Most of all, Chinatowns have rigidly institutionalized political and social structures. These structures have existed, evolved, and been refined since the very beginning of the Chinese presence in this country in the 1850s.

These rigid institutions endure because illegal immigrants compose a substantial portion of Chinatown's labor force. Illegals go to the largest Chinatowns because there they are able to work without English-language skills and their illegal status will be well shielded inside the community. Of course, smugglers and employers also prefer to have the new immigrants concentrated in Chinatowns for easy control, especially when American law-enforcement treats the immigrant enclave as if it is a foreign territory.

The Militancy of
Chinese Immigrant Workers

From previous descriptions, it might seem the hegemony of the Chinese elite in the Chinatown community is complete. Yet Chinese working-class people have never been entirely willing to accept the dominance of the elites. From the very beginning of their arrival in the United States in the nineteenth century, Chinese workers have shown significant labor militancy, even against great odds. In the winter of 1867, for example, five thousand Chinese railroad workers laboring in the high Sierras went on strike to demand that their pay be raised to equal that of white workers and that the workday be reduced to ten hours in the open air and eight hours in tunnels. "Eight hours a day good for white men, all the same good for Chinamen," a spokesman for the workers reportedly said. Workers also called for the abolition of whipping and the freedom for any worker to quit, if and when he chose (Montgomery 1987, 67). In response, the railroad's management cut off the supply trains entering the camps where the Chinese worked. Forced into starvation, the strikers surrendered within a week. Though widely reported in the San Francisco papers, the incident elicited no reaction from either labor unions or the government (Chiu 1963, 47).

In another labor action, in 1884, Chinese tobacco workers in San Francisco successfully struck for increased pay, in the process forming a union called Tang Dak Tong, or Hall of Common Virtue. In the fall of the same year they struck again, this time demanding the dismissal of two Chinese workers who were not members of the union. The Hall of Common Virtue was probably the first Chinese union formed in North America, and the first to make demands for fair wages and an all-union shop. As one scholar has noted, it must have been quite a "source of irritation for the white employers . . . that the Chinese learned to use the strike as a means of exacting higher wages and improved conditions of employment" (Saxton 1971, 104). But be that as it may, these actions on the part of Chinese workers did not receive any support from white trade unions; rather, the Chinese won scorn from white unions for beginning "to feel overbearing in their strength" (Saxton 1971, 214).

Chinese immigrants' struggles were not limited to conflicts with white employers. Because they were often working for Chinese contractors, any demand pressed on the employers inevitably would lead to conflict with their Chinese overseers as well. These often ended up in bloody internecine disputes. One such incident occurred in 1876, when Chinese laborers at the shoe factories owned by two firms in San Francisco—Einstein Brothers and Buckingham, Hecht and Company—felt that management and their Chinese contractors had defrauded them. The workers struck, without results. The laborers finally armed themselves and attacked the contractors, initiating bloody battles that roiled San Francisco's Chinatown for weeks (Saxton 1971, 9).

Today, Chinese workers holding manufacturing and service jobs still labor under an ethnic subcontracting system that helps to keep them isolated in their own ethnic community. Equally unfortunate, Chinese immigrants entered the American labor market in significant numbers at the moment that American organized labor began to seriously decline. Unions have made little attempt to integrate the Chinese into the American labor movement, and they certainly have not encouraged the Chinese to build crossethnic alliances with other immigrant groups.

The first contemporary Chinese immigrant workers to be organized inside their ethnic enclaves by American unions were those working in the garment industry, who were brought into the fold by the International Ladies' Garment Workers Union (ILGWU). Most of the Chinatown garment shops were organized in the mid-1970s, when Chinese contractors agreed to allow the ILGWU to organize their shops in exchange for a promise that the union would help persuade large clothing manufacturers to provide Chinese contractors with a steady supply of job orders. From the beginning, then, Chinatown factories were unionized from the top down, without the ILGWU ever having to actually mobilize Chinese workers to organize in the factories (today, almost 90 percent of Chinese garment workers in Manhattan's Chinatown, both legal and illegal, belong to the ILGWU's present incarnation, UNITE).

The ILGWU-UNITE has since made very little effort to involve Chinese workers on individual shop floors directly. In fact, many Chinatown factories have no shop representative to whom workers can report their grievances, despite a provision in the union contract that makes the union responsible for appointing one in every shop. Without a shop representative, the business agents—the union's overseers of individual shops—become the only union presences in the factories. The most commonly voiced complaint among Chinese immigrant seamstresses is expressed in a labor newsletter: "The business agent rarely visits our shops, and when he/she does come, he/she never talks to the workers" (Chinese Staff and Workers' Association 1988). In some factories, the UNITE business agents get along better with the owners than with their own union members. This is not surprising, as the success of the union is based on its ability to maintain a dues-paying membership, and that depends more on the cooperation of Chinese owners than on the rank and file. This being the case, the owners' power is dominant in the factory, and workers cannot be expected to speak up and risk retaliation from their bosses and betrayal by union officials (Kwong and Lum 1988, 899).

The explanation the union offers for its passivity is that the Chinese women are docile and tied to Chinatown's political and social structure. This image, however, was shattered in the summer of 1982, during negotiations for a new labor contract in the Chinatown garment factories. The negotiations involved the renewal of a three-year contract and called for the standard wage increase. The garment manufacturers signed the contract; in fact, the same contract had already been signed to cover 120,000 non-Chinese garment workers on the East Coast. But the Chinese subcontractors balked. They were angry because even though 85 percent of the firms affected by the contract in the Local 23-25 were Chinese-owned, there were no Chinese on the negotiating team. The subcontractors expected the community to rally behind them, particularly in this clear case of "racial discrimination." To their workers, these contractors said, "We are all Chinese and should be able to settle this in our own house; there is no need to go to the white man's union" (Kwong and Lum 1988, 152).

The union, meanwhile, had to head off the confrontation and called for a demonstration by its membership in Chinatown. Within the union, officials had no idea how the Chinatown women would react, because their staff of business agents had not been close to the membership. Some even doubted that the Chinese would turn out at all. Rank-and-file Chinese ILGWU union members quickly mobilized, however, and dozens of women volunteered to operate phone banks to contact individual members, urging them to turn out. Others wrote bilingual leaflets, banners, and propaganda material. On the day of the demonstration, twenty thousand Chinese workers turned out. After the demonstration, the Chinese contractors backed off, and the workers won a new contract.

This militant demonstration by Chinese garment workers indicated that the Chinese could be more conscious of class than ethnicity when it came to issues relating to their objective interests, especially if they could feel that they were given a chance to participate in the process. Unfortunately, the ILGWU did not take advantage of the workers' activism to build a strong rank-and-file base among Chinese workers. In the aftermath of the demonstration, the union coopted the most active members into managerial positions and continued to treat its members as "clients" rather than as potential labor activists and to operate primarily as a social agency for them.

Another recent case of labor activism among Chinese immigrants involves illegal immigrants from China's Fuzhou and Wenzhou provinces. These immigrants reputedly have very strong kinship ties and indeed, they use kinship networks to find jobs and to raise funds to pay off their high smuggling fees. However, as the number of illegals entering this country increased in the 1990s, these kinship networks were overburdened with debts and unable to handle further demands. As a result, the usefulness of kinship networks declined, and Fuzhounese illegals began to turn to other means to address their needs and interests. In one such case, for example, they resisted the common employer practice of withholding back wages from workers. This is done in hundreds of Chinatown factories and restaurants, where managers count on the fact that labor laws on this issue are hardly ever enforced and assume that Chinese workers, particularly the undocumented, would not fight back. However, in recent years, garment workers and employees of a number of uptown Manhattan Chinese restaurants have gone on strike—often without help or even encouragement from the labor department and the unions—to demand the payment of back wages (Kwong 1987).

Conclusion

Chinese immigrant workers, at this juncture, hold the unpleasant distinction of occupying one of the lowest rungs on the American labor ladder. They are not in the position to form interethnic coalitions with other workers and will not be until they can break up, or break out of, the structure of the ethnic enclave. To do that would require not only the workers' own initiative, but, among other things, that American authorities enforce labor standards and civil rights in Chinese immigrant workplaces. However, the authorities are unlikely to act without political pressure from the workers themselves. Chinese workers, the undocumented included, have fought for their rights despite having to confront Chinese business owners, the threat of gang violence, indifferent labor officials, and even the possibility of deportation. A key problem facing them is the reluctance of organized labor to mobilize them. This is why the small but ongoing struggles for back wages at various garment factories and restaurants are so significant.

Sources

Chinese Staff and Workers' Association. 1988. *The Chinese Staff and Workers' Association Newsletter.* New York: Chinese Staff and Workers' Association.

Chiu, Ping. 1963. *Chinese Labor in California, 1850–1880: An Economic Study.* Madison: The State Historical Society of Wisconsin for the Department of History, University of Wisconsin.

Kwong, Peter. 1987. *The New Chinatown.* New York: Hill and and Wang.

Kwong, Peter, and JoAnn Lum. 1988. "How the Other Half Lives Now." *The Nation,* June 18, 1988, p. 899.

Mahler, Sarah J. 1995. "The Dysfunctions of Transnationalism." Working paper 73. New York: Russell Sage Foundation.

Montgomery, David. 1987. *The Fall of the House of Labor.* New York: Cambridge University Press.

Ong, Paul. 1984. "Chinatown Unemployment and the Ethnic Labor Market." *Amerasia Journal* 11(1): 35–54.

Portes, Alejandro, and Robert Bach. 1985. *Latin Journey: Cuban and Mexican Immigrants in the United States*. Berkeley: University of California Press.

Saxton, Alexander. 1971. *The Indispensable Enemy: Labor and the Anti-Chinese Movement in California*. Berkeley: California University Press.

Weisman, Rachel X. 1997. "Reaping What They Sew." *Brooklyn Bridge* 2(9): 52–53.

Zhou, Min. 1992. *Chinatown: The Socioeconomic Potential of an Urban Enclave*. Philadelphia: Temple University Press.

Chapter 3

Korean Americans and the Crisis of the Liberal Coalition: Immigrants and Politics in Los Angeles

EDWARD J.W. PARK AND JOHN S.W. PARK

O N APRIL 17, 1997, under the sponsorship of the City of Los Angeles, the University of Southern California hosted a "Day of Dialogue" to foster interracial understanding. As the discussion quickly balkanized around the topic of minority political empowerment in Los Angeles, an elderly African American man admonished the participants with some historical perspective. After recounting his experience as a grassroots organizer in Tom Bradley's 1969 and 1973 mayoral campaigns, he counseled, "Blacks alone could not have elected Tom Bradley to the mayor's office. We needed the support of whites from the Westside, Hispanics from the Eastside, and Asians from the Southside. Unless we can come together again in mutual trust and understanding, all of the minority communities will just continue to fight each other for the crumbs of this city." After a brief pause, a young Latina student quipped: "That was the sixties, this is now."

That exchange encapsulates a major shift in urban politics. In fact, the grassroots organizer had invoked one of the most enduring assumptions in the literature on urban politics since the civil rights movement: that success in local politics for racial minorities is inextricably linked with their participation in multiracial, liberal coalitions, an awkward approach known as the liberal coalition model

(Browning, Marshall, and Tabb 1984; Sonenshein 1993, 1994). This assumption, and the political strategies flowing from it, have been fundamental and pervasive not only in practice but also in studies of race and power in contemporary American cities, for compelling reasons. For much of American urban history, governing coalitions actively sought to exclude racial minorities from the political process, with devastating consequences not only for minority political rights but also for minorities' economic development and social lives. Faced with the hostility and recalcitrance of these governing coalitions, racial minorities found a measure of political unity among themselves and worked with white-liberal allies to challenge the status quo (see Boussard 1993 and Taylor 1994). Working in coalitions with their white liberal allies during the 1960s and 1970s, racial minorities—under the leadership of African Americans—ushered in some of the most dramatic changes in the history of American urban politics (Browning, Marshall, and Tabb 1984). While many have questioned the terms and parameters of cooperation and cohesion between racial minorities and white liberals, many liberals—much like the elderly African American activist from the Day of Dialogue—have continued to view the political incorporation of racial minorities as going hand in hand with integration into broader liberal coalitions (Carmichael and Hamilton 1967; Browning, Marshall, and Tabb 1984; Sonenshein 1996; Brackman and Erie 1995, 1998). However, since the civil rights movement of the 1960s and 1970s, other major social and political changes have unfolded in American cities. Most striking is the fact that millions of new immigrants have settled in the United States. These newest Americans bring a set of multiracial complexities and challenges to the urban political process, and they pose daunting challenges for liberals wishing to maintain their traditional claim on racial-minority incorporation. They are neither "black" nor "white," and, as a newer immigrant group, bear few long-term cultural or political attachments to American society. At the same time, on an even broader scale, racial politics have gradually moved from the simplicity of white dominance over blacks to the more nuanced and complex dynamics of "post–civil rights" politics (Omi and Winant 1994; Marable 1995; Portes and Stepick 1993). Since the 1970s, the very same political changes that the civil rights movement unleashed have opened the way for the rearticulation of racial politics, such that charges of "reverse discrimination" and "black racism" now permeate American political discourse. As liberals find themselves struggling with these new challenges, some conservatives have attempted to reconfigure their relationship with racial minorities and have reached out for their votes and support (Omi and Winant 1994; Marable 1995). In the face of demographic change, conservatives are increasingly eager to recruit racial minorities politically, especially in large cities and diverse states, where racial-minority voters can shift the electoral balance. As the Latina student at the Day of Dialogue observed, the signs everywhere seem to indicate that new realities bring into question the traditional liberal assumptions of race, power, and coalition building, assumptions predicated on the realities of another generation.

Within this context, this chapter seeks to outline specific challenges to the liberal coalition model by examining the experience of Korean Americans in Los Angeles. The political participation of Korean Americans poses an important and difficult problem to those who remain committed to that model. First, Korean Americans, like other immigrants of color, complicate the relationship between race and politics by introducing greater multiracial complexities in American cities (Omi 1993; Marable 1995; Freer 1994). Furthermore, Korean Americans have entered the political process with a diverse set of interests, some of which pit them in a very visible and direct way against African Americans who have traditionally been the most important and senior partners in urban liberal coalitions (Chang 1994; Min 1996; Cho 1993). Conflict between Korean-American merchants and African American residents has received a great deal of attention as a metaphor for urban interminority strife, but other, less-publicized conflicts between a variety of new immigrants and African Americans over a wide range of issues have sparked violence in Miami, New York, Washington, D.C., and Chicago (Portes and Stepick 1993; Rodriguez 1995; Rosenfeld 1997). These intense differences ostensibly leave little room for the interracial unity that must be achieved for the liberal coalition model to work.

In addition, like most post-1965 immigrant groups, Korean Americans bring with them diverse class backgrounds and political visions that shape their politics. For this reason if no other, it remains an open question whether *any* existing political coalitions can absorb, in toto, Korean Americans or other similarly situated new immigrant groups characterized by dramatic intragroup diversity and differences (Min 1996; Abelmann and Lie 1995). On the axis of class alone, while they have one of the highest rates of college education (33 percent), Korean Americans living in Los Angeles's Koreatown suffer from one of the city's highest poverty rates (26 percent) (Ong and Umemoto 1994). And though models of racial and ethnic *group* incorporation have been central in the study of urban politics (Glazer and Moynihan 1963; Browning, Marshall, and Tabb 1984; Brackman and Erie 1998), the intragroup diversity and difference among Korean Americans, as well as other new immigrants, pose a challenge to this method of understanding political mobilization and participation. Finally, the participation of a new generation of Korean Americans in the political process offers insights into the problem of intergenerational politics, particularly in new-immigrant communities. Intergenerational conflicts do not by themselves alter the basic aim of coalition politics, but they can potentially change the political trajectory of an immigrant community, including its likelihood of participating in liberal coalitions.

This chapter begins with an introduction to Korean-American politics in Los Angeles, and then turns to the impact of the city's 1992 civil unrest on the Korean-American community. We analyze how the event consolidated alliances, but also revealed hidden cleavages within the community. By focusing on the Korean American community in particular, we can reflect upon the long-term prospects for the liberal coalition model in American urban politics.

Korean Immigration, Settlement, and Diversity

As the full effect of the immigration reforms of 1965 took hold, Koreans immigrated to the United States in astonishing numbers (Hing 1993; Sabagh and Bozorgmehr 1996). Like most post-1965 immigrants, Koreans were attracted to urban areas that had large and dynamic economies, but they also looked for places where there were previous settlements of Korean Americans, who, they hoped, could help them adjust to their new lives. With its booming and diverse economy, and with the largest established Korean-American community in the country, the City of Los Angeles quickly became the center for a new, burgeoning Korean immigrant and Korean-American population (Chang 1994; Min 1996). From 1970 to 1990, the Korean-American population in the City of Los Angeles grew over sevenfold, from 9,395 to 72,970. By 1990, Los Angeles County was home to 145,431 Korean Americans, representing close to 20 percent of all U.S. residents of Korean heritage. In Los Angeles, the center of Korean settlement is a twenty-square-mile area just west of downtown. In 1978, that area acquired the official designation of Koreatown from City Hall. Despite its ethnic moniker, however, the subsequent and rapid movement of Korean Americans into traditionally white suburbs has left Koreatown home to a largely Latino population, with Korean Americans making up less than 15 percent of its residents (Min 1996). Nonetheless, with over three thousand Korean-American-owned businesses and over a hundred community organizations, Koreatown remains the social, economic, cultural, and psychological center for Korean Americans in Southern California, if not the nation. For many Korean Americans, the urban politics of Los Angeles have become the foremost site to pursue their political hopes and dreams (Abelmann and Lie 1995).

The timing of the Korean migration to Los Angeles coincided with the most dramatic change in the city's recent political history. After decades of white conservative rule, a coalition of liberals finally succeeded in electing Tom Bradley mayor in 1973: that coalition would control the city's government for the next two decades (Sonenshein 1993). In the two city council districts that divide Koreatown and its immediate areas, key members of the "Bradley coalition" held public office, and even today, both districts are represented by liberal minority politicians: Nate Holden, an African American, and Mike Hernandez, a Latino. Beyond the city, Koreatown has been represented in Sacramento and Washington, D.C. by liberal politicians including Maxine Waters and Art Torres, both powerful figures within the Democratic Party. In addition to fostering the careers of many liberal minority elected officials, the Bradley coalition also actively diversified city agencies through political appointments and by aggressively pursuing affirmative action hiring in all areas of public employment (Guerra 1987).

Still, the Bradley coalition remained predominantly one of African Americans and white liberals, which in part reflected the decisive role of African American and Jewish voters in electing Bradley to power (Sonenshein 1993). While Latinos gained some prominence in the Bradley coalition as their numbers in the city increased and as individual Latino political leaders emerged (Regalado 1994), Asian Americans (especially newer immigrants) remained somewhat peripheral to the concerns of the established liberal political leadership (Brackman and Erie 1998). Indeed, on the eve of the Los Angeles civil unrest, not one Korean American was serving in any significant political or appointed office, and most of the social service agencies within the Korean-American community looked to the community's own resources, rather than City Hall, to fund programs.

From the point of view of many Korean Americans, then, the face of political power in the city had always been ideologically liberal and racially diverse—yet it did not include them. They often felt far removed from the liberal political leaders who controlled much of Los Angeles politics, at least throughout their community's short history. Many believed that these leaders expressed little interest and provided even less in the way of substantive political outreach to the Korean community (see Browning, Marshall, and Tabb 1984). Liberal political leaders—and more specifically African American political leaders who had the highest visibility in the community—did not appear, at first glance, to be an insurgent political force that toppled the conservative and racist Sam Yorty–William Parker (popularly known as "Yorty-Parker") regime; rather, they seemed like an entrenched and imposing power that ultimately cared little about the Korean-American community.

The apparent indifference of the liberal coalition persisted despite the presence of working-class and poor Korean Americans in Los Angeles, persons who were most likely to be allied with liberal leaders. For although the media has focused on Korean Americans as a predominantly entrepreneurial group, class diversity, not homogeneity, characterizes the community. This is especially true in the City of Los Angeles, where decades of suburbanization have left the city with Korean Americans who predominantly fall into two groups: poorer, newer, younger immigrants and the elderly (Ong and Umemoto 1994; Lee 1994). Min (1996), in his research on Koreatown's ethnic economy, echoes charges familiar to almost any inner city: a clear majority of the businesses in Koreatown are owned by Korean Americans who live outside of boundaries of the community and the city; most of the jobs in Koreatown businesses are in low-paying, service and retail sectors; those who reside in Koreatown now are more likely to be recently arrived immigrants, most of whom are younger and less acculturated that their predecessors; and the elderly, who live in the community's numerous subsidized housing complexes on the edge of poverty. Indeed, while much is made of Korean Americans' 30 percent self-employment rate, larger numbers of Korean Americans work in low-paying jobs with little or no benefits and severely limited opportunities for mobility (Light and Bonacich 1988; Abelmann and Lie 1995). This class diversity among Korean Americans has played a significant role in the community's politics, resulting in incidents ranging from highly publicized labor conflicts to battles over relief money in the aftermath of the civil unrest (Lee 1994).

Diversity also marks the Korean-American political sphere. In part, Korean Americans' political diversity can be traced back to South Korea and its unique and troubled history (Abelmann and Lie 1995; Chang 1988). On the one hand, right-wing dictatorships there during the 1970s and early 1980s have "pushed" Koreans with more liberal ideals to emigrate to the United States. In contrast, though, during the same period, many middle-class Koreans—persons with clear expectations of social mobility—came to the United States in search of economic opportunities, and once settled in this country, they favored policies, such as lower taxes and limits to government regulation, that fall more in line with conservative politics. Yet whether of liberal or conservative inclination, almost all Korean immigrants came to the United States in the aftermath of the Korean War, when the United States emerged as a principal military and political ally of South Korea and Koreans themselves became increasingly familiar with various aspects of American culture. These circumstances surrounding Korean immigration in turn shaped the immigrants' expectations, especially in terms of their economic and class aspirations (Chang 1988; Abelmann and Lie 1995; Kim and Yu 1996).

Perhaps more important than "homeland" influences on Korean immigrants, however, were the contexts and histories of Koreans and other Asians in the United States. From one perspective, as racial minorities, Korean Americans shared a long history of racial oppression with other racial-minority groups. For instance, Korean Americans were one of the very last two groups (along with Japanese Americans) to be granted the right to naturalized citizenship, in 1952 (Choy 1979). At various times and in different localities, Koreans faced discriminatory treatment from the United States government, including laws that restricted immigration, banned owning real property, and discriminated against them in housing markets and educational opportunities (Takaki 1989). In recent years, as Korean Americans began to participate politically, this history resonated with the community's liberals and progressives in particular: before Korean American audiences, these activists constantly drew on this history to argue for the necessity of contemporary coalition politics. In a similar fashion, they linked contemporary political issues—ranging from immigration restrictions, welfare reform, and anti-Asian violence— to broader historical narratives, and they suggested that Korean Americans could best guard their hard-won rights and ensure future racial equality by working together with other members of the liberal coalition (Kang et al. 1993; Cho 1993; Oh 1993; Kim 1994).

At the same time, though, another perspective was being voiced too. An emergent group of Korean-American conservative activists argued, and has continued to argue with increasing strength, that the community as a whole has class-based interests and commitments to "traditional values" that put them squarely at odds with prevailing liberal sentiments. They have argued that the Korean-American community remains a community of entrepreneurs, and have also contended that even working-class Korean Americans will benefit most from a strong and vibrant ethnic economy. By insisting that small-business interests are consonant with community interest, they have rallied the community's support for traditionally conservative economic and social policies that include fiscal conservatism, as well as an emphasis on law and order (Steel and Park-Steel 1994).

It is perhaps that last issue, law and order, that has gained Korean-American conservatives the most support. For while fiscal conservatism addresses the economic interests of the community, the issue of law and order touches Korean Americans more viscerally than any other. Vivid and regular reports in both the ethnic and mainstream media—of horrific crimes against Korean-American shop owners and residents—touch a raw nerve, and Korean conservatives in the community have often been the ones to propose tough justice and righteous vengeance (Yi 1993; Doherty 1992a). If a common history of racism has provided the emotional touchstone for Korean-American liberals, then the issue of crime has served a similar function for conservatives. In a community where a significant number of people has been touched personally by violent crime, many Korean Americans view liberals as, at best, soft on crime and, at worst, excusing criminal behavior with pious structural explanations that ignore or dismiss who the true victims of crime really are. In addition, some Korean-American conservatives have suggested that such liberal justifications exemplify a set of generally more permissive attitudes that stand in opposition to "traditional" Korean culture—a culture that is based on "Confucian values," among them respect for elders and respect for traditional gender roles. Indeed, liberals, especially liberal and progressive women, in the community have been routinely chastised as being "too assimilated," having abandoned Korean ways for the permissive allures of American society.

Among Korean Americans, debates about "Americanization" and political assimilation have taken on an intergenerational dimension, related in large part to a relatively new pattern of migration. More than three decades have passed since reforms in American immigration law triggered a new wave of migrants. This recent wave has been characterized by the immigration of families, including women and children, not just male laborers (Portes and Rumbaut 1996). Two significant results of this immigration pattern are a high naturalization rate among immigrants and the rapid formation of a postimmigrant generation. Bearing this out are numbers from the 1990 census: of the 797,304 Korean Americans enumerated, 27.3 percent were born in the United States and 36.3 percent were naturalized citizens with full political rights (Shinagawa 1996). During the 1990s, the pace of immigration from Korea waned dramatically, while the rate of naturalization greatly increased. Together, these trends signal even more dramatic changes in the citizenship rates for Korean Americans and, with that, greater potential for their political participation.

In addition, because the recent migration of Koreans involved entire families, there arrived, in one fell swoop, a new generation altogether. The so-called 1.5 ("one-point-five") generation denotes Korean Americans who were born in Korea but raised in the United States. While their acculturation and English fluency mark them as different from their parents, their greater familiarity with Korean culture and language, as well as their immigrant experience, distinguish them from their American-born, second-generation counterparts. Within the Korean American community, it is this 1.5 generation that has provided much of the leadership (Park 1994; Kim and Yu 1996). As in most ethnic communities, the intergenerational relationship—here between adult Korean immigrants and their children—has often been difficult, and it has been shaped in part by competition over resources and claims of ethnic authenticity and in part by conflicts among personalities and organizations. In Los Angeles, prior to the civil unrest of 1992, most of these tensions remained latent, lacking a clear public issue to bring out what were in fact becoming very serious differences stretching across political positions in the Korean-American community.

Korean-American Politics in Post–Civil Unrest Los Angeles

The Los Angeles civil unrest of 1992 stands as the single most important event in the history of Koreans in the United States. Confronted with the greatest crisis they had ever faced as a community, Korean Americans were forced to quicken the pace of their political development, and they participated vigorously in Los Angeles politics for the first time. In the process, such action has forced the community to confront its internal tensions and divisions while also pushing various actors into involvement in mainstream politics, all of which necessarily requires engaging other groups and communities. To date, in contrast to the experiences of other racial and ethnic groups that have mobilized politically in response to crises (see Portes and Stepick 1993; Taylor 1994; Boussard 1993), this political mobilization of Korean Americans has not brought unity to the community or community consolidation; rather, the crisis sharpened political divisions and differences. Here, two case studies drawn from the aftermath of the civil unrest lend insight into why the Korean American community remains a community divided, and why the question of coalition building within the community, as well as with outside groups in multiracial coalitions, remains unresolved.

In the first case, the interests of Korean business owners stood in stark contrast to the desires of African American communities in the city, the traditional heart of the Bradley coalition. During the unrest, some two hundred liquor stores—187 of which were owned by Koreans or Korean Americans—were destroyed. In the ensuing discussions over whether such businesses, especially those in predominantly poor, African American and Latino neighborhoods, should be rebuilt, the hopes of some Korean-American and African American progressive activists—that the two communities could begin to work together to build a more just and harmonious Los Angeles—came to a crashing halt. The heavy concentration of liquor stores in such inner-city communities had long been a sensitive political issue for Los

Angeles liberals. Many inner-city residents saw the preponderance of liquor stores in their neighborhoods as evidence of just one way in which their concerns had been betrayed by liberal politicians who apparently cared only about the tax revenues that these stores created. Sympathetic—not to mention uncomfortably sensitive—to such criticism, L.A.'s liberal politicians saw the sudden destruction of these enterprises as a unique opportunity for the city to do something about the situation. However, when it became clear how many of these stores were owned by Korean Americans, the issue of race took on added volatility.

As Sonenshein (1996) has described in detail, local political leaders, working with Democratic leaders in Sacramento, succeeded in passing an ordinance that imposed strict conditions on the reopening of liquor stores, including a requirement that all such businesses provide security and parking. These and other restrictions were so severe that only a handful of stores were able to reopen even two years after the civil unrest (Kang 1994a, 1994b). And while some opponents of the liquor stores valiantly worked with sympathetic members of the Korean-American community to "deracialize" the issue (Chavez 1994), these efforts were hampered by others who relied on explicit racial labels and imagery to rally political support (Sonenshein 1996). Meanwhile, given the volatile nature of the liquor-store controversy, many liberals who were not directly supportive of the restrictions remained quiet in the debate, fearing the anger and hostility of the African-American community should they appear to support the Korean-American liquor-store owners (Sonenshein 1996).

In this time of desperation, many Korean-American entrepreneurs found their only willing allies among political conservatives. When the Republican-led effort to overturn the restrictions finally failed in Sacramento, Korean-American community leaders, side by side with business-association members from the Korean American Grocers' Association (KAGRO) and Republican activists, charged African Americans with "black racism" and blamed liberal Democrats for using Korean Americans as scapegoats for decades of failed liberal inner-city policies (Kang 1994a, 1994b; Gladstone 1994). In a terse editorial in the *Korea Times*, two Republican activists aimed their comments directly at the liberal coalition and implored the readers to carefully rethink "who are their friends and who are their enemies" (Steel and Park-Steel 1994). Although they lost this particular policy battle, the conservatives within the Korean-American community won an important victory by revealing what they perceived to be a fundamental, if not fatal, antagonism between the Korean-American community and the liberal coalition. Even years after the controversy, the liquor-store issue remained a key metaphor among many Korean

Americans who felt that they had been victimized by African American and liberal politicians (Park 1996).

In contrast to this, in the second examination of the changes in Korean American political participation since the civil unrest, we see the ways in which elements of the Korean-American community used national and statewide issues to make a case for liberal multiracial coalitions. Clearly, while the liquor-store controversy energized conservatives within the Korean-American community, changes to federal and state immigration, hiring, and education policies inspired liberal and progressive Korean Americans to take political action. Through the 1990s, Korean-American activists participated in political organization and grassroots mobilizations in Los Angeles (Freer 1994; Regalado 1994; Park 1996; Brackman and Erie 1998), largely in response to what liberals and progressives regarded as a series of policies designed to undermine the political gains of racial minorities and immigrants on both the state and national levels. On such contentious issues as immigration law, affirmative action, and bilingual education, liberals and progressives see recent conservative activism threatening the central gains made during the civil rights era. California's Propositions 187 and 209 that sought to ban undocumented immigrants from social programs and undermine affirmative action programs, and the Republican-led effort in Congress to bar legal immigrants from some social security programs, provided powerful impetus for liberals to work together across racial lines (Saito and Park 2000).

In Los Angeles, a city with a growing minority electorate and a liberal city council, conservative and centrist political leaders, including Mayor Richard Riordan, did not support the anti-immigrant initiatives of the 1990s. Nonetheless, Korean-American liberals and progressives successfully portrayed these initiatives as broad-based conservative attacks on immigrants and civil rights gains made by racial minorities. In particular, Korean-American activists succeeded in convincing voters in the Korean community to reject Proposition 209, even though its proponents argued that Korean Americans, indeed Asian Americans in general, would be some of its chief beneficiaries. In addition, liberal Korean-American activists sounded the alarm against the Republican-led push in 1996 to eliminate legal immigrants from federal-level assistance programs, including supplemental Social Security income and food stamps, measures that would have had an inordinately negative impact on Koreatown's poor, with its large concentrations of elderly Korean Americans and newer immigrants. With the Latino community providing the political leadership, Korean Americans joined in a vigorous grassroots campaign to challenge these initiatives (*Crosscurrents* 1996; Saito and Park 2000).

So, at a moment when they were on the defensive because of the liquor-store controversy, Korean-American liberals and progressives rallied the Korean community against these state and national initiatives. For conservative Korean Americans, the explicit anti-immigrant sentiment of these policies—particularly those designed to cut immigrants from social-welfare programs—proved embarrassing. For a time, Korean-American conservatives were in the awkward position of having to defend newfound political allies who seemed hostile to new immigrants. Lamenting the politics surrounding the elimination of supplemental Social Security income and food stamps for elderly legal immigrants, a conservative activist expressed the dilemma vividly in a conversation: "How can I ask Korean Americans to support the Republican Party when they are being told that it wants to yank the food out of their grandparent's mouth?" (Jeon 1999). On the opposing side, in a similar exchange, the progressive head of a Korean-American social-service agency wondered, "I don't get it. While one segment of the Republican Party puts out the welcome mat for Korean Americans, another segment hangs out the sign 'Koreans Go Home!'" (Kim 1999).

The increasing political mobilization of the Korean-American community has been followed by a generational transfer of political leadership within the community. In contrast to their predecessors, these new Korean-American political leaders are characterized by their willingness to go beyond their ethnic boundaries and to participate in the mainstream political process (Park 1996). Even though, as a group, they hold views that span the political spectrum (among their number are officers of the Korean American Republican Association who are well networked in the Republican Party at the state and national levels), the high visibility of two leaders in particular, Angela Oh and Bong Hwan Kim (a member of President Clinton's Commission on Race Relations and the executive director of the Korean Youth and Community Center [KYCC]—the largest social service agency in Koreatown—respectively) created a perception within the Korean-American community that this new generation of leaders was ideologically liberal (Oh 1993; Kang 1992, 1993; Dun et al. 1993; Chavez 1994).

This perception triggered a very public and polemical debate within the Korean-American community during the fifth anniversary of the civil unrest. In a scathing editorial that was timed to coincide with a conference organized by the community's leading liberal and progressive organizations (the KYCC, Korean Immigrant Workers Advocates, and the University of California at Los Angeles's Asian American Studies Center), Kapson Yim Lee, the editor of the *Korea Times* English edition, openly charged "English-speaking" community leaders and intellectuals of "[continuing] to make fame and money on the backs of nameless victims, whose knowledge of English is limited" and thus using the community's "tragedy to enhance their personal and organizational agendas" (Lee 1997). She reserved her harshest criticism for Kim and the work of the KYCC during the liquor-store controversy (KYCC was one of the few Korean American organizations to attempt to work with African American community organizations to deracialize the issue [Sonenshein 1996; Chavez 1994]), arguing that they "were on the other side, holding hands with black leaders." The intensity of Lee's anger was reflected in the conclusion of her article, a rebuke to the new generation of liberal and progressive leaders: "Stay away from us. With friends like [you], who needs enemies."

This open attack on the post-immigrant generation's most visible leaders was met head-on by Angela Oh at the conference itself. In an emotionally charged speech, she began by claiming her right, and the right of other members of her generation, to the "us"—the "real" Korean Americans—in Lee's editorial. Oh declared that her politics would not be compromised by Lee's claims of ethnic authenticity or her charges of opportunism, and she concluded with a promise that she, and the thousands of new-generation Korean Americans like her, would not go away. Rather, she stated, they would continue to participate in the community's political process, a commitment that included representing its interests in the broader political system. By not focusing on a defense of liberal politics as her main point, but rather by broadly defending the right of members of the 1.5 and second generations to participate in the Korean community's politics, Oh staked out a claim for inclusion rather than appearing as a partisan advocate. Her defense left even 1.5- and second-generation conservative activists cheering, sending the powerful message that generational issues in Korean-American politics were here to stay.

Conclusion

This excursion into Los Angeles's Korean-American politics reveals some important ways in which new multiracial realities challenge the liberal coalition model of urban politics. First, it is important to recognize that the model's central assumption of power relations in American cities can no longer be taken for granted. On the one hand, new immigrant groups, even those that are racial minorities, lack the personal experience of de jure racism that served as such a powerful unifying force a generation ago. For them, the faces of conservative urban politicians—among them Richard Riordan in Los Angeles and

Rudolph Giuliani in New York City—no longer represent recalcitrant defenders of white supremacy. Instead, they are perceived as competent managers who will lower taxes, grow the economy, fight crime, reduce bureaucracy, and even celebrate the multiculturalism of their cosmopolitan cities. For Korean-American entrepreneurs and the middle class of any race or ethnicity, this is a very compelling vision of urban governance.

These circumstances have forced liberals to rethink what they have to offer—in terms of both policies and leadership—to new immigrants, as well as to other constituents, to win their political support. In this context, the new immigrants can either revitalize the liberal coalition by helping to build a new vision of urban America, or bury it under the weight of its own recalcitrance toward shedding an ideology that no longer reflects urban realities. As was evident in Los Angeles, African Americans can—within the urban political context— appear to the new immigrants to be an imposing and entrenched political power rather than the polity's most important agents of progressive change. Broadening existing liberal coalitions will not be easy; it is already made difficult by the current political and economic crises faced by African American communities (Marable 1995) as well as by decades of mistrust and animosity between African Americans and new immigrants (Rodriguez 1995; Portes and Stepick 1993; Oliver, Johnson, and Farrell, 1993). Perhaps the greatest challenge for the liberal coalition will be to articulate a vision that will move urban politics beyond the zero-sum game that has thus far pitted these groups against one another.

Finally, the class and generational diversity within new immigrant groups poses another set of issues that must be addressed by prospective liberal coalitions. Class divisions within the new immigrant communities provide opportunities for liberals who have traditionally garnered support among the working class and the poor. However, because race and ethnicity no longer have the same leveling effect that they once did in minority political mobilization, liberals cannot simply pursue a "one-class" strategy that focuses on the working class to win the political support of new immigrant groups, as they did a generation ago. Likewise, generational transitions of leadership within new immigrant communities will not by themselves create conditions for political consolidation. Rather, intergenerational transitions may exacerbate political divisions within a given ethnic or racial community, as each side claims legitimacy, authenticity, and belonging as bases for political mobilization. Altogether, these dynamics will no doubt complicate urban politics in the United States for the foreseeable future. Urban politics, altered once again by mass migration, will never be the same.

References

Abelmann, Nancy, and John Lie. 1995. *Blue Dreams: Korean Americans and the Los Angeles Riots*. Cambridge, Mass.: Harvard University Press.
Boussard, Albert S. 1993. *Black San Francisco: The Struggle for Racial Equality in the West, 1900–1954*. Lawrence: University of Kansas Press.
Brackman, Harold, and Steven P. Erie. 1995. "Beyond 'Politics by Other Means'?: Empowerment Strategies for Los Angeles' Asian Pacific Community." In *The Bubbling Cauldron: Race, Ethnicity, and the Urban Crisis*, edited by Peter Smith and Joe R. Feagin. Minneapolis: University of Minnesota Press.
———. 1998. "At Rainbow's End: Empowerment Prospects for Latinos and Asian Pacific Americans in Los Angeles." In *Racial and Ethnic Politics in California*, vol. 2, edited by Michael B. Preston, Bruce E. Cain, and Sandra Bass. Berkeley, Calif.: Institute of Government Studies Press.
Browning, Rufus, Dale Rogers Marshall, and David Tabb. 1984. *Protest Is Not Enough: The Struggle of Blacks and Hispanics for Equality in City Politics*. Berkeley: University of California Press.
Carmichael, Stokely, and Charles V. Hamilton. 1967. *Black Power: The Politics of Liberation in America*. New York: Random House.
Chang, Edward T. 1988. "Korean Community Politics in Los Angeles: The Impact of Kwangju Uprising." *Amerasia* 14(1): 51–67.
———. 1994. "America's First Multiethnic 'Riots.'" In *The State of Asian America*, edited by Karin Aguilar San-Juan. Boston: South End Press.
Chavez, Lydia. 1994. "Crossing the Culture Line." *Los Angeles Times Magazine*, August 28, 1994: 22–24.
Cho, Sumi K. 1993. "Korean Americans vs. African Americans." In *Reading Rodney King/Reading Urban Uprising*, edited by Robert Gooding Williams. New York: Routledge.
Choy, Bong-Youn. 1979. *Koreans in America*. Chicago: Nelson-Hall.
Crosscurrents 19(2). 1996. "Affirmative Action Controversy in California."
Doherty, Jay. 1992a. "Korean Americans Hail Kim's Victory." *Los Angeles Times*, November 8, 1992: A11.
———. 1992b. "Black-Korean Alliance Says Talk Not Enough, Disbands." *Los Angeles Times*, December 24, 1992: B1.
Dun, A., P. J. McDonnell, K. C. Kang, and J. L. Mitchell. 1993. "Ethnic Groups Look to Future as Crisis Passes." *Los Angeles Times*, April 19, 1993: A1.
Espiritu, Yen Le. 1992. *Asian American Panethnicity: Bridging Institutions and Identities*. Philadelphia: Temple University Press.
Freer, Regina. 1994. "Black-Korean Conflict." In *The Los Angeles Riots: Lessons for the Urban Future*, edited by Mark Baldassare. Boulder, Colo.: Westview Press.
Gladstone, M. 1994. "Bill to Ease Rebuilding of Korean American Stores Fails." *Los Angeles Times*, August 30, 1994.
Glazer, Nathan, and Daniel P. Moynihan. 1963. *Beyond the Melting Pot*. Cambridge, Mass: MIT Press.
Guerra, F. J. 1987. "Ethnic Office Holders in Los Angeles County." *Sociology and Social Research* 71: 89–94.

Jeon, Laura. Interview with Edward J.W. Park. Los Angeles, California, 24 March 1999.

Hing, Bill Ong. 1993. *Making and Remaking Asian America Through Immigration Policy, 1850–1990*. Palo Alto, Calif.: Stanford University Press.

Kang, K. Connie. 1992. "Understanding the Riots—Six Months Later; Touched by Fire." *Los Angeles Times*, November 19, 1992: JJ8.

———. 1993. "Asian Americans Seek Role in L.A. Renewal." *Los Angeles Times*, May 29, 1993: B2.

———. 1994a. "Store Owners Fight Restrictions on Reopening." *Los Angeles Times*, July 21, 1994: B3.

———. 1994b. "Asian American Groups Organize to Fight Measure." *Korea Times* (English edition), September 2, 1994: B1.

———. 1995. "L.A. Hilton Owner Will Keep Service Workers." *Los Angeles Times*, January 10, 1995: B1.

Kang, Miliann, Juliana J. Kim, Edward J. W. Park, Hae Won Park. 1993. *Bridge Toward Unity*. Los Angeles: Korean Immigrant Workers Advocates.

Kim, Elaine H. 1993. "Home Is Where the Han Is." In *Reading Rodney King/ Reading Urban Uprising*, edited by Robert Gooding Williams. New York: Routledge.

———. 1994. "Between Black and White." In *The State of Asian America*, edited by Karin Aguilar San-Juan. Boston: South End Press.

Kim, Elaine H., and Eui-Young Yu. 1996. *East to America: Korean American Life Stories*. New York: The New Press.

Kim, Youngbin. Interview with Edward J.W. Park. Los Angeles, California, 16 March 1999.

Lee, Hoon. 1994. "4.29 Displaced Workers Justice Campaign." *KIWA News* 1: 6–13.

Lee, Kapson Yim. 1997. "Sa-ee-gu (April 29) Was a Riot, Not 'Civil Unrest.'" *Korea Times*, English edition, March 26–April 29, 1997: 3–4.

Light, Ivan, and Edna Bonacich. 1988. *Immigrant Entrepreneurs: Koreans in Los Angeles, 1965–1982*. Berkeley : University of California Press.

Marable, Manning. 1995. *Beyond Black and White: Rethinking Race in American Politics and Society*. New York: Verso.

Min, Pyong Gap. 1996. *Caught in the Middle: Korean Communities in New York and Los Angeles*. Berkeley: University of California Press.

Morrison, Peter A., and Ira S. Lowry. 1994. "A Riot of Color: the Demographic Setting." In *The Los Angeles Riots: Lessons for the Urban Future*, edited by Mark Baldassare. Boulder, Colo.: Westview Press.

Oh, Angela E. 1993. "Rebuilding Los Angeles: Why I Did Not Join RLA." *Amerasia Journal* 19: 157–60.

Oliver, Melvin L., James H. Johnson, and W. C. Farrell. 1993. "Anatomy of a Rebellion." In *Reading Rodney King/Reading Urban Uprising*, edited by Robert Gooding Williams. New York: Routledge.

Omi, Michael. 1993. "Out of the Melting Pot and into the Fire: Race Relations Policy." In *Policy Issues to the Year 2020*. Los Angeles: LEAP Asian American Public Policy Institute.

Omi, Michael, and Howard Winant. 1994. *Racial Formations in the United States*, 2nd ed. New York: Routledge.

Ong, Paul, and Karen Umemoto. 1994. "Life and Work in the Inner-City." In *The State of Asian Pacific America: Economic Diversity, Issues and Policies*, edited by Paul Ong. Los Angeles: LEAP Asian Pacific American Public Policy Institute.

Park, Edward J. W. 1996. "Our L.A.?: Korean Americans in Los Angeles After the Civil Unrest." In *Rethinking Los Angeles*, edited by Michael J. Dear, H. Eric Schockman, and Greg Hise. Thousand Oaks, Calif.: Sage Publications.

Park, Kyeyoung. 1996. "Use and Abuse of Race and Culture: Black-Korean Tension in America." *American Anthropologist* 98(3): 492–99.

Park, Winnie. 1994. "Political Mobilization of the Korean American Community." In *Community in Crisis: the Korean American Community After the Los Angeles Civil Unrest of April 1992*, edited by George O. Totten and H. Eric Schockman. Los Angeles: Center for Multiethnic and Transnational Studies, University of Southern California.

Portes, Alejandro, and Rubén G. Rumbaut. 1996. *Immigrant America: A Portrait*, 2nd ed. Berkeley: University of California Press.

Portes, Alejandro and Alex Stepick. 1993. *City on the Edge: The Transformation of Miami*. Berkeley: University of California Press.

Regalado, James A. 1994. "Community Coalition-Building." In *The Los Angeles Riots: Lessons for the Urban Future*, edited by Mark Baldassare. Boulder, Colo.: Westview Press.

Rodriguez, Nestor P. 1995. "The Real 'New World Order': The Globalization of Race and Ethnic Relations in the Late Twentieth Century." In *The Bubbling Cauldron: Race, Ethnicity, and the Urban Crisis*, edited by Michael Peter Smith and Joe R. Feagin. Minneapolis: University of Minnesota Press.

Rosenfeld, Michael J. 1997. "Celebration, Politics, Selective Looting, and Riots: A Micro-Level Study of the Bulls Riot of 1992 in Chicago." *Social Problems* 44: 483–502.

Sabagh, Georges, and Mehdi Bozorgmehr. 1996. "Population Change: Immigration and Ethnic Transformation." In *Ethnic Los Angeles*, edited by Roger Waldinger and Mehdi Bozorgmehr. New York: Russell Sage Foundation.

Saito, Leland T., and Edward J.W. Park. 2000. "Multiracial Collaborations and Coalitions." In *The State of Asian Pacific America; Transforming Race Relations*, edited by Paul M. Ong. Los Angeles: LEAP Asian Pacific American Public Policy Institute and the UCLA Asian American Studies Center.

Shinagawa, Larry Hajime. 1996. "The Impact of Immigration on the Demography of Asian Pacific Ameicans." In *Reframing the Immigration Debate*, edited by Bill Ong Hing and Ronald Lee. Los Angeles: LEAP Asian Pacific American Public Policy Institute.

Sonenshein, Raphael J. 1993. *Politics in Black and White: Race and Power in Los Angeles*. Princeton, N.J.: Princeton University Press.

———. 1994. "Los Angeles Coalition Politics." In *The Los Angeles Riots: Lessons for the Urban Future*, edited by Mark Baldassare. Boulder, Colo.: Westview Press.

———. 1996. "The Battle over Liquor Stores in South-Central Los Angeles: The Management of an Interminority Conflict." *Urban Affairs Review* 31(6): 710–37.

Steel, Shawn, and Michelle E. J. Park-Steel. 1994. "Outcome of AB 1974: Korean-Americans Strangled Again." *Korea Times* (English edition), September 7, 1994: 3.

Stewart, Ella. 1993. "Communication Between African Americans and Korean Americans." *Amerasia Journal* 19: 23–54.

Takagi, Dana Y. 1992. *The Retreat from Race: Asian American Admissions and Racial Politics.* New Brunswick, N.J.: Rutgers University Press.

Takaki, Ronald. 1989. *Strangers from a Different Shore.* Boston: Little, Brown.

Taylor, Quintard. 1994. *The Forging of a Black Community: Seattle's Central District from 1870 through the Civil Rights Era.* Seattle: University of Washington Press.

Yi, Daniel. 1993. "From NAFTA to Immigration: Rep. Kim Speaks Out Before KA Republicans." *Korea Times* [English edition], (October 6): 1.

PART II

COMPETITION AND CONFLICT

Chapter 4

Racial Minority Group Relations in a Multiracial Society

PAULA D. MCCLAIN AND STEVEN C. TAUBER

T HE UNITED States Census Bureau estimates that by 2005, Latinos will displace blacks as the largest racial-minority group in the United States (U.S. Bureau of the Census 1996a). The Bureau also estimates that by 2015, several states, California and New Mexico foremost among them, will become majority-minority, with members of racial-minority groups, as opposed to whites, constituting the majority of their populations (U.S. Bureau of the Census 1996b). This changing racial dynamic raises important questions for the nation concerning the relationship patterns that will evolve among these various groups. These changes are also forcing scholars in urban politics, and scholars of American politics in general, to move beyond the white-black dynamic that has historically structured race-relations scholarship and dialogue. Researchers recognize that Latinos, Asians, American Indians, and other populations of color must be included in discussions about race and how it is viewed in the United States. Still, however, the importance of the white-black dynamic cannot be overlooked because it permeates white relationships with virtually all other groups in this country: as Dr. John Hope Franklin, the chair of President Bill Clinton's "One America" Initiative on Race, said during one of the Initiative's hearings, "This country cut its eyeteeth on racism with black-white relations . . . They [whites] learned to do this to other people at other times because they had already become experts" (Baker, 1997).

As the country becomes increasingly multiracial, the patterns of racial interaction move from domination by the two-way black-white interaction to a series of multigroup interactions with any number of permutations. Various racial and ethnic groups—Asians, Latinos, American Indians, to name a few—are rapidly finding voices and beginning to participate with blacks and whites in the political process, thus initiating contact, expanding discourse, and, at times, coming into conflict. Many scholars have assumed that because blacks, Latinos, and Asian Americans share a racial-minority status, they are likely to form political coalitions. Coalition theory views the relationship between the various racial-minority groups as one of mutual respect and shared political goals and ideals. Indeed, there is ample evidence of multiracial coalitions in a number of American cities (Sonenshein 1990, 1993; Henry 1980; Henry and Muñoz 1991; Browning, Marshall, and Tabb 1984).

However, in many urban areas, conflict and competition among racial-minority groups has been increasing. Some of the more conspicuous conflicts include tensions between blacks and Koreans in New York City and Los Angeles, between Latinos and blacks in Washington, D.C., and, in Miami, between Puerto Ricans and blacks on one side and Cuban Americans on the other. Research also indicates that competition is emerging among minority groups over socioeconomic, political, and public-employment issues. Moreover, in some cities, the coalition model may be irrelevant for some minority groups: what interest do Cubans in Miami, for instance, or blacks in Camden, New Jersey, have in coalitions when their numbers are sufficient to achieve electoral success on their own? (See McClain and Tauber 1998; McClain and Karnig, 1990; McClain 1993; Oliver and Johnson 1984; Johnson and Oliver 1989; Meier and Stewart 1990; Falcon 1988; Warren, Corbett, and Stack 1986, 1990.) Yet even so, one must remember that the context in which racial-minority groups interact with one another cannot be viewed separately from the patterns established by the black-white dynamic. As Professor Franklin reminds us, the black-white dynamic created the framework that determines the attitudes and behaviors of each group toward others.

This chapter addresses many of the issues involved in past, present, and future patterns of interminority-group relationships in the United States in general, with a particular focus on data from ninety-six American cities.[1] Several questions structure our analysis, the first of which speak to patterns of interminority relations: Will America's changing demographics provide a basis for coalitions among blacks, Latinos, and Asian Americans, or will they result in competitive behaviors? Or, will we see that interactions are governed by political, economic, and social conditions? We will attempt to address these coalition-versus-competition questions using 1990s aggregate census data for a set of American cities. The second set of questions, discussed in the latter part of this chapter, explores the perceptions that minority groups harbor of others and extrapolates about the potential influence these perceptions exert on prospects for coalition or competition. Using 1995 and 1993 survey data and recent anecdotal evidence, we will speculate on the effect that these perceptions might have on tensions among racial-minority groups.

Coalition or Competition Politics?

The possibilities for coalitions between racial minorities, principally blacks and Latinos, has been a dominant theme in urban-politics research over the past several decades. Although discussing African Americans specifically, Stokely Carmichael and Charles V. Hamilton (1967, 79–80) in their seminal work, *Black Power*, offer four bases on which viable biracial coalitions (white and blacks, though these conditions presumably also apply to other biracial coalitions) may be formed: 1) parties entering into a coalition must recognize their respective self-interests; 2) the belief that each party will benefit from a cooperative relationship with the other or others; 3) each party has its own independent power base and control over its own decision making ; and 4) the recognition that the coalition is formed with specific and identifiable goals in mind. Accordingly, in Carmichael and Hamilton's rendering, interests rather than ideology provide the most substantial basis for the most productive biracial coalitions.

This interests-versus-ideology argument lies at the heart of the debate concerning a theory of biracial coalitions (Sonenshein 1993). One side of the argument sees interests as the ties binding together biracial coalitions, which are, at best, short-lived tactical compromises between self-centered groups. Conversely, those who emphasize ideology contend that the essential character of biracial coalitions is common beliefs. This perspective of coalition theory holds that preexisting attitudes on racial issues shape political views and subsequent political actions. The most likely coalition, according to this perspective, will be between groups close in ideology even when another union might be more strategically advantageous.

During the black and Chicano civil rights movements of the 1960s, numerous coalitions between the two groups existed. Latinos participated in the March on Washington in 1963 and in the Poor People's Campaign in 1968, for instance, while blacks lent their support to César Chavez's farmworkers' campaign. Shared concerns, such as poverty and discrimination, underpinned these unions between blacks and Latinos, especially blacks and Mexican Americans (Estrada, Garcia, and Marcias 1981), and there is clear evidence of coalition building between these two racial-minority groups (Browning, Marshall, and Tabb 1984, 1990; Henry and Muñoz 1991; Sonenshein 1993). There is also evidence from this era of coalitions between Asians and Latinos. Then, during the immigration debates of the late 1980s, Asians and Latinos coalesced to oppose the Simpson-Mazzoli immigration bill, a bill that required employers to report illegal aliens and established sanctions for employers who employed illegal aliens (Espiritu 1992). And in 1993, Asians and Latinos in Oakland, California, allied to force the creation of two city council districts in which each group constituted a plurality of the population (Fong 1998, 271). More recently, in California, blacks, Latinos, and Asians came together in unsuccessful attempts to defeat both Proposition 187, aimed at denying services to illegal immigrants, in 1994, and Proposition 209, abolishing affirmative action in state government and public university admissions, in 1996 (McClain and Stewart 1999).

Despite these examples of cooperation, however, the coalitions between blacks and Latinos break apart when policies designed to promote equality for one group conflict with the interests of the other group. In just one case, in the 1990s blacks and Latinos clashed over bilingual education, with blacks believing that it would shift resources from desegregation efforts (Falcon 1988, 178). Many black groups alienated Latinos by supporting the "English only" movement and sanctions on employers who hired illegal immigrants, and opposing the extension of the Voting Rights Act to cover Latinos (National Council of La Raza 1990).

Thus, among racial-minority groups, competition rather than coalition building may well be the dominant factor structuring intergroup relationships. Competition exists when two or more groups strive for the same finite objectives, such that the success of one group implies reduced possibilities for another. One could view minority-group competition as power contests among rival groups rooted in different cultures. And just like coalitions vary in composition, duration, and scope, the form of competition among groups with differing goals may also vary. Competition may only occur in selective areas, leaving open the possibility of coalitions in other areas. On the other hand, though, competition may be present in virtually all aspects of socio-economic and political life, leading all groups to regard one another on an "enemies-always" basis (Eisinger 1976, 17–18). In this situation, the possibility of coalitions is nonexistent. Furthermore, the greatest perceived competition may occur among near-equal groups: this framework, while addressed primarily to white-black relations, also is useful in examining relationships among minority groups if one recognizes that in addition to status differences, status similarities may become bases for conflict (Blalock 1967).

Research from selected cities finds that blacks, Latinos, and Asians in fact do compete for scarce jobs, housing, and government services (Oliver and Johnson 1984; Johnson and Oliver 1989; Falcon 1988; Mac-Manus and Cassel 1982; Welch, Karnig, and Eribes 1983; Mollenkopf 1990). Competition also arises among the various groups when their goals differ, when there is distrust or suspicion among the groups, or when the size of one group obviates the need to form coalitions with other minority groups (McClain 1993; McClain, and Karnig 1990; Falcon 1988; Warren, Corbett, and Stack 1990; Meier and Stewart 1990). Further conflict can result when particular groups begin to associate themselves, with justification or not, with the majority: recent survey data, for example, have indicated that Latinos and Asians believe themselves to have more in common with whites than with other racial-minority groups (National Conference 1993). (Blacks felt they had more in common with Latinos than with any other group [National Conference 1993].) Examining these phenomena, earlier survey data from the 1980s have shown an emerging hostility and distrust among blacks, Asians, and Latinos (Oliver and Johnson 1984; Johnson and Oliver 1989), with a majority of Mexican Americans opposed to building coalitions with blacks (see also Ambrecht and Pachon 1974; Browning, Marshall, and Tabb 1984; Grebler, Moore, and Guzman 1970; Henry 1980). Quite simply, then, all of this shows there is an underlying basis for hostilities among the groups. A final question concerns the extent to which blacks, Latinos, and Asians struggle for scarce resources in urban areas. There is evidence that competition occurs at the individual level, competition that may give rise to perhaps more important macro-level consequences.

The first part of this chapter explores the extent to which blacks, Latinos, and Asians compete for socioeconomic resources and political position, focusing on whether the political and socioeconomic resources of one racial-minority group facilitate or impede the other groups' ability to achieve political ends. Several possible intergroup patterns exist: one group may do well at the expense of the other groups; the successes of each group may be independent of one another but dependent upon the fortunes of non-Latino whites; and, either through coalitions or a consequence of the aggregate effects of independent actions, black, Latino, and Asian successes may covary positively.

Data and Methods

This study employs a variety of measures to assess socioeconomic and political outcomes (see Karnig and McClain 1985; McClain and Karnig 1990; McClain 1993). Socioeconomic indicators include median education,[2] median income, percent nonpoverty population, and percent employed. Political measures reflected whether members of the three groups hold mayoral offices, the percentage of the city council each groups constitutes, and the proportionality of each group's council representation when standardized by the size of that group in the entire population in the city in question. Our data set consisted of all ninety-six cities in the United States cities with populations over 25,000 that are at least 10 percent black and 10 percent Latino.[3]

Findings

The analyses presented are from the first pass through the data, and thus are very preliminary. These tentative results are subject to refinement as we work our way systematically through our analyses over the next years. In our ninety-six cities taken as a whole, whites constituted 58 percent of the population, blacks 24 percent, Latinos 23 percent, and Asians 5 percent. (These total to more than 100 percent primarily because Latinos can be of any race and hence may be also represented in the figures for whites, blacks, and Asians.) Sample averages from the cities parallel census data for the nation as a whole: Among the socioeconomic indicators, Asian income ($32,881) is the highest, followed in order by white ($31,309), Latino ($26,113), and black income ($24,101). White employment and Asian employment are the highest (both 94 percent), black employment is the lowest (87 percent), and Latino employment (89 percent) falls in between. Whites have the highest level of nonpoverty (89 percent) and blacks the lowest (70 percent), while Asians are second (84 percent) and Latinos third (78 percent). Also congruent with national data is the finding that Asian median education (13.0 years) is the highest, followed in order by white (12.3) and black (12.1), and Latino (10.9) a distant fourth. With respect to political outcomes, whites fare most favorably, winning mayoralties (73 percent), and council seats (71 percent) at rates far in excess of their proportion of the population (1.37 proportionality). Blacks rank second on these representational scores (20 percent mayoralties, 17 percent council seats, and .63 proportional of the population). Latinos are a distant third (7 percent mayoralties, 11 percent council seats, and .43 proportionality), and Asian political fortunes are virtually nonexistent (no mayoralties, .76 of one percent of council seats, and .03 proportionality).

The first column of table 4.1 seeks to test directly whether black, Latino, and Asian successes come either at the expense of one another or at the expense of whites. The results of the socioeconomic outcomes support the positive covariation model: where any group does better on the nonpoverty, income, and employment scales, the other groups—including whites—do significantly better as well. Educa-

Table 4.1   Correlations Among Black, Latino, Asian, and White Socioeconomic and Political Outcomes

Relationships	Simple Correlations	Partial Correlations
Socioeconomic (nonpoverty rates)		
Black-Latino	.41***	—
Black-Asian	.26**	—
Latino-Asian	.49***	—
Black-white	.33***	—
Latino-white	.59***	—
Asian-white	.51***	—
Black-Latino (controlling white)	—	.28*
Black-Asian (controlling white)	—	.12 (ns)
Latino-Asian (controlling white)	—	.28*
Income		
Black-Latino	.68***	—
Black-Asian	.62***	—
Latino-Asian	.74***	—
Black-white	.59***	—
Latino-white	.67***	—
Asian-white	.67***	—
Black-Latino (controlling white)	—	.63***
Black-Asian (controlling white)	—	.45***
Latino-Asian (controlling white)	—	.53***
Education		
Black-Latino	.13 (ns)	—
Black-Asian	−.03 (ns)	—
Latino-Asian	.06 (ns)	—
Black-white	.21*	—
Latino-white	.53***	—
Asian-white	.31**	—
Black-Latino (controlling white)	—	.03 (ns)
Black-Asian (controlling white)	—	−.10 (ns)
Latino-Asian (controlling white)	—	−.13 (ns)
Employment		
Black-Latino	.50***	—
Black-Asian	.33***	—
Latino-Asian	.40***	—
Black-white	.47***	—
Latino-white	.51***	—
Asian-white	.44***	—
Black-Latino (controlling white)	—	.35***
Black-Asian (controlling white)	—	.14 (ns)
Latino-Asian (controlling white)	—	.19 (ns)

(Table continues on p. 118.)

Table 4.1   (*Continued*)

Relationships	Simple Correlations	Partial Correlations
Political (mayors)		
Black-Latino	−.14 (ns)	—
Black-white	−.78***	—
Latino-white	−.46***	—
Black-Latino (controlling white)	—	−.92***
Percent Council		
Black-Latino	−.06 (ns)	—
Black-Asian	−.16 (ns)	—
Latino-Asian	.02 (ns)	—
Black-white	−.70***	—
Latino-white	−.65***	—
Asian-white	−.03 (ns)	—
Black-Latino (controlling white)	—	−.97**
Black-Asian (controlling white)	—	−.26*
Latino-Asian (controlling white)	—	−.001 (ns)
Council Proportionality		
Black-Latino	−.03 (ns)	—
Black-Asian	−.18 (ns)	—
Latino-Asian	.09 (ns)	—
Black-white	−.23*	—
Latino-white	−.25*	—
Asian-white	.04 (ns)	—
Black-Latino (controlling white)	—	−.09 (ns)
Black-Asian (controlling white)	—	−.18 (ns)
Latino-Asian (controlling white)	—	.10 (ns)

Source: Authors' compilation.
*$p < .05$. **$p < .01$. ***$p < .001$.

tional outcomes for blacks, Latinos, and Asians are not significantly related to one another, as increased educational opportunities for one racial-minority group do not significantly affect the educational opportunities of the other racial-minority groups (though there is evidence of an emerging competition between black and Asian education levels, minuscule and clearly not significant as that may be). Outcomes for each group, however, are positively and significantly related to increases in whites' educational opportunities.

The political variables exhibit a somewhat different pattern. In principle, there is no inherent reason for socioeconomic competition among the four groups, because socioeconomic outcomes are limitless: success for one group does not necessarily preclude the potential for increased socioeconomic fortunes for other groups. Conversely, however, political outcomes are finite. Each city has only one mayor and from three to fifty council seats; thus, winning these positions is a zero-sum game (that is, a victory for one group necessarily comes at the expense of another group). Still, though, the results here show no significant relationship between black and Latino elections to mayoral posts or among blacks, Latinos, and Asians for council posts. Such findings suggest neither widespread direct political competition nor mutual support. Nevertheless, it is possible that both exist in different cities but cancel out one another in the aggregate. Moreover, there is evidence of significant political competition between Latinos and whites as well as between blacks and whites. Clearly, if blacks and Latinos are to win political office, they do so at the expense of whites, who hold 73 percent of the mayoralties and 71 percent of the council seats. It bears noting that there is no significant competition between Asians and whites for political outcomes.

Based upon our findings to this point, we cannot conclude that there is a causal relationship between one group's outcomes and the outcomes of other groups. One reason for this may be that the cities in our data set differ in their opportunity structures, and the positive covariation among the groups for socioeconomic indicators may reflect that fact. Moreover, the relationship among the groups themselves may in fact be spurious. For example, New York and Chicago residents on average earn substantially higher salaries than residents of Baytown, Texas, and Wichita Falls, Texas, so we would expect that members of all races have higher incomes in New York and Chicago compared to their counterparts in Baytown and Wichita Falls. To test the possibility of such spuriousness, we used the outcomes for whites to control for the standard in each community.

The final column of table 4.1 shows socioeconomic findings, controlled for white outcomes. There is little evidence of spuriousness in the partial relationship between black, Latino, and Asian income; black and Latino employment; and black and Latino, and Latino and Asian nonpoverty levels. While the partial relationships are lower than their matched simple correlation, all the partials are positively and statistically significant at $p < .05$. Decreases in the size of correlations after controls are introduced signal that economic opportunities are definitely important, but the consistent positive correlations suggest no deleterious interminority competition in income, employment, and nonpoverty. However, the introduction of controls renders the relationship between black and Asian nonpoverty and employment no longer significant. In addition, although still not significant, the negative relationship between black and Asian education outcomes and those of Latinos and Asians become more explicitly negative.

When white outcomes are controlled, there are strong and negative links among certain aspects of black, Latino, and Asian political outcomes. Once results for whites are controlled, the correlation between black and Latino mayoral victory is $-.92$. Likewise, when white presence on city councils is controlled, the relationship between blacks and Latinos for council seats is fiercely competitive, though the same relationship between blacks and Asians is only mildly competitive. When controlling for whites, Latinos and Asians do not appear to compete for council seats.

The evidence to this point in our analysis is mixed. On the one hand, most socioeconomic measures (nonpoverty, income, and employment) of black, Latino and Asian outcomes covary positively with one another and with white outcomes; on the other hand, black, Latino, and Asian educational outcomes appear to be independent of each other, although all three are significantly positively related to white educational outcomes. Finally, black, Latino, and Asian political representation is also largely independent of each group, although representation outcomes for all are significantly negatively related to white representation.

Table 4.2 tests the proposition that an increasing proportion of one minority negatively affects the socioeconomic and political outcomes of the others. It reports simple correlations between each group's percentage of each city's population and the other groups' outcomes. To reduce possible spuriousness, partial correlations controlling for white outcomes were computed.

Still the results remain mixed. Increases in the proportion of a city's Latino population, for instance, do not appear to be related to competition with either blacks or Asians: none of the zero-order correlations between percentage Latino and black and Asian socioeconomic indicators is significant at $p < .05$, and none of the zero-order correlations on the political outcomes is significant either. Of the partial correlations, four are statistically significant—three of them (black and Asian income and Asian nonpoverty) not in the predicted direction. It is important to note that black council representation ($r_{yx1,x2} = -.39$) is significantly negatively related to increases in the Latino proportion of the population. Although not significant, the negative sign on black mayor and black council proportionality provide additional support that Latino population is negatively related to black council representation. In sum, Latino population increases are not injurious to black and Asian socioeconomic development or to Asian political outcomes. Yet when controls are introduced, increasing proportions of Latinos do have negative consequences for black political fortunes, particularly in city council representation.

Blacks and Latinos fare better socioeconomically in cities with higher Asian populations. Specifically, increasing proportions of Asians are significantly and positively related to Latino nonpoverty, black and Latino income, and black and Latino education. Politically, increases in the Asian population are of no consequence for black and Latino mayoral aspirations. But, when controls for white council outcomes are introduced, significant competition is revealed between blacks and Asians for city council seats.

Table 4.2 does, however, suggest possible negative effects of black population size on Latinos, particularly in the area of socioeconomic development. In the zero-order case, the percentage black is negatively and significantly associated with Latino nonpoverty ($r = -.21$) and education ($r = -.28$). When controls for white outcomes are introduced, none of the socioeconomic outcomes continues to be significantly affected by black population size. To be certain that these findings were not consequences of poverty and poor schools in communities with large black concentrations, we created twelve additional comparisons: black-Latino, black-Asian, and Latino-Asian ratios of nonpoverty, income, education, and employment.[4] Simple correlations indicate that as the black portion of the population rises, there is no statistically significant increase in black income versus Latino income, black education versus Latino education, and black employment versus Latino employment. There is, however, a statistically significant increase in black nonpoverty versus Latino nonpoverty, and a decrease in Latino income versus Asian income as the percentage of black population size increases. These relationships are intensified when controls for white outcomes are introduced. There are no negative effects of increasing black population size on Asian socioeconomic and political development outcomes.

Table 4.2 also suggests the possible existence of a competitive relationship concerning political outcomes. Initially, there appears to be no significant negative consequences to Latino mayoral aspirations, city council representation, and council proportionality by increases in black population size. Once again, however, when controls for white outcomes are introduced, the partial correlations suggest a moderate negative effect on Latino mayoral elections ($r_{yx1,x2} = -.43$) and a strong negative association to Latino council representation ($r_{yx1,x2} = -.53$).

These results on the effects of increasing black, Latino, and Asian population sizes suggest three things. First, the data indicate that increases in Latino population size are negatively related to black city council representation when controlling for white city council outcomes. Second, increases in Asian population size are negatively related to black city council representation when controlling for white city council outcomes. And, finally, the results reveal that increasing

Table 4.2 Correlations Among Percentage Groups and Socioeconomic and Political Outcome Measures with and Without Controls for White Outcomes

Outcomes	Controls for White Percentage Black Outcomes		Controls for White Percentage Latino Outcomes		Controls for White Percentage Asian Outcomes	
Socioeconomic nonpoverty rates						
Black	—	—	-.15 (ns)	-.01 (ns)	.16 (ns)	.10 (ns)
Latino	-.21*	.07 (ns)	—	—	.30**	.21**
Asian	-.08 (ns)	.07 (ns)	-.03 (ns)	.25***	—	—
Black-Latino	.38***	.40***	-.07 (ns)	-.13 (ns)	-.01 (ns)	.01 (ns)
Black-Asian	.10	.32**	-.08 (ns)	-.06 (ns)	.002 (ns)	-.01 (ns)
Latino-Asian	.07 (ns)	.10 (ns)	-.07 (ns)	-.05 (ns)	.006 (ns)	-.01 (ns)
Income						
Black	—	—	.03 (ns)	.15 (ns)	.29**	.28*
Latino	-.18 (ns)	-.07 (ns)	—	—	.21*	.23*
Asian	-.06 (ns)	.29**	-.08 (ns)	.24*	—	—
Black-Latino	.15 (ns)	.23 (ns)	.001 (ns)	.02 (ns)	.16 (ns)	.11 (ns)
Black-Asian	-.12 (ns)	-.16 (ns)	-.06 (ns)	-.09 (ns)	.09 (ns)	.11 (ns)
Latino-Asian	-.30*	-.39**	-.06 (ns)	-.13 (ns)	-.002 (ns)	.03 (ns)
Education						
Black	—	—	-.15 (ns)	-.01 (ns)	.30**	.24*
Latino	-.28*	.01 (ns)	—	—	.24*	.07 (ns)
Asian	-.12 (ns)	.06 (ns)	-.19 (ns)	.07 (ns)	—	—
Black-Latino	-.29**	.02 (ns)	.49***	.17	-.11 (ns)	.09 (ns)

Black-Asian	.10 (ns)	.02 (ns)	.06 (ns)	−.08 (ns)	.21*	.29**
Latino-Asian	−.19*	−.03 (ns)	−.40***	−.24***	.26*	.18 (ns)
Employment						
Black	—	—	.11 (ns)	.16 (ns)	.10 (ns)	.05 (ns)
Latino	−.17 (ns)	.11 (ns)	—	—	.07 (ns)	.02 (ns)
Asian	−.18*	−.03 (ns)	.01 (ns)	.20*	—	—
Black-Latino	−.05 (ns)	.02 (ns)	−.03 (ns)	.04 (ns)	.05 (ns)	.04 (ns)
Black-Asian	−.03 (ns)	.11 (ns)	−.09 (ns)	−.02 (ns)	−.005 (ns)	−.02 (ns)
Latino-Asian	.07 (ns)	.011(ns)	−.09 (ns)	−.08 (ns)	−.05 (ns)	−.05 (ns)
Political Mayors						
Black	—	—	.05 (ns)	−.18 (ns)	−.07 (ns)	−.11 (ns)
Latino	−.13 (ns)	−.43***	—	—	.08 (ns)	.10 (ns)
Percentage Council						
Black	—	—	.02 (ns)	−.39***	−.18 (ns)	−.29**
Latino	−.13 (ns)	−.53***	—	—	.12 (ns)	.13 (ns)
Asian	−.04 (ns)	−.07 (ns)	−.0045(ns)	−.01 (ns)	—	—
Council Proportionality						
Black	—	—	−.02 (ns)	−.06 (ns)	−.13 (ns)	−.13 (ns)
Latino	−.12 (ns)	−.12 (ns)	—	—	.27**	.28**
Asian	−.06 (ns)	−.06 (ns)	−.01 (ns)	−.01 (ns)	—	—

Source: Authors' compilation.
*p < .05. **p < .01. ***p < .001.

black population size is negatively related to Latino mayoral and city council representation when controlling for white city council and mayoral outcomes. That said, it must be noted, however, the analysis thus far has not directly tested the dominance proposition, which contends that when a group reaches majority or plurality status in a metropolitan area, it begins to obtain a disproportionate share of favorable outcomes, especially with respect to other minorities.

To examine more satisfactorily this dominance hypothesis, the sample was divided into cities with and without black and Latino majorities or pluralities. Additionally, although no cities in the sample have an Asian plurality or majority, there are three cities with Asian populations that constitute between 25 and 33 percent of the population. Thus, we thought that it would be useful to divide the data into cities with a quarter or more Asian population and those with less than a quarter. When all of this division was complete, twelve cities fell into the black-majority or -plurality; they ranged from Saginaw, Michigan, at the low end, with its 40 percent African-American plurality, to Irvington, New Jersey, at 70 percent.[5] Nine cities qualified as Latino-majority or -plurality cities; the extremes in this category were Paterson, New Jersey (40 percent Latino) and Miami, Florida (62 percent Latino). Finally, the populations of three cities were at least a quarter Asian; Carson, California, was 25 percent Asian while Gardena, California, was 33 percent Asian.[6] With so few majority-plurality cases, it was impossible to test for statistically significant differences. Still, though it provided only modest exploratory information, it may be instructive to focus on the data yielded by this sample as displayed in table 4.3.

Examination of the means displayed here demonstrates that in black-majority or -plurality cities, Latinos fare as well as or better than blacks on three socioeconomic indicators—nonpoverty, employment, and income. Education is the only area in which Latinos fared less well, lagging approximately two years behind blacks and Asians. On the other hand, Latinos do even better on all dimensions in cities with black minorities—they show an increase of 5 percent in nonpoverty levels, an $549 income increase, a 2 percent increase in employment levels, and a one-half-year increase in median years of education in such cities. Meanwhile, in the black-majority or -plurality cities, Asians show higher nonpoverty, education, employment, and income levels than both blacks and Latinos. Asians generally fare even better in cities with black minorities. Surprisingly, however, Asian income is $661 lower in black minority cities than it is in black-majority or -plurality cities.

The picture with respect to political success is markedly different in the black-majority or -plurality cities. Where they hold a majority or plurality, blacks overwhelm Latinos and Asians politically, holding

92 percent of mayoral posts and 58 percent of the city council seats, both of which are slightly in excess of their proportion in the population (1.09 proportionality). These outcomes are considerably higher compared to the figures for black-minority cities: there, blacks hold 11 percent of mayoralties and 12 percent of council seats, which is substantially less than their proportion in the population (.57 proportionality) would suggest. There are no Latino or Asian mayors in black-majority or -plurality cities, and Latinos hold only 4 percent of the council seats—which equates to a .16 proportionality—in such cities. Asians have not been elected to city councils in any of the black-majority or -plurality cities, but they fare no better in black-minority cities, having captured less than 1 percent of the council posts (a paltry .03 proportionality) there. Latinos, on the other hand, do somewhat better politically in black-minority cities, occupying 8 percent of the mayoralties and 12 percent of the city council seats (.46 proportionality) in those communities.

While socioeconomically Latinos fare as well as or, in some instances, better than blacks in black-majority or -plurality cities, blacks fare less well than Latinos in income, employment, and nonpoverty levels in Latino-majority or -plurality cities. Although still higher than that of Latinos, the black median education level is still less than a high school diploma in Latino-majority or -plurality cities, which is lower than it is in Latino-minority cities. Latinos enjoy a greater proportional share of the political outcomes in Latino-majority or -plurality cities than their proportion of the population—44 percent of mayorships, 40 percent council seats for .74 proportionality.[7] It is worth noting that blacks fare better politically in Latino-majority or -plurality cities than Latinos do in black-majority or -plurality cities. Asian political outcomes in Latino-dominated cities are comparable to Asian political outcomes in black dominated cities—virtually nonexistent.

Asians, in fact, while doing well socioeconomically, do not fare well politically in either black- or Latino-majority or -plurality cities. Asian-American political prospects improve, however, in cities that are at least one-quarter Asian. In these cities, Asians occupy 20 percent of the city council positions for their highest proportionality level (.69 proportionality) in any of our analyses. In terms of council-proportionality, Asian political outcomes in these cities surpass the outcomes for both blacks and Latinos in communities where they constitute majorities or pluralities.

Interestingly, and perhaps paradoxically, in cities where Asians constitute at least 25 percent of the total population, black income is second to Asian income and higher than it is in cities with other population compositions. These are the only cities in which black income is greater than Latino income. Latino income, while in the aggregate is third behind whites and Asians, is also at its highest level in cities

Table 4.3 Socioeconomic and Political Outcomes in Cities with and Without Black-Latino Majorities or Pluralities, and Cities with Twenty-five Percent or More Asian Population

Outcomes	Black Majority or Plurality Cities (n = 12)	Black Minority Cities (n = 84)	Latino Majority or Plurality Cities (n = 9)	Latino Minority Cities (n = 87)	Asian 25 Percent Cities (n = 3)	Asian < 25 Percent Cities (n = 93)
Socioeconomic (nonpoverty rates)						
Black	74%	70%	69%	70%	86%	70%
Latino	74	79	77	78	86	78
Asian	79	85	85	84	92	84
Income						
Black	$25,411	$23,952	$24,305	$24,116	$37,092	$23,716
Latino	$25,619	$26,168	$26,339	$26,074	$32,487	$25,893
Asian	$33,462	$32,801	$34,202	$32,725	$40,721	$32,508
Education (in years)						
Black	12.10	12.15	11.79	12.18	12.68	12.13
Latino	10.36	10.95	9.57	11.01	11.14	10.87
Asian	12.53	13.07	12.86	13.02	12.68	13.02
Employment						
Black	85%	87%	85%	87%	90%	86%
Latino	88	90	88	90	91	89
Asian	89	94	91	94	96	93
Ratios (nonpoverty)						
Black-Latino	1.00	.89	.89	.90	1.00	.90
Black-Asian	.97	.82	.82	.85	.94	.84
Latino-Asian	.97	.93	.91	.94	.94	.94

Income						
Black-Latino	.93	1.12	.93	.92	.92	.99
Black-Asian	.78	.89	.79	.74	.80	.74
Latino-Asian	.82	.81	.83	.76	.83	.73
Education						
Black-Latino	1.13	1.14	1.11	1.28	1.12	1.20
Black-Asian	.94	1.00	.94	.92	.94	.97
Latino-Asian	.84	.88	.85	.74	.84	.83
Employment						
Black-Latino	.97	.99	.97	.96	.97	.97
Black-Asian	.93	.94	.93	.94	.92	.96
Latino-Asian	.96	.95	.96	.97	.96	.99
Political (mayor)						
Black	22%	00	21%	22%	11%	92%
Latino	8	00	3	44	8	00
Percentage Council						
Black	18	00	17	20	12	58
Latino	11	8	8	40	12	4
Asian	13	20	0.82	0	0.85	0
Council Proportionality						
Black	.66	.00	.64	.55	.57	1.09
Latino	.43	.36	.39	.74	.46	.16
Asian	.01	.69	.03	.00	.03	.00

Source: Authors' compilation.

where Asians constitute at least 25 percent of the population. (We recognize that the presence of San Francisco as one of the three "Asian" cities probably accounts for the extremely high median income levels because of its higher income levels. Nevertheless, the means provide a sense of the dynamics in these varied sets of cities.)

Given the simplicity of our analyses, we are reluctant to cast these findings in any definitive fashion. More rigorous examination is needed before we can develop firm generalizations. Nevertheless, the preliminary research does suggest some interesting patterns concerning socioeconomic and political competition among blacks, Latinos, and Asians. But because the data used in these analyses are aggregate level, it is impossible to employ it to explain individual-level behavior. Thus, for another view of the potential for coalition or competitive behavior among blacks, Latinos, and Asians, we examine survey data in the next section. Survey data provide insight into the attitudes of these groups toward one another and may give us a basis for speculating about the future of relationships among the groups.

Racial Minorities' Perceptions of One Another

In our introduction to this chapter, we stated that although the United States was becoming increasingly multiracial, the black-white paradigm still structured the way in which white Americans perceive Latinos and Asian Americans. Likewise, this paradigm also structures how blacks, Latinos, and Asians view one another. In this section, we examine this idea more fully.

In 1968, the Kerner Commission warned that the United States was moving in the direction of becoming two nations, one white, the other black. Scholars may disagree as to whether this has actually come to pass, but a national survey conducted by the *Washington Post*, Harvard University, and the Kaiser Foundation in 1995 found that the chasm between whites and blacks was so great that the groups did indeed appear to live in two different countries (Morin 1995). That survey found that a majority of white Americans believed that blacks fared as well as or better than whites economically, had an equal chance to succeed, and had achieved equality with whites. The majority of whites also believed that racism was not a major problem in America, that whites bore no responsibility for the problems blacks face today, and that the federal government had no responsibility to ensure economic equality for racial minorities. In stark contrast, most blacks surveyed felt that racism and discrimination had increased over the last decade, posing serious problems to the ability of blacks to succeed. Most blacks also believed that they were economically disadvantaged and that the federal government had an obligation to

equalize outcomes as well as opportunities. Large majorities of Latinos and Asian Americans also agreed that blacks were worse off
than whites in terms of income, jobs, housing, and education (National Conference 1993).

A 1993 report called "Taking America's Pulse: The National Conference Survey on Inter-Group Relations" also found that blacks, Latinos, and Asians held similar perceptions of race relations. Majorities
of all three groups believed whites to be insensitive to other people.
All three groups described whites as having "a long history of bigotry
and prejudice," although while three-fourths of blacks felt this way,
only slightly more than half of Latinos and Asian Americans agreed.
Also, four-fifths of blacks, two-thirds of Latinos, and three-fifths of
Asian Americans believed that they lack the same opportunities enjoyed by whites. Whites in the survey, as in the 1995 *Washington Post*
survey, believed that blacks, Latinos, and Asian Americans enjoyed
the same opportunities as they (National Conference 1993).

Yet, despite agreement on broad notions concerning fewer opportunities afforded to members of minority groups, blacks, Latinos, and
Asian Americans hold views of one another that may open the door
to increasing conflicts among them. When asked, for instance, the
groups with which they felt they had most in common, blacks responded that they had most in common with Latinos and least in
common with whites and Asian Americans. Latinos believed that
they had more in common with whites and least in common with
blacks, and Asian Americans felt they had the most in common with
whites and the least in common with African Americans (National
Conference 1993).

Survey data also offer evidence that Asians, blacks, and Latinos
each harbor racial stereotypes about the other groups. A plurality of
blacks and Latinos, for example, consider Asian Americans to be "un-
scrupulous, crafty and devious in business" and see them as "be-
liev[ing] they are superior to people of other groups and cultures."
Two-thirds of Asian Americans and slightly less than 50 percent of
blacks, meanwhile, believe that Latinos "tend to have bigger families
than they are able to support," and one-third of Asian Americans and
a quarter of blacks believe that Latinos "lack ambition and the drive
to succeed." A third of Asian Americans and a quarter of Latinos
believe that blacks "want to live on welfare" and that "even if given
a chance, [blacks] aren't capable of getting ahead." Some, if not
many of these views may not be shared by a majority of a group, but
nevertheless it is well known that the perceptions of a few mani-
fested in the right situations can easily result in exacerbating any
already-existing tensions among the groups (Bobo and Hutchings
1996).

Two incidents from late 1999 illustrate problems that arise from

Table 4.4 Negative Stereotypes of Minorities by Other Racial Minorities

| | Group Stereotypes | | | | | |
| | Asian American | | Latinos | | African Americans | |
	Crafty in Business	Unfriendly to Non-Asians	Overly Large Families	Lack Ambition	Like Living on Welfare	Cannot Get Ahead on Own
Group response						
Blacks	41%	44%	49%	24%	—	—
Latinos	46	44	—	—	26	33
Asians	—	—	68	35	31	21

Source: National Conference 1993.

these stereotyped perceptions. And although both anecdotes focus on blacks, other minority groups have received the same treatment at the hands of rival groups. We chose these accounts because they are the most recent events to have received widespread media exposure.

The first incident occurred in Miami Beach, Florida, during the first week of November. After dining at the Thai Toni restaurant, Charles Thompson, a black travel consultant for American Express, noticed that a 15 percent gratuity had been added to his bill. To determine whether this was a common practice at the restaurant, he asked the white couple at the table next to him if he could see their bill. It did not include the gratuity. When Mr. Thompson confronted the restaurant owner, Hiromi Takarada, Takarada responded, "Black people don't tip well." Mr. Thompson was so furious that the only thing he could think to do was to dial 911. When the police arrived and the officer asked the owner why he had added 15 percent to the bill, the owner told the officer the same thing: "Black people don't tip well." So convinced was he of the accuracy of his stereotype, Mr. Takarada assumed that the police officer would support him. The officer, however, became one of the primary witnesses against the restaurateur.

Mr. Thompson filed a civil rights–violation complaint with the Florida Commission on Human Relations. State Attorney General Robert Butterworth, in turn, filed suit charging Mr. Takarada with violating Florida's Unfair Trade Practices Act. In the ensuing fallout, Thai Toni has been dropped from the Miami Beach Chamber of Commerce and removed from the city's Web site. Of the situation, Attorney General Butterworth is quoted as saying, "We've made great strides in this country to make sure that restaurants, public places, are open to everyone. This is like being told to move to the back of the bus. It's kind of ironic, [because] this guy [Mr. Takarada] has benefited because of the openness of this country" (Bragg 1999). To date, Mr. Takarada has settled the state's suit for $15,000 and agreed that he and his employees would undergo sensitivity training (*New York Times* 1999). Meanwhile, Mr. Thompson's complaint is still pending. Clearly, Mr. Takarada held negative stereotypes about blacks and felt justified in treating his black customers in a discriminatory fashion based on those stereotypes.

Around the same times as this Miami Beach incident, the actor Danny Glover complained to the New York City Taxi and Limousine Commission that five cabs failed to stop for him. When one finally did pick up Glover, his daughter, and her friend, Glover, who suffers from a hip ailment that would prevent him from sitting comfortably in the backseat, was not permitted to sit in the front seat—despite taxi rules allowing it. Given the black-white dynamic that has historically framed race relations in the United States, one might initially expect these cab drivers to be white. Yet 70 percent of New York's cab drivers are nonwhite, mostly immigrants from nonwhite countries: upwards of 50 percent are of South Asian descent, predominantly immigrants from India, Pakistan, and Bangladesh (Duke 1999). Still, one could argue that the racist views about blacks held by white Americans have been internalized by nonwhite immigrants to this country, who then behave toward blacks in a discriminatory fashion.

Conclusion

This chapter has focused on the extent to which racial-minority groups cooperate or clash in urban settings. Scholars have traditionally examined race relations in terms of a black-versus-white dichotomy, but more recently, a growing body of research has recognized that Latinos and Asian Americans also affect racial politics in United States cities—though they too are influenced by the black-white dichotomy. In order to advance the nascent study of the relationships among multiminority groups, we statistically analyzed black, Latino, and Asian-American socioeconomic and political outcomes in a set of cities. We found that for many socioeconomic indicators (such as income, employment, and nonpoverty), the increased success of one group means increased success for all. Therefore, for the most part, there is cooperation among the minority groups in terms of socioeconomic indicators. However, we found that for political positions, there is a tremendous amount of competition among the groups. One racial minority group's political success comes at the expense of another racial minority group.

We also explored the extent to which racial stereotypes among the minority groups affect their actions. Survey data suggest that many blacks, Latinos, and Asian Americans hold negative stereotypes of one another. Two anecdotes offered here, while not indicative of widespread tensions and conflict among communities of color, illustrate that the potential for conflict does exist. Perhaps a systematic, statistical analysis of the connection between racial stereotypes and tensions among the groups is in order.

In closing, we believe that understanding immigration is the key to predicting the future of interminority group relations. As more Latino and Asian immigrants enter American economic, social, and political life, the potential for conflicts with blacks and each other certainly increases. The negative stereotypes of immigrants harbored by many native-born Americans (including blacks) may influence the way in which blacks interact with immigrant minority groups. Moreover, the negative stereotypes that immigrants hold about blacks may affect the way in which they will interact with them. It is not clear whether immigrants, such as Mr. Takarada, developed their negative stereo-

types of blacks in their native land or whether they learned that behavior upon arriving on American soil. Either way, it appears that
many immigrants' stereotypes of other racial minority groups will
only lead to increased tension. Perhaps through intergroup dialogue
and education the stereotypes and potential conflict might be eliminated, or, at a minimum, reduced.

Notes

1. The cities are: Freeport, Haverstraw, Hempstead, Newburgh, New Rochelle,
    New York City, Ossining, White Plains, and Yonkers, NY; Sierra Vista, AZ;
    Homestead, Lake Worth, Miami, Miramar, North Lauderdale, North Miami,
    North Miami Beach, Oakland Park, Tampa, and West Palm Beach, FL; Aurora,
    Chicago, Chicago Heights, Joliet, and Waukegan, IL; East Chicago, IN; Kenner,
    LA; Boston, and Springfield, MA; Saginaw, MI; Las Vegas, and North Las
    Vegas, NV; Lorain, OH; Lancaster, PA; Providence, RI; Austin, Baytown, Bryan,
    Conroe, Dallas, Fort Worth, Galveston, Houston, Killeen, Temple, Texas City,
    Waco, and Wichita Falls, TX; Bridgeport, Hartford, New Haven, New London,
    and Waterbury, CT; Denver, CO; Carson, Compton, Culver City, Fairfield,
    Gardena, Hawthorne, Highland, Inglewood, Long Beach, Los Angeles, Lyn-
    wood, Marina, Monrovia, Moreno Valley, Oakland, Paramount, Pasadena,
    Pittsburg, Pomona, Rialto, Richmond, Sacramento, San Bernardino, San Fran-
    cisco, San Pablo, Seaside, and Vallejo, CA; Atlantic City, Camden, Elizabeth,
    Hackensack, Irvington, Jersey City, Long Branch, Newark, New Brunswick,
    Passaic, Paterson, Perth Amboy, Plainfield, Trenton, and Vineland, NJ.

2. The Census Bureau no longer provides median years of education; the
    measure is the percent of the population twenty-five years of age and
    older that completed high school. The figures used in this analysis for
    median years of education were calculated from grouped data reported in
    the 1990 Census (U.S. Bureau of the Census 1990).

3. Information on socioeconomic indicators were taken from the U.S. Bureau
    of Census (1990). Data on black elected officials were drawn from the
    Joint Center for Political and Economic Studies (1993), and information on
    Latinos elected officials was drawn from the National Association of La-
    tino Elected and Appointed Officials (1993). Data on Asian elected offi-
    cials were collected through phone calls to the city clerk's office in all of
    the cities. Professor Don Nakanishi of the Asian American Studies Center
    at the University of California at Los Angeles assisted us in identifying
    Asian elected officials. We verified the data when the UCLA Center for
    Asian American Studies published a directory of Asian American elected
    officials (1995). Municipal or county executive directors (1990 to 1991)
    provided data on city council size and type of governmental and electoral
    structure; phone calls were made to collect information on cities that were
    not listed and to verify data about which there were questions.

4. The ratios were constructed by dividing each group's outcomes for the
    indicators by the appropriate outcomes for the others—for instance, black
    income was divided by Latino income to arrive at the ratio of black to

Latino income. When black and Latino outcomes are equal, then, the ratio is 1.0; when blacks do better, the ratio exceeds 1.0; where Latinos are more successful, the ratio is below 1.0.

5. Interestingly, Chicago, which was a black-plurality city in 1980 with a black population of slightly over 40 percent, no longer meets our threshold because its black population percentage dropped to 39 percent in 1990. Compton, California, which in 1980 had a black population of 74 percent and was the city with the largest percentage of black residents, experienced a drop in the black population percentage to 55 percent.

6. The population of San Francisco, the third city, was 29 percent Asian.

7. The less-than-equitable representation could be the result of the presence of a sizable proportion of noncitizens in the Latino population, as these people are counted in the population but are not eligible to participate in the political process.

References

Ambrecht, Beliana, and Harry P. Pachon. 1974. "Ethnic Political Mobilization in a Mexican American Community: An Exploratory Study of East Los Angeles, 1965–1972." *Western Political Quarterly* 27: 500–19.

Baker, Peter. 1997. "A Splinter on the Race Advisory Board." *Washington Post*, July 15, 1997, p. A04.

Blalock, Herbert M. 1967. *Toward a Theory of Minority-Group Relations*. New York: John Wiley and Sons.

Bobo, Lawrence, and Vincent L. Hutchings. 1996. "Perceptions of Racial Group Competition: Extending Blumer's Theory of Groups Position to a Multiracial Social Context." *American Sociological Review* 61 (December): 951–72.

Bragg, Rick. 1999. "Restaurant's Added Gratuity Leads to Discrimination Claim." *New York Times*, November 10, 1999, p. A16.

Browning, Rufus P., Dale Rogers Marshall, and David H. Tabb. 1984. *Protest Is Not Enough*. Berkeley: University of California Press.

———. 1990. "Has Political Incorporation Been Achieved? Is It Enough?" In *Racial Politics in American Cities*, edited by Rufus P. Browning, Dale Rogers Marshall, and David H. Tabb. New York: Longman.

Carmichael, Stokely, and Charles V. Hamilton. 1967. *Black Power: The Politics of Liberation in America*. New York: Random House.

Cohen, Gaynor. 1982. "Alliance and Conflict Among Mexican Americans." *Ethnic and Racial Studies* 5: 175–95.

Duke, Lynne. 1999. "'Hailing While Black' Sparks a Cab Crackdown." *Washington Post*, November 16, 1999, p. A03.

Eisinger, Peter K. 1976. *Patterns of Interracial Politics: Conflict and Cooperation in the City*. New York: Academic Press.

Espiritu, Yen Le. 1992. *Asian American Panethnicity: Bridging Institutions and Identities*. Philadelphia: Temple University Press.

Estrada, Leobardo, F. Chris Garcia, and Reynaldo F. Marcias. 1981. "Chicanos in the United States: A History of Exploitation and Resistance." *Daedalus* 110: 103–32.

Falcon, Angelo. 1988. "Black and Latino Politics in New York City." In *Latinos in the Political System*, edited by F. Chris Garcia. South Bend, Ind.: University of Notre Dame Press.

Fong, Timothy P. 1998. *The Contemporary Asian American Experience: Beyond the Model Minority*. Upper Saddle River, N.J.: Prentice Hall.

Grebler, Leo, Joan Moore, and Ralph Guzman. 1970. *The Mexican American People*. New York: Free Press.

Henry, Charles P. 1980. "Black and Chicano Coalitions: Possibilities and Problems." *Western Journal of Black Studies* 4: 222–32.

Henry, Charles P., and Carlos Muñoz Jr. 1991. "Ideological and Interest Links in California Rainbow Politics." In *Racial and Ethnic Politics in California*, edited by Bryan O. Jackson and Michael B. Preston. Berkeley: Institute of Governmental Studies.

Jennings, James. 1992. "Blacks and Latinos in the American City in the 1990s: Toward Political Alliances or Social Conflict." *National Political Science Review* 3: 158–63.

Johnson, James H., and Melvin L. Oliver. 1989. "Inter-Ethnic Minority Conflict in Urban American: The Effects of Economic and Social Dislocations." *Urban Geography* 10: 449–63.

Joint Center for Political and Economic Studies. 1993. *Black Elected Officials: A National Roster*. Washington, D.C.: Joint Center for Political and Economic Studies Press.

Karnig, Albert K. 1979. "Black Representation on City Councils." *Urban Affairs Quarterly* 11: 223–42.

Karnig, Albert K., and Paula D. McClain. 1985. "The New South and Black Economic and Political Development: Changes from 1970 to 1980." *Western Political Quarterly* 38: 537–50.

MacManus, Susan, and Carol Cassel. 1982. "Mexican Americans in City Politics: Participation, Representations, and Policy Preferences." *Urban Unrest* 4: 57–69.

McClain, Paula D. 1993. "The Changing Dynamics of Urban Politics: Black and Hispanic Municipal Employment—Is There Competition?" *Journal of Politics* 55: 399–414.

———. 1994. "Coalition and Competition: Patterns of Black-Latino Relations in Urban Politics." Paper presented to the Wellesley College Conference on Conflicts and Coalitions Among Minorities: The Crisis of Ethnic and Racial Tribalism in Cities. Wellesley, Mass. (April 9–11, 1994).

McClain, Paula D., and Albert K. Karnig. 1990. "Black and Hispanic Socioeconomic and Political Composition." *American Political Science Review* 84: 535–45.

McClain, Paula D., and Joseph Stewart Jr. 1999. *"Can't We All Get Along?" Racial and Ethnic Minorities in American Politics*, 2nd edition update. Boulder, Colo.: Westview Press.

McClain, Paula D., and Steven C. Tauber. 1998. "Black and Latino Socioeconomic and Political Competition: Has a Decade Made a Difference?" *American Politics Quarterly* 26 (April): 237–52.

Meier, Kenneth J., and Joseph Stewart Jr. 1990. "Interracial Competition in Large Urban School Districts: Elections and Public Policy." Paper presented to the annual meeting of the American Political Science Association, San Francisco.

Mollenkopf, John H. 1990. "New York: The Great Anomaly." In *Racial Politics in American Cities*, edited by Rufus P. Browning, Dale Rogers Marshall, and David H. Tabb. New York: Longman.

Morin, Richard. 1995. "A Distorted Image of Minorities: Poll Suggests That What Whites Think They See May Affect Beliefs." *Washington Post*, October 8, 1995, p. A01.

National Association of Latino Elected and Appointed Officials. 1993. *National Roster of Hispanic Elected Officials*. Washington, D.C.: NALEO Educational Fund, Inc.

National Conference. 1993. *Taking America's Pulse: The Full Report of the National Conference Survey on Inter-Group Relations*. New York: L. H. Harris.

National Council of La Raza. 1990. "Background Paper for Black-Hispanic Dialogue." Unpublished paper.

New York Times. 1999. "Restaurateur Settles Discrimination Suit." November 26, 1999, p. A27.

Oliver, Melvin L., and James H. Johnson. 1984. "Inter-Ethnic Conflict in an Urban Ghetto: The Case of Blacks and Latinos in Los Angeles." *Social Movements, Conflicts, and Change* 6: 57–94.

Robinson, Theodore, Robert E. England, and Kenneth J. Meier. 1985. "Black Resources and Black School Board Representation: Does Political Structure Matter?" *Social Science Quarterly* 66: 976–82.

Ruane, Rosalie, et al., editors. 1991. *Municipal/County Executive Directory*. Washington, D.C.: Carroll Publishing.

Sonenshein, Raphael J. 1990. "Biracial Coalition Politics in Los Angeles." In *Racial Politics in American Cities*, edited by Rufus P. Browning, Dale Rogers Marshall, and David H. Tabb. New York: Longman.

———. 1993. *Politics in Black and White: Race and Power in Los Angeles*. Princeton, N.J.: Princeton University Press.

UCLA Center for Asian American Studies. 1995. *1995 Directory of National Asian Pacific American Political Almanac*. 6th ed. Los Angeles: UCLA Center for Asian American Studies.

U.S. Bureau of the Census. 1990. *Census of Population: 1990 (CP-1; CP-2; STF3A)*. Washington: Government Printing Office.

———. 1996a. "Population Projections of the United States by Age, Sex, Race, and Hispanic Origin: 1995 to 2050." Available on the World Wide Web at: *www.census.gov/population/projections/nation/nsrh/sprh0610.txt*

———. 1996b. "Population Projections for States, by Age, Sex, Race, and Hispanic Origin: 1995 to 2025." Available on the World Wide Web at: *www.census.gov/population/projections/state/stpjrace.txt*

U.S. Riot Commission Report. 1968. *Report of the National Advisory Commission on Civil Disorders*. New York: Bantam.

Warren, Christopher L., John G. Corbett, and John F. Stack. 1986. "Minority Mobilization in an International City: Rivalry and Conflict." *PS: Political Science and Politics* 19: 626–34.

———. 1990. "Hispanic Ascendancy and Tripartite Politics in Miami." In *Racial Politics in American Cities*, edited by Rufus P. Browning, Dale Rogers Marshall, and David H. Tabb. New York: Longman.

Welch, Susan, Albert K. Karnig, and Richard Eribes. 1983. "Changes in Hispanic Local Employment in the Southwest." *Western Political Quarterly* 36: 660–73.

Chapter 5

Blacks and Cubans in Miami: The Negative Consequences of the Cuban Enclave on Ethnic Relations

GUILLERMO J. GRENIER AND MAX CASTRO

IN THE fall of 1990, Arthur Teele got to know Miami's Calle Ocho very well. Teele, an African American Republican who had made his name as a functionary in Ronald Reagan's Department of Transportation, was running for Dade County commissioner. His opponent, the incumbent commissioner Babara Carey, was well known and respected in the black community. Teele did the numbers and decided that his best chance to win the at-large seat was by focusing on the Cuban community. He said as much: "[W]e felt that the only place that we could not beat Commissioner Carey was in the black community. She put most of her resources in one place and I didn't" (Viglucci 1990). Thus Teele made the rounds of the Cuban organizations, restaurants, and the elderly activities centers known as comedores, courting Cubans, most of whom were (and still are) registered Republicans with a generally sterling record of turning out to vote. Teele was particularly welcomed in the comedores, where the elderly Latinos were pleased to have him recognize their importance. The comedores were important to Teele, in turn, because they provide transportation to the voting booth to those who needed it—and in a close race, these several thousand votes could be essential. The strategy paid off: Teele won an election in which he received two of three Cuban votes while losing four out of five black votes. In doing to, he became the black community's representative without receiving the majority of its vote.

Fast forward to 1996. Teele was on the campaign trail again after serving five successful years as a commissioner. This time, though, he was aiming to become the first strong mayor of Dade County, a newly created office replacing the weak mayor system that had existed since the county's 1960 "good government" restructuring. Teele's opponent this time around was Alex Penelas, who had entered county government in 1992, when he joined Teele as a commissioner. Back in 1992, Penelas had run a campaign emphasizing his Cubanness. He had to: his opponent, Carlos Valdes, was an old-guard Cuban who made ethnic purity a major theme of his own campaign, mocking Penelas as a "Cuban wannabe" and saying that it took more than eating chicken and rice in a Calle Ocho restaurant to be a real Cuban. Penelas, young and born in Hialeah, fought back feebly, defending his bona fides. At one point, even his mother appealed to the public during a popular Cuban radio talk show, saying, "It's not his fault that he was born in this country." Penelas won the commission seat, but split the Cuban vote. Had it not been for the Anglo vote, he might not have had the opportunity to face Teele in the 1996 race for control of the largest metropolitan area in the fourth-largest state in the union.

In 1996, both candidates returned to their ethnic roots. Teele, though still a Republican, had built a solid record of addressing the concerns of the African American community and had gained the respect of many of its civic leaders. For his part, Penelas, though a Democrat, had become the darling of the Cuban American community, a young rising star whose political future some saw leading to the governor's mansion. And in the race, while discussion and debates were heard on the issues and the candidates' experience, the bottom line to many voters was ethnicity. Penelas was the Cuban candidate, Teele the African American candidate. Each community was expected to support its own—and did. Both the Hispanic and black communities mobilized forces and got out the vote for "its" candidate.

The result of the 1996 election is significant for the stark evidence it provides of polarization along ethnic lines. Penelas garnered a little over 60 percent of the total vote, and an estimated 60 percent of the Hispanic vote, but only 3 percent of the black vote. As for Teele, the overwhelming 84 percent support he received from the African American community was not enough to carry him to victory; he won but 2 percent of the Hispanic vote. "Even when African Americans turn out," remarked one Teele campaign worker in an interview with the author, "we can't put one of ours in office."

These two cases years, six apart, show the significance of the Cuban American population in Miami's local politics, as well as the African American community's inability to counterbalance it. This state of affairs—a conflict, really—is rooted in the entrenchment of the Cuban American population as the dominant force in the political, cultural, economic, and social development of Miami-Dade County and the entire South Florida region.

This chapter explores the dynamics of Miami's Cuban enclave and its impact on black-Latino relations in the region. The emphasis is on how the enclave, while increasing the opportunities for Cubans, Cuban Americans, and other Latinos to become incorporated into the American political system, has created social, political, cultural, and economic structures and dynamics that segregate the Latino community from the African American community. The separation that results increases the solidarity of the Cuban American and Latino communities of the Greater Miami area but also increases the friction between Latinos and African Americans. In short, "Blacks and Cubans in Miami" presents some negative consequences of the ethnic enclave.

Creation and Characteristics of the Cuban Enclave

Miami's Cuban community is regarded as America's foremost example of a true ethnic enclave, which Portes and Bach (1985, 203) define as "a distinctive economic formation, characterized by the spatial concentration of immigrants who organize a variety of enterprises to serve their own ethnic market and the general population." The creation of the enclave began in the early 1960s, as the first wave of Cuban exiles found its way to Miami. The Cubans in this first wave, which arrived between 1959 and 1961, is often referred to as the Golden Exiles. As a group, the Golden Exiles included a large swath of the 1950s Cuban elite: a large proportion of the island's successful entrepreneurs, physicians, lawyers, engineers, managers, accountants, and architects. The entrepreneurial base of the Miami Cuban community was thus established largely by these Cuban immigrants who possessed the skills and attitudes that eventually enabled many of them to establish themselves as self-employed tradespeople in a wide range of businesses (Portes 1987). Most shared a belief in the superiority of capitalism, a confidence in their own abilities, and a positive regard for the United States. As members of Cuba's precommunist professional, economic, and social elite, exiles arriving in the early 1960s often had close personal and family ties to other exiles who had arrived earlier. Some of these early arrivals had managed to get money out of Cuba; some had been able to land jobs with American companies. Yet even if they could not transfer their investments, these Cubans' human capital—their knowledge and experience—came with them.

The Golden Exiles came from the part of Cuban society most immediately threatened by a socialist revolution. Accordingly, their opposition to the revolution and its leader served as a unifying force and lent them a sense of identity as the concentration of Cubans in the Miami area increased. Anti-Castro organizations proliferated and established themselves as the voice of the Cuban community in exile, and the failure of the Bay of Pigs invasion served to solidify the exile identity as the primary characteristic of the Miami population. The return to the island, not necessarily becoming an assimilated part of American society, was the goal of the exiles, and this was to be achieved not through alliances with the United States, but through solidarity and persistence of the Cuban community in exile. The early waves of Cubans provided the core of the Cuban enclave, and they reinforced it with the welcome given newcomers: in the context of the Cold War, Cubans were officially welcomed as refugees fleeing the scourge of communism. The U.S. government viewed the immigration of tens of thousand of some of the ablest Cubans as an economic and propaganda blow against the Castro regime, as well as a potential exile army to be deployed against it.

Not all established resident Anglos opened their arms and hearts to the new immigrants, however, and Cubans did encounter a measure of prejudice and discrimination. Nevertheless, given the nature of racism in the United States and in Miami, white Anglo employers would often prefer to hire a white former Cuban teacher, pharmacist, or office worker with a heavy Spanish accent, for instance, than an African American. Moreover, American attitudes toward immigration were fairly positive in the early 1960s. The country was in the midst of postwar prosperity, immigration was very low, and there was a special sympathy for refugees feeling from communism.

Whatever the feelings of the populace, the federal government rolled out the welcome mat to these Cold War refugees and established a comprehensive agenda to assist the Cubans. The Cuban Refugee Program spent nearly $1 billion in direct assistance to Cuban exiles between 1965 and 1976 (Pedraza-Bailey 1985, 41). Furthermore, the federal government provided transportation costs from Cuba, financial assistance to needy refugees as well as to state and local public agencies that provided services for refugees, and employment and professional training courses for refugees. Cubans also benefited disproportionately from programs not specifically designed for them: from 1968 to 1980, Latinos (almost all of them Cubans) received 46.9

percent of all Small Business Administration loans granted in Dade County (Porter and Dunn 1984, 196).

Indirect assistance was even more significant. Through the 1960s, the University of Miami had the largest Central Intelligence Agency station in the world outside of the organization's headquarters in Reston, Virginia. With perhaps as many as twelve thousand Cubans in Miami on its payroll at one point in the early 1960s, the Agency was one of the largest employers in the state of Florida. It supported what was described as the third-largest navy in the world and over fifty front businesses: CIA boat shops, CIA gun shops, CIA travel agencies, CIA detective agencies, and CIA real estate agencies (Didion 1987, 90–91; Rieff 1987, 193–207; Rich 1974, 7–9). This investment was far more successful in giving Cubans in Miami an economic boost than it was in destabilizing the Castro regime (Grenier and Stepick 1992).

Cubans arriving in the United States in the 1960s came at the best of times. That decade marked the apex of the most vigorous economic expansion in American history: the post–World War II boom. It was also the beginning of the restructuring and globalization of the American economy. Those Cubans who could not be absorbed in Miami's labor market were relocated to other areas where work was plentiful, while those who stayed in Miami contributed to the globalization of the Miami economy as well as to the development of the enclave.

Cuban American family and class structures also contributed to the development of the economic enclave and, more generally, to Cuban economic successes. Families of Cuban origin in the United States tend to have few children, high female labor-force participation, and third and fourth earners in many households, all characteristics that contributed to their economic advantage. A final key factor in the development of the Cuban enclave is the continued flow of Cubans into the Miami area. While the first wave was rich in human and financial capital, subsequent waves contributed the labor for the burgeoning Cuban enclave. Indeed, the success of the Cuban enclave partly results from the re-creation of a complete class structure within the exile community, allowing Cubans to exploit fellow Cubans. There are poor Cubans (19 percent of Cuban Americans in Dade County are below poverty level), middle-class Cubans, and working-class Cubans as well as wealthy and elite Cubans. The key elements of this class structure were in place by the 1970s and only solidified with the post-1980 waves of primarily working-class Cubans. And while compensation may not be higher in the enclave than elsewhere, ethnic bonds provide for informal networks of support that facilitate the learning of new skills and the overall process of economic adjustment, thereby blurring the usual differences between the primary and secondary labor markets. The enclave's positive implications for economic adjustment are seen as a factor that has maintained the Cubans' relatively high socioeconomic position, particularly in comparison with many other immigrant groups (Portes 1981, 290–95; Portes 1982, 106–9).

Class stratification and strong and diversified entrepreneurial activity are the two factors most responsible for the enclave's key feature: institutional completeness. While it is rare that Latinos in Miami-Dade can live their lives only within the Hispanic community, the completeness of Miami's Latino enclave is impressive. The wide range of sales and services, including professional services, available within the community testify to the enclave's institutional breadth. The completeness of the enclave has geographic and demographic aspects as well: over 56 percent of the population of the Miami metropolitan area is of Hispanic origin, and this population and its enclaves are dispersed throughout Dade county. This pervasiveness has its limits, however. Because of the sheer size of the Latino population, Hispanic-Anglo segregation is not as high as one would expect. That is not the case, though, for Hispanic-black segregation. These two populations in fact exhibit considerable spatial distance. None of Miami-Dade's African American concentrations are contiguous. As a result of being spread throughout the county, it is much more difficult for African Americans to develop common agendas and unified political action. Hispanic communities, by comparison, are joined in a wide band that extends westward from downtown Miami.

All of these factors—the human capital Cubans brought with them and their geographical concentration in Miami, the role of the federal government in providing aid to the arriving Cuban refugees, and the creation of a collective Cuban American identity arising from the interplay of the CIA and Cuban exile counterrevolutionary organizations—have contributed to the creation of the Cuban enclave and its impact on the Miami area.

Negative Consequences of the Enclave on Interethnic Relations

As may be imagined, the idea that a newly arrived ethnic group has reshaped the city in its own image does not sit well with other groups of longer standing in Miami-Dade. This is particularly true of the black population, and currently, black-Hispanic relations in Miami are shaped by the dramatic demographic, economic, political, and cultural changes brought on by the Cuban migration. Of pivotal importance in this relationship is that in this city alone among American urban areas, a Hispanic population—recently arrived in historical terms—has swiftly overtaken a large and established black minority demographically, politically, and economically, while simultaneously transforming the very cultural and linguistic character of the community. The Hispanic population has very literally made Miami its own. In 1960, black Americans greatly outnumbered Hispanics in Miami-Dade; by 1990 there were considerably more than twice as many Hispanics (987,394) as non-Hispanic blacks (371,691) in Dade County. In 1990, half of the metropolitan area's population area was Hispanic, while blacks accounted for about only one in every five residents.

These demographic changes were more than proportionately reflected in Miami's economy, politics, and culture. In addition, to a far greater degree than is the case in most other urban areas, black Americans and Hispanics in Miami are divided by class, power, ideology, language, color, and place of birth and political affiliations.

Since the early and mid-1980s, when Cuban Americans began to make major inroads in the local political arena, blacks have increasingly regarded Cuban Americans as competitors and even adversaries in a struggle for power in Miami-Dade. There has also been a corresponding intensification of African American alarm about the growth of Cuban American power and a growing dismay at the consequences for blacks when that power is exercised.

Specifically, black complaints about Cubans and other Hispanics have centered on a consistent set of themes and issues, all of which relate to the creation, characteristics, and consequences of the ethnic enclave. Particular issues include perceived preferential treatment given by the government to Cubans, Nicaraguans, and other Hispanics over blacks and Haitians; political competition, or the "Cuban takeover" of Miami-Dade politics; and conflicts over police-community relations, with Hispanic police portrayed as prejudiced toward and abusive of blacks. Further sources of discontent are economic competition over jobs and other resources, with Cubans—thanks to their reputed unwillingness to hire blacks—sometimes portrayed as unfair competitors; differences in ideology and political culture, with occasional criticism of Cuban ideological intransigence and intolerance of free speech; and language issues, particularly bilingualism as an unfair job requirement.

The balance of this chapter will deal with two points of conflict between the African American and Cuban communities: political empowerment and economic opportunity, both of which are inextricably linked to the Cuban enclave. In addition, the public perception that each group has of the other will be examined in light of some recent research, and, finally, some arenas in which cooperation between the groups has occurred will be presented.

Political Empowerment

Despite the fact that for many Cuban Americans participation in the American political system at any level has traditionally taken a back seat to the politics of the homeland, the 1980s saw the rapid and substantial entry of Miami's Cubans into the realm of electoral politics. That entry, however, was not entirely unrelated to, nor did it signal a departure from, traditional exile politics. One factor encouraging Cubans in Miami to become citizens and register to vote, in fact, was the 1980 presidential candidacy of Ronald Reagan. A Republican, Reagan espoused a strong anticommunist ideology and activist foreign policy that was appealing to many Cubans, and this served to link exile politics with registration and voting in the U.S. Participation in the American political system, therefore, was seen not as an abandonment of the homeland, but as an extension of exile concerns (de la Garza, et al. 1994).

During the 1980s, then, Cubans in Miami established local power and exercised it through an increasing number of elected officials and such organizations as the Cuban American National Foundation, Latin Builders Association, Hispanic Builders Association, and the Latin Chamber of Commerce. The size of the Cuban community in Greater Miami and its fairly high turnout rates during elections produced a boom in the number of Cubans in elected positions at all levels of government. So, by the late 1980s, the City of Miami had a Cuban-born mayor, and the city manager and the county manager were both Cuban-born. Cubans controlled the City Commission and constituted more than one-third of the Dade delegation to the state legislature. And after Claude Pepper died in 1989, his seat in the U.S. House of Representatives was won by Ileana Ros-Lehtinen, a Cuban American.

By the 1990s, the mayors of the incorporated areas of Miami, Hialeah, Sweetwater, West Miami, and Hialeah Gardens, all within Greater Miami-Dade, were all Cuban Americans and Cuban Americans hold majorities in the commissions or councils of those cities as well. Six of thirteen Miami-Dade County commissioners are Cuban, as is the mayor, Alex Penelas. On top of that, when the 1990s began, there were already ten Cubans in the Florida legislature: seven in the House and three in the Senate. Then, during the 1992 election cycle, Ileana Ros-Lehtinen was joined in Congress by another Cuban, Lincoln Diaz-Balart. Thus, as Arthur Teele recognized very well in 1990, so great is the political involvement of Cubans in Miami that the Cuban voting block has to be considered by any candidate seeking countywide office.

In contrast to this Cuban American case, the quest by black Miamians for political strength has traditionally confronted two debilitating conditions: weak community leadership and an unresponsive political system. The first was a byproduct of typical 1960-era urban-renewal programs, especially freeway construction. Such Great Society initiatives, in the interest of a greater good, eliminated one positive result of segregation: cohesive, vibrant urban centers of black culture and business. In Miami, the pre–civil rights era saw the emergence of Overtown, a hub of black culture and small businesses and professionals serving the local black population. Urban renewal virtually destroyed Overtown by displacing much of the African American middle class to newly desegregated suburbs, new black suburban developments such as Richmond Heights, or away from Miami altogether—often to other Southern cities such as Atlanta, which offered greater economic opportunity. The net result was a split between more-affluent black suburbs and an inner-city black underclass.

Exacerbating the damage of urban renewal, Dade County's metropolitan governance system has traditionally provided few possibilities for redressing black concerns. This too may be the product of a "renewal": it is argued that the late-1950s movement to reform Miami's local politics by developing the nation's first metropolitan government, including at-large elections for all commissioners, effectively squelched any effective forum for neighborhood and minority concerns (Stack and Warren 1992). And with some 60 percent of the area's African American population residing in unincorporated Dade County, and much of the remainder in the City of Miami amid a large Hispanic majority, the chance of generating effective black political representation was nonexistent.

The situation was remedied somewhat in the early 1990s, a fragile black-Latino coalition managed to overturn the county's at-large system in favor of thirteen single-member districts. The subsequent elections established a more representative mix of four African Americans (including the chair), six Hispanics, and three Anglos. Yet although this restructuring enhanced black representation in regional politics, increased representation did not easily translate into black political power—as was made abundantly clear during the 1994 elections for a new Metro-Dade county manager.

Current trends clearly favor the Hispanic electorate. The importance of the Hispanic vote that Arthur Teele recognized in 1990 continues to be reinforced in recent elections and received empirical verification on November 5, 1996, when Dade's total electorate reached 849,046 registered voters—39 percent of whom are Hispanic, making

Latinos the largest voting block in the county. White non-Hispanics make up 38 percent of the electorate and black non-Hispanic voters stand at 20 percent.

The prospects for bridging these gaps in political empowerment through coalitions are small. As mentioned, Cuban Americans are overwhelmingly Republicans, and at least at the state level, all Cuban American legislators are Republicans as well, while all black legislators in Florida are Democrats. Despite an initial flirtation with the possibility of a united stand on a minority-reapportionment proposal, black and Cuban legislators ultimately clashed over reapportionment during the 1992 session of the Florida legislature. Today, these representatives are fighting over the creation of a new state-chartered law school. Black legislators argue that it should be given to Florida A&M in Tallahassee, a historically black school, and Cuban American legislators are lobbying for Miami's Florida International University, which has a heavily Hispanic enrollment. Party affiliation and the partisan conflicts that result from them broaden the scope of conflict between the groups and illustrate the structural dimensions of the gulf between Cubans and blacks.

Entering the year 2000, these communities again found reason to disagree, this time over the plight of Elian Gonzalez, a Cuban boy rescued from the sea on Thanksgiving Day 1999 after his mother and other rafters had perished attempting the hazardous crossing from Cuba. Enraged that the Immigration and Naturalization Service (INS) ordered the return of the six-year-old to his father in Cuba, hundreds of Cuban Americans in Miami took to the streets in civic protests that stopped traffic and inconvenienced drivers throughout the downtown area. When some Cuban leaders claimed that their actions were similar to those employed by Martin Luther King Jr. and the civil right activists of the 1960s, African Americans were quick to point out that effective civil protests do not inconvenience the people whose opinion they are trying to influence. To most African Americans, this was more than a tactical critique: the Cuban actions were seen as a manifestation of the Cubans unwillingness to forge links across communities. As an African American writer for the *Miami Herald* noted at the time,

> Since emerging as a significant presence here, Cubans have not particularly needed allies. They've prospered, placing their cultural and political stamp on Miami-Dade County largely by using their own resources and determination.
>
> In addition, many have set the bar of friendship too high for most non-Cubans to reach. . . . Many older Cubans view non-Cubans as irrelevant to their lives.

But inevitably, there comes a day when any community needs support from outside—from ethnic and cultural communities that don't share its history and passions. Elian Gonzalez's future is such an issue. (Steinback 2000)

In the predawn darkness of the Saturday before Easter 2000, federal marshals stormed the home of Elian's Miami relatives and initiated a process which resulted in the boy returning with his father to Cuba. The Cuban American community was shocked at the raid, as were many other observers, and many people took to the streets again. The limited demonstrations did little to divert the course of event, however: the courts supported the government's position that Elian belonged with his father and not with his Miami relatives. On June 28, 2000, he boarded a plane back to the island, leaving behind him a deeply divided Miami.

The Florida International University Cuba Poll, conducted in August and September of 2000, showed communities to be deeply divided over the fate of the child. Over 78 percent of Cuban Americans believed that Elian Gonzalez should have stayed in Miami, a view shared by only 33 percent of non-Cuban Americans. While time alone will tell the direct impact that the Elian case will have on ethnic relations in Miami, it is certain that at least in the short run, it will not have a positive effect. Thirty-one percent of Cuban Americans and 37 percent of non–Cuban Americans, for example, felt that the Elian affair worsened ethnic relations in the county. Although these might seem to be disheartening figures, perhaps more telling of the continuous tensions in Miami are the following: nearly 60 percent of Cubans and 54 percent of local non-Cubans felt that the Elian case had not changed relations at all. So, while the future of Elian Gonzalez in Cuba may be uncertain, his legacy in Miami-Dade County seems to be a Cuban American community that has increased its already significant isolation from the area's other communities.

Economic Opportunity

In the economic sector, gains by black Miamians over the past few decades have paled in comparison with the successes of the Cuban community. When Martin Luther King Jr. visited Miami in 1966, he noted Miami's racial hostility and warned against pitting Cuban refugees against blacks in competition for jobs (Porter and Dunn 1984). In that warning was the implicit understanding that given the intractability of racism, white, educated Cubans, providing cheap labor, might replace African Americans in the labor market. This kind of displacement is difficult to document, but displacement did indeed occur, as Portes and Stepick (1993, 43) explain: "There was no one-to-one substitution of blacks by Cubans. . . . There was, however, a new urban economy in which the immigrants raced past other groups, leaving the native minority behind."

In the area of government contracts and disbursements earmarked for minority-run enterprises, Cubans clearly prevailed over blacks. Between 1968 and 1980, for instance, the Small Business Administration (SBA) cumulatively dispersed 46.6 percent of its Dade County loans to Hispanics and only 6 percent to blacks. The situation actually worsened after the riots of the 1980s, when nearly 90 percent of SBA loans in Miami-Dade were awarded to Hispanics or whites. Meanwhile, the Metro Miami Action Plan, created to tap public and private resources for the development of Miami's black community, achieved only modest success and saw its elite Anglo participants soon lose interest (Dugger 1987).

Four riots during the 1980s crystallized a widespread anger among black Miamians over both their failure to keep pace economically with other groups and their lack of political voice (Herman 1995). The response of city elites—most of them white or Latino—was to initiate a series of economic and social programs designed to shore up black neighborhoods (Reveron 1989). The task of rejuvenating the black community was daunting, but there were some successes. By 1987, for example, the number of black-owned businesses in Miami-Dade was more than triple the number from a decade earlier (U.S. Bureau of the Census 1990). Furthermore, under a special set-aside program, black contractors began receiving county work. And in a gesture that might well symbolize what it takes to develop successful businesses in Miami's African American communities, in 1990 a man named Otis Pitts received a MacArthur Foundation "genius grant" for building a shopping center that provided jobs for 130 people on the border of Liberty City and Little Haiti (Viglucci 1990). In Miami's black community, development projects have met with limited success and gains in employment have been modest (Dunn and Stepick 1992). It could be generalized that most of the limited benefits from special programs and incentives had gone to black professionals and middle-class businesspeople.

Beyond opportunities and contracts, another area of conflict and division is business activity. According to the Minority Business Report of 1992, the latest figures available, there are 926 black-owned businesses with paid employees in Dade County. Their sales and receipts totaled $626.5 million, .5 percent of the total sales and receipts in Dade County—a considerably lower share than is typical of black-owned business statewide or nationwide. Compare that to the area's 7,949 Cuban firms, which had sales and receipts of more than $7 billion. Even these figures, however, underestimate the stagnation within the black business community: In 1982, African Americans owned 1 percent of all businesses in Miami-Dade; twenty years later, the number stands at 1.5 percent. Hispanics, on the other hand, already owned 11 percent of all businesses in 1987 and now own almost 17 percent. This disparity has repercussions throughout the community, influencing the black legislative agenda and strongly affecting how blacks view Latinos. Until recently, black leaders at county and state levels persistently argued that Hispanics should not be included in minority set-asides. And when a Cuban American woman was named to succeed Janet Reno as the state attorney for Dade County, a prominent black leader was quoted in the *New York Times* to the effect that Hispanics are merely whites who speak Spanish.

The Public Discourse: The Issue of Perceptions

Given the effectiveness of the Cuban enclave in separating the Cuban and African American communities, it is not surprising that each has only partial knowledge of the other. In such an environment, stereotypes develop. To investigate the level of stereotyping among Cubans and African Americans in Miami specifically, the authors conducted content analysis of the ethnic press from 1960 to 1992 and found that each community developed public perceptions of the other, perceptions that served as bases for conflict.

Black Perceptions of Latinos

The social distance created by Miami's Cuban enclave between itself and other groups has contributed to changing perceptions of Cubans by the black community in Dade County. Recent evidence indicates that during the 1960s and early 1970s, black Miami viewed Cubans as possible allies in the battles for minority empowerment in Dade County, but by the 1980s, this view was replaced by one of clear antagonism (Grenier and Castro 1998).

Analysis of editorials from the Hispanic and black press and interviews reveals the following pattern in the evolution of the black-Latino relationship. In the 1960s, the black community was focused on civil rights concerns and the arrival of Cubans had relatively little relevance and thus received scant attention: for Miami as elsewhere, the 1960s were marked by classic civil rights struggles over desegregation. The coming of tens of thousands of Cuban refugees was noted and commented upon in the black press and on occasion sympathy for the plight of the refugees was expressed, but the issue was peripheral to blacks in comparison to issues such as school integration.

Yet although black attention to the Cuban refugee issue may have been limited during the civil rights era, that is not to say that Cuban immigration was not an issue. Even from the onset of large-scale Cuban immigration in the early 1960s, concerns were voiced about possible adverse consequences that competition for jobs and preferential treatment for Cubans by local officials could pose for African Americans. Since the 1970s, and especially since the 1980s, the African American community in general and the black press specifically has taken increasing note of the growing presence and political and economic power of Cubans. As one indicator, editorials in the weekly *Miami Times* (Miami's black newspaper of record, published since 1923) that mention Cubans critically appeared with increasing frequency through the 1970s and even more often in the 1980s.

Such criticism is directed at Cubans; by contrast, blacks view Puerto Ricans and Mexicans much more sympathetically. One African American civic leader interviewed by this researcher, for example, characterized Puerto Ricans in Miami as "an invisible community" and described blacks and Puerto Ricans as "natural allies" who nonetheless hardly ever worked together. Another African American political leader, from the rural southern end of Miami-Dade, which contains the area's largest concentration of Mexicans, ascribed similar cultural characteristics to blacks and Mexicans, while a Mexican-American woman who works for a migrant advocacy organization in the same area stated that blacks and Mexicans get along because of shared economic circumstances.

Not only is the prevailing African American discourse about Cubans generally adversarial, but it has become more so over time. In the 1960s and 1970s, the black press bore scattered references to Cubans as a minority or underrepresented group or as objects of prejudice, but these virtually disappear in the 1980s. Over the past two decades, *Miami Times* editorials have become increasingly critical, persistently questioning the legitimacy of the status of Cubans as a minority and intensifying a portrayal of Cubans as the new masters. In the black press, the shift toward a harder line on Hispanics extends even to some civil rights issues. As an example, in 1975 a *Miami Times* editorial supported bilingualism and advised blacks to learn Spanish; in 1980 the paper opposed an English-only referendum, condemning it as racist. By 1988, however, the paper advised its readers that conditions had changed: with Hispanics now holding "oppressive power," the paper declined to oppose an amendment to the state constitution that would enshrine English as Florida's official language.

Latino Perception of Blacks

Unlike the black alarm vis-à-vis Cubans, the Latino community evidences little overt concern that the African American community could adversely affect the fate of the Cuban and Nicaraguan communities—except through riots that could damage Miami's image and economy. Negative judgments, when rendered, are usually oblique. If the black press increasingly reflects and reinforces an openly adversarial discourse toward Cubans and some other Hispanics, the Spanish-language daily press is marked by a seeming inattention or disinterest to conflicts with African Americans. Given the black perceptions and expectations elicited from that community's press, the Latinos' attitude is interpreted as lack of empathy or outright hostility to black concerns.

Alongside this apparent indifference, however, there is a more covert Hispanic discourse toward blacks, and it emerges more clearly through other media and channels: in the pages of tabloids and newsletters, on radio talk shows, and in daily conversations and interactions. The elements of this discourse include the denial of racism and of any responsibility in redressing its toll; strong support for police and the association of blacks with crime; and an invidious comparison between Hispanic economic advancement—attributed to hard work, family values, and self-reliance—and black dependency on welfare and other social programs. Illustrative of the veiled nature of some of this discourse, as well as its major themes, is *Hispanews,* an unsigned 1993 newsletter issued by a previously unknown group, the Federation of Hispanic Employees of Dade County. One passage, a response to a *Miami Times* editorial accusing Cubans of insensitivity to blacks, brings together denial of racism and invidious comparison:

> Under this label (insensitivity), the newspaper launches against Cubans the variety of rockets usually reserved for Anglos. Our answer is that it may be okay with Anglos, since, historically, they are guilty of enslaving and degrading blacks for centuries; they owe blacks. But, folks, we Hispanics owe blacks nothing: what are we guilty of? Of hard work, not only as bankers and entrepreneurs, but also as humble laborers and peddlers? Keep it clear in your head that we have never coerced assistance from anyone, but much rather roam the streets of Miami selling limes, onions, flowers, peanuts, etc. Some folks should try this, it is hard work, but not bad.

Elements of Cooperation

Within the context of a generally adversarial relationship, there are nevertheless opportunities for common action and empathy. In one instance, from 1992, a fragile black-Hispanic coalition successfully sued Metropolitan Dade County and overturned the at-large voting system that had limited black and Hispanic participation to a single member each on a nine-member commission. Instituted in the at-large system's place were today's thirteen districts, a restructuring that enhances black representation in the politics of the region. Such may be seen in the next election, which produced a new Metropolitan Dade County Commission comprising four African Americans (including the chair), six Hispanics, and three Anglos. African American political gains have not stopped there: South Florida currently has two African Americans, Carrie Meeks and Alcee Hastings, serving in Congress, and six blacks sit on the state legislature. Blacks also serve on the current city commissions or councils of Miami, El Portal, Opa Locka, and Florida City—the latter two predominantly black communities also have black mayors (Metro Dade County 1994).

Teamwork similar to that which changed the voting system in 1992 resurfaced in the spring of 1993. At that time, after lengthy discussions with leaders of the Spanish American League Against Discrimination, the Miami-Dade branch of the National Association for the Advancement of Colored People (NAACP) supported a successful attempt to abolish the county's English-only ordinance, which Hispanics had vehemently opposed. The NAACP cited, along with other reasons of principle, the adverse impact of the ordinance on the large Creole-speaking Miami Haitian community. The four black county commissioners voted for repeal of English-only.

These are not the only examples of cooperation; there have been other sporadic instances of cooperation as well. In one, visible support from more politically moderately Cuban leaders for restoration of Haitian democracy and against deportation of Haitians has brought some black and Cuban leaders together, albeit briefly, and helped to momentarily assuage, at least to some degree, resentment over the disparate treatment of Cuban versus Haitian refugees. Then, when Cuban American pop star Gloria Estefan gave a benefit concert in March 1992, the United Negro College Fund was one of four charities to share the proceeds. Earlier, black lawyers and their Cuban American counterparts together organized a fundraising ball. And in yet another example of cooperation, an organization of black Cubans, formed in the 1990s, has attempted to serve as a bridge between white Cubans and African Americans, with limited success.

Efforts to improve black-Cuban relations continue. The Community Relations Board of Miami-Dade County government, a triethnic committee that conducts activities designed to develop joint agendas among whites, blacks, and Latinos, initiated a Maceo-King Initiative bringing together the Cuban Civic Council and the NAACP. Named after a black hero of the Cuban war for independence, Antonio Maceo, and the black civil rights leader, the program seeks to facilitate joint ventures and business partnerships between Cuban and African Americans in South Florida. Other examples of cooperation between Hispanics and African Americans include a June 1989 fundraiser organized by the Black Lawyers Association and the Cuban American Bar Association for the benefit of the Liberty Mart, a small grocery store in Liberty City that had burned down the previous January. The nonprofit minimart was a celebrated part of the Liberty Square public-housing community because it employed welfare mothers and served as gathering place for children. In another effort, in 1987, the Transit Workers Union organized a triethnic coalition to fight, with mixed success, the privatization of the county transit system.

In the late 1990s and early 2000s, the City of Miami is working its way through a series of scandals and elections that collectively might produce conditions favorable to the creation of interethnic political coalitions. In October 1999, for instance, Miller Dawkins, the city commission's sole African American member, resigned amid charges of corruption. Required to appoint a replacement to serve until elections could take place in early November, Miami's new mayor, Joe Carollo, a Cuban American, consulted with black leaders and appointed Marvin Dunn to the vacant seat. During the brief campaign, Carollo openly supported Dunn, pleading with the Cuban voting majority to elect an African American to the seat to "preserve full representation of all of the citizens of Miami." He did not stop there, however: in public pronouncements, Carollo reminded Cuban American voters that the African American community stepped up to the plate to support single-member districts in countywide elections. "This is something that clearly benefited the Hispanics of Dade County, yet the African American community went into it with us, arm in arm. Now, we have to be supportive of them," Carollo declared in a personal discussion with this researcher. Dunn's strongest opponent, a Cuban American lawyer named Humberto Hernandez, argued that he, Hernandez, could represent all of the constituents of Dade County. "This is not an African American seat. It is a seat for the citizens of Miami," he stated. If elected, he promised to make immediate recommendations to the city commission that it implement a process of reapportionment into single-member districts. Following the mayor's lead, various Cuban American community leaders openly supported Dunn. Nevertheless, the election was not even close. Hernandez won easily. While conditions favorable to black-Cuban political coalitions may exist, their achieving success is still an uphill battle.

Insight into the limits of cooperation may be gleaned by examining those occasional editorials in the black press that are favorable to Cu-

bans. These most frequently pertained to instances in which prominent Cuban leaders, such as former Miami Mayor Xavier Suarez, Florida International University President Modesto Maidique, or former
Miami-Dade County Manager Joaquin Avino, reached out directly to
blacks or supported black causes. Such examples indicate that the
African American press is not uniformly or reflexively negative to
Hispanics. Rather, to the extent that blacks perceive that Hispanics
have risen to political and economic leadership in Miami, they expect—at a minimum—that Hispanic leaders will behave in the same
manner that the most racially progressive Anglo civic and corporate
leaders do. In cases where this expectation is met, Hispanics receive
kudos. But most Hispanic businessmen and civic leaders differ from
racially progressive Anglo corporate leaders in their structural position, historical experience, culture, and ideology. To state the matter
bluntly, they do not generally have the resources that Anglo corporate
leaders can rely on and they feel little or no moral obligation to re-
dress grievances rooted in American race relations, with which they
do not identify. And they are more interested in spending their time,
money, and energy in catching up to the Anglos and in attempting to
overthrow Fidel Castro than in helping African Americans. Therefore,
black expectations of Cubans are generally not met.

Conclusion

In many respects, the Cubans of Miami-Dade are exceptional among
Latinos in the United States: Their average income is relatively high
and the poverty rate is relatively low. They have achieved economic
and political success essentially within the first generation, a dramatic
departure from immigrant communities' experiences, and they have
contributed in important ways to the transformation of Miami into
the economic capital of the Caribbean.

These accomplishments arose from three forms of capital possessed by the first wave of Cuban immigrants, the Golden Exiles. Economically, Cubans brought diverse capital with them from Cuba. The
first waves came with not only an unusual amount of financial wealth
but skill wealth as well. The immigrants included a high percentage
of professionals and businessmen who could relatively easily use
their skills in the United States. Then, subsequent flows of working-
class immigrants furnished low wage, pliant labor to emerging Cu-
ban-enclave firms and created a community with a broadly diverse
class structure. Socially, Cuban family structure facilitated the most
productive use of the immigrants' economic capital: relatively few
children, women in the labor force, and three-generation families
combined to create a very efficient means to use resources and gener-

ate wealth. And finally, politically, no other Latino group has bene-fited so extensively from American government aid all the way from the White House down to the Miami school district. These three forms of capital have combined in a peculiar way to produce extraor-dinarily high ethnic solidarity that both ameliorates and masks class exploitation within the community while providing a basis for ethnic political power.

While the Cuban community has prospered, Miami's African American community has felt left behind. Although many African Americans have advanced into professional and executive positions during the decades since Cubans began arriving in Miami, the major-ity of Miami-Dade blacks remains poor and is increasingly welfare-dependent. Equally important, in spite of the lack of evidence, many African Americans blame the Cubans for the relative failure of Afri-can Americans to have gained more economically and politically. Meanwhile, Miami's Latino community ostensibly ignores or covertly disparages African Americans—which only exacerbates African Americans' negative feelings toward the Cubans.

Hence, ethnic tensions in Miami are extreme, seething constantly and fuming periodically. The contrast between Miami's Cuban and African American communities and an examination of the Cuban case in particular reveals just how unique and special it indeed is—and how much luck it has benefited from. The original immigration by an elite class was initiated by a Cold War confrontation, circum-stances that elicited a generous welcome in the form of massive state aid and settlement in a city geographically poised for a new role as a nexus to Latin America. Moreover, the original immigrants of upward social and economic bias were followed by controlled and limited waves of working-class immigrants, which, coupled with an internal right-wing hegemony, produced extraordinarily high community trust and internal cooperation for those who submitted to the domi-nant ideology. The absence of any one of these factors easily could have changed the entire profile of the community.

Developing harmonious black-Latino relations in Miami in the im-mediate future poses an enormous challenge, for the main black and Latino communities are divided by space, class, political party, ideol-ogy, and language. The task ahead for leaders and citizens is to show how such divisions can be overcome under the most difficult of cir-cumstances. For example, the Miami African American community perceives the American government's differing approaches to immi-gration—Cuban versus Haitian, for example—reflecting racist dis-crimination. This situation increases black-Cuban tensions and en-genders Haitian resentment of Cubans and other Latinos. Thus, while this perception of unjust national politics has produced some solidarity between African Americans and Haitians, it has increased the distance, resentment, and tension between blacks and both the non-Hispanic whites who make immigration policy and the Latinos who benefit from it.

The conflict in Miami might seem more intense and its sources more intractable than in other regions of the country, but national trends suggest that black-Latino relations may follow the Miami model unless national and local leadership intervene to avert such circumstances. The Latinization of the United States, as well as urban decay, unclear national immigration policies, and underfunded social programs, are all factors that alone or in combination could lead to increased tensions between these two largest ethnic minorities in many urban settings. The case of Miami is not a hopeful one. In a metropolitan area where ethnic groups—especially blacks—are spatially segregated, the existence of an institutionally complete community among Cuban Americans makes it even less likely that the mutual understanding necessary to work toward a common agenda will be realized.

References

Allman, T. D. 1987. *Miami: City of the Future.* New York: Atlantic Monthly Press.

Branch, Karen. 2000. Hispanics, Non-Hispanics at Odds About Boy's Fate. *Miami Herald,* January 8, 2000: 1B.

de la Garza, Rodolfo, Martha Menchaca, and Luis DeSipio, editors. 1994. *Barrio Ballots: Latino Politics in the 1990 Elections.* Boulder, Colo.: Westview Press.

Didion, Joan. 1987. *Miami.* New York: Simon & Schuster.

Dugger, Cynthia. 1987. "MMAP Losing Punch, Leaders Say." *Miami Herald,* July 17, 1987: 5C.

Dunn, M., and Alex Stepick, III. (1992). "Blacks in Miami." In *Miami Now! Immigration, Ethnicity, and Social Change,* edited by Guillermo Grenier and Alex Stepick. Gainesville: University of Florida Press.

Filkins, D. 1994. "A New Leader for Metro: Latin Bloc Prevails in Manager Vote." *Miami Herald,* December 16, 1994: 1A.

Grenier, Guillermo J., and Max Castro. 1998. "The Emergence of an Adversarial Relation: Black-Cuban Relations in Miami, 1959–1998." In *Research in Urban Policy,* edited by Fred W. Becker and Milan J. Dluhy. Vol. 7. Stamford, Conn.: JAI Press.

Grenier, Guillermo J., and Alex Stepick, editors. 1992. *Miami Now! Immigration, Ethnicity, and Social Change.* Gainesville: University of Florida Press.

Herman, M. 1995. *A Tale of Two Cities: Testing Explanations for Riot Violence in Miami, Florida, and Los Angeles, California, 1980, 1992.* Washington, D.C.: American Sociological Association.

Massey, Douglas, and Nancy Denton A. 1993. *American Apartheid.* Cambridge, Mass.: Harvard University Press.

Metro Dade County. 1993. *A Minority-Owned and Women-Owned Business Discrimination Study: Executive Summary*. Miami: Miami-Dade County.

———. 1994. *Black Elected Officials in Dade County*. Miami: Office of Black Affairs, Miami-Dade County.

Metro Dade County Planning Department. 1996. *Population Projections by Minor Statistical Area and Census Tract, Dade County, Florida, 1970 to 2015*. Miami: Miami-Dade County Planning Department.

Muir, H. 1990. *Miami, USA*. Miami: Pickering Press.

Parks, A. M. 1991. *Miami: The Magic City*. Miami: Centennial Press.

Pedraza-Bailey, Sylvia. 1985. *Political and Economic Migrants in America: Cubans and Mexicans*. Austin: University of Texas Press.

Peters, T. 1984. *Miami, 1909*. Miami: Banyan Books.

Porter, Bruce, and Marvin Dunn. 1984. *The Miami Riot of 1980: Crossing the Bounds*. Lexington, Mass.: D. C. Heath.

Portes, Alejandro. 1981. "Modes of Structural Incorporation and Present Theories of Labor Immigration." In *Global Trends in Migration: Theory and Research of International Population Movements*, edited by Mary M. Kritz, Christopher B. Keely, and Silvio M. Tomasi. New York: Center for Migration Studies.

———. 1982. "Immigrants' Attainment: An Analysis of Occupation and Earnings Among Cuban Exiles in the United States." In *Social Structure and Behavior: Essays in Honor of William Hamilton Swell*, edited by R. M. Hauler. New York: Academic Press.

———. 1987. "The Social Origins of the Cuban Enclave Economy of Miami. *Sociological Perspectives* 30(October): 340–72.

Portes, Alejandro, and Robert Bach. 1985. *Latin Journey: Cuban and Mexican Immigrants in the United States*. Berkeley: University of California Press.

Portes, Alejandro, and Alex Stepick. 1993. *City on the Edge: The Transformation of Miami*. Berkeley: University of California Press.

Reveron, D. 1989. "Violence, Delays Hurt Renewal in Black Dade." *Miami Herald*, February 13, 1989: 1A, a.

Rich, Cynthia. 1974. "Pondering the Future: Miami's Cubans after 15 Years." *Race Relations Reporter* 5(21): A-1.

Rieff, David. 1987. *Going to Miami: Exiles, Tourists and Refugees in the New America*. Boston: Little, Brown.

Stack, John, and Christopher L. Warren. 1992. "The Reform Tradition and Ethnic Politics: Metropolitan Miami Confronts the 1990's." In *Miami Now! Immigration, Ethnicity and Social Change*, edited by Guillermo Grenier and Alex Stepick. Gainesville: University of Florida Press.

Steinback, Robert. 2000. "Cuban Exiles in Need of Allies." *Miami Herald*, January 9, 2000, p. 1B.

Stepick, Alex. 1992. "Haitians in Miami." In *Miami now! Immigration, Ethnicity, and Social Change*, edited by Guillermo Grenier and Alex Stepick. Gainesville: University of Florida Press.

U.S. Bureau of the Census. 1990. *Survey of Minority-Owned Business Enterprises, 1987/Blacks*. Washington: U.S. Department of Commerce.

———. 1992. *Current Population Reports*. Washington.: U.S. Department of Commerce.

Viglucci, A. 1990. "Liberty City Rises Like the Phoenix." *Miami Herald*, July 22, 1990, pp. 1B, 7B.

Chapter 6

Protest or Violence: Political Process and Patterns of Black-Korean Conflict

PATRICK D. JOYCE

I N THE early 1990s, devastating civil unrest in Los Angeles and a
contentious boycott in New York City alerted the nation to a puz-
zling new feature of race relations in its largest cities: tensions
between African Americans and Korean Americans. Each of these
cities, however, expressed these tensions differently. In Los Angeles,
legal scholar Reginald Robinson noted that an inescapable "violent
reality" existed for these two groups, both before and during the 1992
riots: "The violence between African- and Korean Americans reflects
their inability to find an alternative bridging language by which each
group can peacefully co-exist with the other," he wrote (Robinson
1993). In New York, sociologist Heon Cheol Lee reported that conflicts there exhibited the more peaceful dynamic of organized protest:
"The key defining element of black-Korean conflict is the black boycott of Korean stores in black neighborhoods" (Lee 1993). The same
latent tensions had translated into different forms of overt conflict.
Why?

The most prominent cities were not the only sites of these conflicts.
Incidents of violence, and even instances of looting and arson, were
reported elsewhere as well. But even more striking has been the boycotting in other cities. Black-led boycotts of Korean-owned businesses
happened at a beauty shop in Indianapolis, an entire block of stores
in Chicago, a flea market in Miami, a shopping center in Dallas, and a

minimart in Philadelphia. None of these actions against Korean-owned establishments received the nationwide attention that the conflicts in New York City and Los Angeles did. Nevertheless, expanding the focus from New York and Los Angeles to examine the broader patterns of these conflicts across cities can tell us as much or more about the causes of tension between Korean Americans and African Americans, and, specifically, why in some instances conflicts took the form of protest and in others violence.

These patterns tell us that where and when boycotts happen has more to do with the nature of local political systems than with the sociological phenomena typically presumed to generate intergroup tensions. Incidents of violence between blacks and Koreans, on the other hand, are unrelated to politics and more strongly related to competition over community businesses. Although violence and boycotts are somewhat related to each other, these two expressions of intergroup conflict follow different causal dynamics.

This chapter uses statistical analysis to test the empirical validity of various theories of racial and ethnic conflict. The findings suggest that sociological explanations—such as cultural differences, competition theory, or middleman-minority theory—fail to account for the distribution of collective action across time and space. Overt, nonviolent conflicts, in the form of black-led boycotts of Korean stores, take place more often in cities where traditional political organizations have strong roots and where African Americans have greater political representation. Both factors—organization and representation—lend structure to political life in communities and represent signs that greater resources are available for the kind of grassroots organization necessary for one group to engage another in protest.

The chapter begins by briefly describing data collection for the study and then lays out the observable implications of various theories that may explain black-Korean conflicts, making each theory measurable in quantitative terms. Following that, I use statistical analysis to address two questions: Why do conflicts happen where they do? And, why does violence occur sometimes and protest other times?

Data Collection

In order to identify incidents of black-Korean conflict, I conducted a comprehensive search of local newspapers using three electronic databases that offer national coverage: Lexis-Nexis, Ethnic News-Watch, and FirstSearch Abstracts. I searched these electronic databases first (with the keywords "black" and "Korean") and used paper indexes and archives to supplement the electronic searches. One reason for this method was the efficiency and convenience it affords a single researcher seeking to identify incidents of conflict across large expanses of time and space.

Once relevant newspaper stories were sorted out, I used a systematic coding scheme to extract specific information on each event found. In the newspaper stories found, I identified events in which members of one group confronted members of the other, individually or collectively, in a public location.[1] Because I am concerned with the relationship between protest and violence, I distinguished between these two types of events.

As commonly conceived, protest consists primarily of nonviolent forms of collective action such as demonstrations, pickets, and marches. This study deals with one particular type of protest: the boycott. I define a boycott as a campaign that mobilizes participants to protest publicly at the scene of a targeted establishment, with the stated goal of denying patronage to the store in order to shut it down or extract other concessions. A campaign that merely issues a call to boycott, without actively mobilizing protesters, falls outside this definition, and thus would not be counted in this study. Specifically, my study focuses on boycotts led by African Americans against establishments owned by Korean Americans.

Violence consists of reports of interpersonal violence (such as shootings, assaults, and other physical disputes) or property damage (such as looting or arson) in which the perpetrator and victim are each positively identified as either black or Korean.[2]

The sample of cities for the statistical analysis was determined mainly by the availability of substantial newspaper coverage in the electronic databases and paper indexes used. Still, the cities included in the sample meet three criteria. First, each city is located in an area defined by the Census Bureau as a "primary metropolitan statistical area" (U.S. Bureau of the Census 1980, 1990) served by one of the daily newspapers in my search. Second, each city is covered by at least five years of newspaper content. Third, each has a population of at least 100,000. The resulting sample consists of thirty-nine cities.[3] This sample includes cities from each region of the mainland United States: the Northeast (seven cities), the Midwest (eight cities), the Southeast (seven cities), the Southwest (eight cities), and the West (nine cities).

My search found forty boycotts and sixty-nine reports of violence.[4] The boycotts are distributed across thirteen cities: Atlanta, Berkeley, Chicago, Dallas, Fort Worth, Indianapolis, Inglewood, Los Angeles, Miami, New York City, Orlando, Philadelphia, and Washington, D.C.[5] The reports of violence are distributed across sixteen cities: Atlanta, Baltimore, Berkeley, Boston, Chicago, Dallas, Fort Worth, Inglewood,

Long Beach, Los Angeles, New York City, Orlando, Philadelphia, San Francisco, Tacoma, and Washington, D.C.[6]

Figure 6.1 displays the occurrence of boycotts and incidents of violence by year, excluding black and Korean participation in the 1992 rioting in Los Angeles (which is difficult to measure accurately, due to the participation of other groups besides blacks and Koreans). For each year, the total number of incidents is reported, with boycotts in dark shading and violence in light.

One crucial matter addressed in figure 6.1 is whether the conflict data is biased over time—whether the media tended to report more conflicts in the wake of the two nationally televised events (the civil unrest in Los Angeles and New York City's 1990 boycott). As shown, reports of violence between blacks and Koreans built to a peak in 1991, before the riots of the following year, then dropped afterward. Hence it does not appear that the riots increased the media's reporting of violence. Reports of violence did, however, increase after the 1990 boycott.

The level of boycotting is low in the first half of the period shown, with no more than one boycott reported per year, but then increases during the second half, when between two and seven boycotts are reported each year. Because this increase took place prior to both of the nationally televised events, it does not appear that the data on boycotting was biased upward in their aftermath.

Independent Variables

Cultural Difference

The cultural-differences explanation for black-Korean conflicts proposes that tensions are rooted in preexisting group differences. Korean immigrants to the United States bring with them customs and values that contrast with those of African Americans living around them, which leads to misunderstandings when members of the two groups encounter each other. Applying this idea here, if cultural differences imply a single "Korean" culture and a single "African American" culture, no variation in the conflict levels or expressions would be seen across cities. However, because barriers to communication lie at the heart of this problem, the linguistic abilities of Korean Americans can serve as a measure of cultural distance—and this factor does vary across the sample cites. Immigrants acquire the language of their host country, and through it the customs as well, to different degrees and at different rates. As a result, some Korean communities may be more linguistically insulated, and thus more culturally distant from African American residents, than others. Census data indicate the

Figure 6.1   Boycotts and Violence by Year, 1980 to 1995

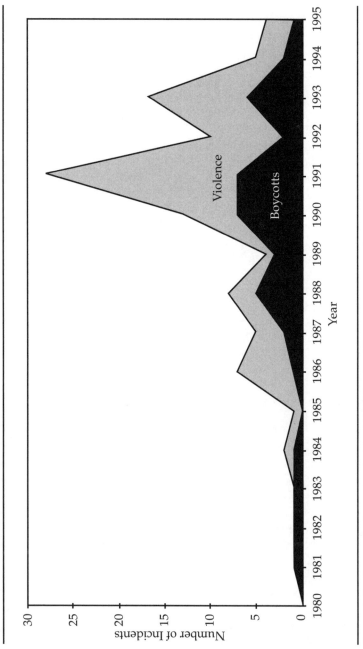

Source: Author's survey of newspapers covering thirty-nine cities.

variation that exists in the ability of Korean Americans to speak English. For instance, whereas only 24 percent of Korean Americans living in the Minneapolis area in 1990 were reported by the U.S. Census Bureau as not speaking English "very well," the figure was 81 percent for Korean Americans living in Los Angeles–Long Beach in 1980. The average percentage of Korean Americans not speaking English "very well" in the cities sampled is 53 percent, Baltimore's rate.

Ideology

According to ideological explanations of black-Korean conflict, boycotts and violence occur because members of the two groups subscribe to different social and political ideologies, which leads to disagreement (Chang 1991; Cheng and Espiritu 1989; Light, Har-Chvi, and Kan 1994; Min 1996). Korean Americans are said to believe more strongly in the "American dream," while African Americans purportedly adhere to some form of black nationalism. For this analysis, measures of ideology would have to come from intercity surveys focused on the beliefs of Korean Americans and African Americans. Although national-level surveys of black Americans include questions about nationalism, I am not aware of any surveys that do this for a large number of cities.[7] Thus, no indicator for ideology is included in the statistical analysis.

Competition

Competition theory suggests that black-Korean conflicts arise over a perceived imbalance in business ownership in inner-city neighborhoods (Blalock 1967; Freer 1994; Olzak 1992). Following this, then, the level of conflict should be higher in cities where black business ownership is small relative to Korean business ownership. As a measure of this theory, I used data from the *Survey of Minority-Owned Business Enterprises* (U.S. Bureau of the Census 1987) to construct an index of competition that compares the ratio of black-owned firms to Korean-owned firms.[8] To provide support for competition theory, this variable should correlate negatively with intergroup conflict. The data indicate that in the Seattle and Los Angeles–Long Beach metro areas, the places with the lowest ratios in the sample, there are 1.4 black-owned firms for every Korean-owned firm. By contrast, in the Miami-Hialeah metro area, the ratio is about forty-seven black-owned firms for every Korean-owned firm. Houston and Orlando fall closest to the mean, which is about eleven black firms per Korean firm.[9]

Middleman-Minority Theory

Some scholars argue that disputes between blacks and Koreans represent a form of class conflict, in which a culturally distinct immigrant group is subjected to scapegoating by a host group due to its vulnerable, intermediate position in the class structure (Bonacich 1994; Light and Bonacich 1991; Min 1996; Ong, Park, and Tong 1994). Two empirically measurable factors can be identified as working to make Korean merchants vulnerable, as a so-called middleman-minority group, to targeting by black residents or activists: first, the extent to which Korean merchants fill the traditionally defined niche of the middleman and, second, the presence of economic strain on black residents that would exacerbate class tension. What makes a group a middleman minority? A major factor is articulated by Light and Bonacich (1991, 18) as "self-employment within the immigrant group at a rate much in excess of the general rate."[10] In the United States, Korean Americans are self-employed at a higher rate than the general population, but the difference varies from city to city. The indicator of Korean middleman-minority status I use is the ratio of the Korean self-employment rate to a city's overall self-employment rate, based on metro-area data from the 1980 and 1990 censuses.[11]

Korean Americans range from a middleman-minority status of 0.7 in Minneapolis (actually indicating that Koreans are not a middleman group, as the value is less than one) to 6.2 in Baltimore (indicating Korean self-employment is over six times the general rate), with a mean of 2.9, represented by Korean Americans in the Los Angeles–Long Beach metro area in 1980. The only places in the sample besides Minneapolis where Koreans are not a middleman minority, as measured here, are Columbus and Boston. Koreans in New York City in 1990 fell closest to the mean. Economic strain is represented by the black unemployment rate in 1990. Black unemployment ranges from 1.7 in Scottsdale, Arizona, to 22.2 in Detroit, with a mean of 13.0. A positive correlation of Korean self-employment and black economic strain with the level of conflict in a city would lend support to the economic-scapegoating explanation for black-Korean conflict suggested by middleman-minority theory.

Political Process

Political process theory hypothesizes that protest requires activists to mobilize support and is thus a function of higher levels of political organization and resources. More precisely, black-led boycotts of Korean stores should occur not only where social forces produce tensions between the two groups (explained by other theories), but also where the political system as a whole encourages the proliferation of organizational activity, and where black communities in particular possess greater political and organizational resources than elsewhere. The existence of these factors in the formal political sphere allows and encourages their replication outside that sphere as well. A context in which there are greater political and organizational resources allows latent ethnic tensions to be expressed through overt, organized protest.

Unlike the other theories of conflict, however, the political-process explanation hypothesizes that violent conflict follows a different dynamic than protest: according to political-process theory, intergroup violence should not be related to political and organizational factors—if anything, it should be greater where these factors are present in lesser degrees. In contrast, none of the sociological theories reviewed suggests different causes for these two forms of conflict.

For the purposes of this analysis, the degree of black political resources is derived from black representation on city councils.[12] Higher levels of representation are associated with higher levels of political efficacy, sophistication, and resources, which in turn facilitate collective mobilization for protest activities. Greater black representation also reflects a shift in the structure of political opportunities, or system-level balance of power, signaling to black activists that the political system is more open to their demands (Eisinger 1973). Under such conditions, activists might be more likely to mobilize neighborhood residents to protest. Black political representation on city councils for the sample ranges from no representation to 85 percent of council membership, with a mean of 27 percent and a standard deviation of 20 percentage points. A positive correlation of black political resources with protest would support a political-process explanation.

With regard to the second component of political process, political structure, the overarching pattern of political institutions in a city is hypothesized to shape behavior *outside* as well as within electoral politics. Reform-style political institutions tend to be more insulated from community pressures and thus less encouraging of community organization. Traditional organizations, by contrast, which in the past were highly centralized (in the form of political machines) and thus may have been able to absorb or suppress overt group conflict, today persist in a fragmented form; the high degrees of organization remain, but without the high degrees of control (Wolfinger 1972). Due to the legacies of the machine era, traditional cities today tend to have larger numbers of public offices and resources and more active intermediate institutions (such as political parties and neighborhood councils) between formal political institutions and residents.

For this study, traditional political structure—as opposed to reform-style structure—was measured based on the strength of local traditional party organizations (TPOs) in the state, using Mayhew's (1986) scale. Mayhew's TPO scores range from 1 to 5, with 5 representing strong parties.[13] The mean for the sample is 2.36 and the standard deviation 1.61. A positive correlation with protest and a negative correlation with violence would lend support for political process theory.

Control Variables

The cities in the sample vary widely in their demographic attributes. To control for these attributes, the following variables are included: the natural log of the city population, the percentage of blacks in the total population, and the percentage of the population that is Korean. Also considered is the rate of violent crimes per 100,000 population.[14] The reason for including the latter is that some cities might be more prone to conflict in general than others. In such places, a social environment laced with higher levels of apprehension might generate overt intergroup conflict simply as a matter of course. If this is the case, it would be best to separate this factor out from other city or group characteristics to which it is unrelated. Finally, a control variable is included to represent the possible contagion effect of previous conflict.

Findings

Two regression models provide the findings for this study—one with boycotts as the dependent variable and the other with incidents of intergroup violence as the dependent variable. Both models use pooled time-series data. The unit of analysis is a "city-year"; each data point thus represents one year for each of the thirty-nine cities. The number of years for each city is at least six (1990 to 1995) and as many as eleven (from 1985 to 1995), depending on the number of years of newspaper coverage available in the electronic databases. The dependent variable is a dummy variable, represented by a zero or a one, which indicates whether or not boycotting occurred in each year in each city. For this reason, logit regression was chosen for the statistical analysis. As a result, what these models predict is the effect that each explanatory variable has on the probability of blacks boycotting Korean stores in a given year in a given city.

To maintain their comparability, both models are virtually identical in the sets of independent variables that they use, the only exception being a contagion variable. In both models, this variable simply indicates whether an incident occurred the previous year—in the boycott model, a previous boycott; in the violence model, a previous report of violence. This controls for the possibility that conflict one year might increase the probability of conflict the next year.[15]

The Occurrence of Boycotts

The results of the boycott model, which are shown in table 6.1, yield two striking findings—one surprising and one expected. The unexpected result is the complete lack of support for any of the sociological theories—cultural differences, middleman minority theory, and competition theory—put forth here to explain boycotts. None of the coefficients for any of the variables representing these theories achieves statistical significance.[16] Although this fact renders each of the coefficients indistinguishable from zero, it is interesting to note that three out of four are not correlated with the probability of boycotts in the expected direction. The coefficients for the percentage of non-English-speaking Koreans, the relative self-employment rate of Koreans, and the unemployment rate of blacks all bear negative signs, whereas their respective theories would predict positive correlations. Only the coefficient for competition theory, the ratio of black- to Korean-owned firms rendered the expected negative sign. This lack of support for any of the sociological theories is surprising because it was expected that they would work in tandem with the political process to increase the likelihood of black boycotts of Korean stores.

The second striking result displayed in table 6.1 is not surprising, for it gives credence to a political process explanation for the distribution of boycotting. The coefficients for traditional party organization and black city council representation both achieve statistical significance here. The substantive significance of variables in a logit model cannot be interpreted directly from their coefficients as in a linear model—the coefficients must first be translated into probabilities.[17]

To facilitate comparison of substantive significance, the third column in the table shows a measure of the relative impact of explanatory variables. The impact represents the difference in probabilities when the value of the explanatory variable is increased, from the mean to one standard deviation above the mean, while all other variables are held constant. Black city council representation has the largest impact on the probability of boycotting, at .08, followed by the population of a city and the violent-crime rate, both at .05. Traditional party organization has an impact score of .03.

The impacts of these variables can be put in terms that have more relevance to the real world. For example, the probability of boycotts occurring in a hypothetical city with all average characteristics but with a TPO score of 1—that is, with little or no traditional political

Table 6.1   Probability of Black Boycotts Against Korean Stores in
Thirty-Nine Cities, 1985 to 1995

Explanatory Variables	Logit Coefficient	Impact
Political process theory		
Traditional party organization (1–5)	**0.36***	**0.03**
Black city council representation (percentage)	**0.05***	**0.08**
Cultural differences		
Proportion of Koreans who don't speak English well (percentage)	0.20	
Middleman minority theory		
Ratio of Korean self-employment to city self-employment	−0.01	
Black unemployment (percentage)	−0.17	
Competition theory		
Ratio of black-owned to Korean-owned firms	−0.01	
Demographics		
Boycott occurrence in previous year	−0.78	
Violent crime rate (per 100,000 population)	**0.001***	**0.05**
Population (ln)	**0.69****	**0.05**
Black population (percentage)	−0.04	
Korean population (percentage)	0.84	

*p < .10 **p < .05.
Number of cases: 284 city-years; significant coefficients in bold.

organization, such as Los Angeles or Miami—is .03, meaning that approximately one out of every thirty-three such cities would experience a boycott in any given year examined. By contrast, a city with a high level of traditional political organization—such as New York or Chicago—has a .12 probability of experiencing boycotting. Other things equal, about one out of every eight of these places would have a boycott. Black boycotting of a Korean store during a given year is thus about four times more likely in a high-organization, traditional-style city than in a low-organization, reform-style city.

A substantive interpretation of the effect of black city council representation reveals a similar relationship. Holding other factors constant, increasing the value of the representation variable by one standard deviation (20 percentage points) produces a roughly threefold increase in the probability of boycotting. When African Americans hold 10 percent of the seats on a city council, as is the case in San Francisco, Long Beach, and Phoenix,[18] the probability of boycotting is .02. When black representation equals 30 percent (which is close to the sample mean of 27 percent), as in Louisville, Columbus, and Phil-adelphia, the probability becomes .06.[19] And when black representa-tion is as high as 50 percent, there is a .15 probability. Cities at this end of the spectrum include Inglewood and Cleveland.[20]

Other than the two political variables, only two other variables give us statistically significant coefficients: two of the controls, the violent-crime rate and the log of the population size. A hypothetical city with all average features, including the mean crime rate of 1,800 crimes per 100,000 population, has a .05 probability of seeing a black boycott of Korean-owned stores in any given year. A similar city with a crime rate of about one standard deviation higher, or 2,060 incidents per 100,000, would exhibit a probability of .10.

The Occurrence of Intergroup Violence

The results from a regression model that tests the same explanatory variables on incidents of violence between African Americans and Korean Americans reveal marked differences from the boycott model. A glance at table 6.2 shows right away that this time, none of the political-process variables yield statistically significant coefficients. Neither traditional party organization nor black council representa-tion explains the probability of intergroup violence.

This lack of support for political factors in violent incidents is not the only departure from the boycott model. In another important con-trast, variables for all of the sociological theories turn up statistically significant coefficients when it comes to violence. This does not, how-ever, translate into support for all of these theories. For instance, the percentage of Korean Americans who do not speak English well is related to the probability of violence, but not in the predicted direc-tion: table 6.2 shows that this variable's coefficient bears a negative sign instead of the expected positive sign. So, rather than supporting the notion that violence is more likely where the linguistic gap is larger, this finding tells us counterintuitively that violence is more likely where Koreans and blacks can communicate *better*.

The probability of violence in the hypothetically average city is about .04. With all other variables held constant, and the percentage of non-English-speaking Korean Americans increased from its mean of 48 percent to 63 percent (one standard deviation, 15 percentage points), the new probability is about .02. The probability of violence occurring is thus half that in the city with the greater linguistic gap. The unemployment rate for blacks also yields a statistically significant coefficient but does not bear the expected sign—it is negative instead of positive. Holding everything else constant at its mean, increasing unemployment by a single standard deviation above the mean results

Table 6.2   Probability of Violence Between Koreans and Blacks in Thirty-Nine Cities, 1985 to 1995

Explanatory Variables	Logit Coefficient	Impact
Political process theory		
Traditional party organization (1–5)	0.25	
Black city council representation (percentage)	0.02	
Cultural differences		
Proportion of Koreans who don't speak English well (percentage)	− 5.15*	− 0.02
Middleman minority theory		
Ratio of Korean self-employment to city self-employment	− 0.31	
Black unemployment (percentage)	− 0.17*	− 0.02
Competition theory		
Ratio of black-owned to Korean-owned firms	− 0.18**	− 0.03
Demographics		
Violence occurrence in previous year	0.32	
Violent crime rate (per 100,000 population)	0.001*	0.03
Population (ln)	0.54*	0.03
Black population (percentage)	0.02	
Korean population (percentage)	0.97	

*p < .10 **p < .05.
Number of cases: 284 city-years; significant coefficients in bold.

in a new violence probability of .02, the same negative impact as language difference.

The only explanatory variable in table 6.2 that yields a coefficient that is both statistically significant and in the predicted direction is the ratio of black-owned to Korean-owned businesses, the indicator for competition theory. As competition theory predicts, the smaller the ratio (and thus the closer Koreans and blacks are to each other in their levels of business ownership), the greater the chance of conflict. The impact of a one-standard-deviation change is just .03, as the table shows. This is similar to the impact of the other variables.

A hypothetical city with a one-to-one ratio of black to Korean firms (close to Los Angeles or Seattle, which both have a ratio of 1.4), and all other variables set to their means, would have a .10 probability of violence. A city with the mean ratio, which is 12.7, would have a probability of about .04. At 11.07 and 11.7, respectively, Orlando and Houston have firm ratios close to this figure. (And a city with roughly one standard deviation higher than that, a ratio of 22.0, has a probability near zero (.004). In the sample, Louisville is closest to that mark with a 22.9 ratio. Two control variables also end up with statistically significant coefficients: the population log and the violent-crime rate. These variables have similar impacts: in each case, raising the value by one standard deviation increases the probability of violence by about .03.

Discussion of Findings

As two different expressions of black-Korean conflict, protest and violence follow different causal dynamics. Although the two are somewhat related to each other (the simple correlation of boycotting and reports of violence in city-years is .25), different factors explain their distribution across time and space. My findings indicate that the political processes of cities influence when and where blacks boycott Korean stores: The more structured the political life in a city, as indicated by the degree of traditional party organization, the more boycotts will happen. And the greater the political resources of African Americans, as indicated by their representation on city councils, the greater the likelihood of boycotts.[21]

The data also suggest that boycotts by African Americans against Korean Americans have nothing to do with the level of competition between the two groups, the degree of their cultural difference, or the middleman-minority status of a city's Korean population. The reasoning behind a political process explanation for protest-oriented conflict has already been laid out, but the reasons why the sociological theories should fail empirically have not. So before attaching any meaning to this surprising finding, the facts surrounding it require deeper examination. Three possible explanations might hold the answer: first, we can accept this finding at face value—that most boycotts really do have nothing to do with the phenomena commonly associated with them; second, there may be a problem with the measurement of the independent variables representing those phenomena; or third, intermediary steps in the puzzle may be missing from the analysis.

Boycotts as a Purely Political Phenomenon

The first possible interpretation of the finding that the distribution of boycotts is not related to the expected social phenomena is that the boycotts are a purely political phenomenon and thus have nothing to do with the sociologically based intergroup tensions that supposedly cause them. That is, the conflicts do not occur as a result of class, competition, or cultural differences. This presents an unlikely scenario, given the remarkable similarity in boycotters' stated motives across cities, which tend to cite all three of these themes (Joyce 1999), and organizers' aims for their efforts, which are mirrored from city to city, across time. It is possible that local activists mimic events that they hear about from other cities, but given the cell-like nature of much local activism, and the fact that a third to a half of all the boycotts occurred *prior* to the most publicized events in New York City and Los Angeles (see figure 6.1), this possibility would not seem to account for all of the boycotts.

Yet even if boycotts are not purely political, the role that political organization and resources play in generating overt conflicts, as suggested by these findings, cannot be denied. Activists in black communities who seek to rally support for their causes, like activists anywhere, must pay heed to the problems of organizational maintenance. Leading a protest not only helps an activist achieve his or her long-term goal—whether that means community control of a neighborhood's economic resources or bringing the alleged perpetrator of a crime to justice. Rallying supporters for a neighborhood boycott also helps to focus public attention and to build an organization with which the activist can compete with other organizations and pursue other issues.

Problems with the Measurement of Independent Variables

Many of the measures of independent variables used in these statistical models were limited by available data and therefore could only serve as rough indicators of the theories they were meant to represent. Indicators for all of the sociological theories—the proportion of non-English-speaking Korean Americans, the ratio of the Korean self-employment rate to that of the general population, and the ratio of black-owned to Korean-owned businesses—rely on data for metro areas rather than for cities. City-level data for these measures were unavailable.[22] So it remains possible—and seems likely—that the lack of precision in the measurement of the sociological variables has affected their explanatory capacities, and thus may be partly responsible for the lack of support for them.

If the imprecision of these independent variables provides reason to doubt their lack of explanatory power, then the same reasoning testifies to the power of the political variables. Neither of the two political variables that yielded significant results—traditional party organization and black representation on city councils, but especially the former—are ideal measures. Traditional party organization is used as a proxy for the level of political organization in a city, which should encompass more than formal political parties. Measures of other political activities, such as interest-group activity and community organizing, reflect other dimensions of political organization that deserve consideration. Moreover, another problem with this variable is its lack of precision: its range from 1 to 5 may not adequately reflect the full range of levels in traditional party organization. In additional, the measure was originally created by David Mayhew to compare average levels of local party organization at the end of the 1960s on a state-by-state basis (Mayhew 1986), so it is hardly ideal. However, I used his rich descriptions of local party systems to tinker with the TPO scores if a particular city seemed to have characteristics different from other localities in the state.

Still, disparaging the use of Mayhew's TPO scoring system distracts from its advantages. Political process theory speaks to the broad nature of the political systems of cities and the implications of this larger configuration of political institutions, so to use measures of smaller components of this larger whole would defeat the purpose of testing for the effects of the broader configuration of urban politics. Hence, Mayhew's traditional party organization is a measure that is meant to say something lasting about the nature of politics in a city, something that does not change from year to year.

Missing Steps in the Puzzle

A third possible explanation—and another likely culprit—for the lack of support for sociological explanations for black-Korean conflict is the fact that an important step in the process of conflict generation is missing. If factors such as competition, middleman-minority status, and cultural differences matter, they most likely produce latent tensions—in the form of attitudes—between the members of different groups. Political and organizational resources then help to determine the form of collective action and severity of conflict that ensues from these tensions. Because intercity measures of tensions—the attitudes of blacks toward Koreans and vice versa, for example—were not available for a large sample of cities, they could not be included in this analysis. Perhaps they would have proven significant were they included.

What effect would including a measure of tensions have on the analysis? Tensions are hypothetically produced by sociological factors. Tensions might not only contribute to the generation of overt forms of conflict, but might also be affected by them, introducing the possibility of feedback effects. Currently, the closest the analysis gets to this is accounting for the possibility of contagion effects from previous conflicts, which do not achieve statistical significance. Another element missing is the lack of an indicator for ideological explanations for conflict. The solution to the problem of missing measures for both tensions and ideology would lie in opinion surveys, were they available for a large sample of cities.[23]

Violence

The support found here for competition theory in explaining the distribution of violence is not an isolated finding. Competition theory has received increased attention in recent years, such as in the work of Susan Olzak (1992). However, an equally plausible explanation is that the indicator representing competition theory merely signals a greater number of locations at which violence between the two groups can take place. Korean-owned stores, after all, constitute one of the few locations where members of the two groups encounter one another. Other things being equal, when crime is constant and the ratio of black to Korean stores decreases, incidents that might otherwise have taken place in black-owned stores might take place in Korean-owned stores instead. In any case, politics does not appear to be related to incidents of violence between blacks and Koreans. Although a negative correlation of political factors with violence might suggest that traditional political structures dampen this form of conflict, that has not been born out here. Instead, politics helps to explain the nonviolent expression of conflict, whereas sociological factors help to explain the violent.

Conclusions

This analysis suggests that the intercity variation in nonviolent conflict between African Americans and Korean Americans might have less to do with the two groups' feelings toward each other and more to do with the nature of the local political system (keeping in mind, though, that sociological variables might have performed better, or at least differently, in the analysis had better data been available). Party organizations play an important role in structuring political life, and black elected officials represent the presence of political resources in black communities. Racial tensions may be more likely to translate into nonviolent collective action where political life is more structured and resource-laden.

The finding that politics is related to protest is not entirely new. For example, in a statistical analysis of black protests against city governments in the 1960s, Peter Eisinger (1973) discovered that the frequency of protest was related to certain features of traditional-style urban political systems and to the representation of blacks on city councils.

Given the evidence of this study, it might be argued that the utility of political variables in explaining the occurrence of boycotts is quite small. It must be remembered, however, that conflicts between African Americans and Korean Americans are relatively rare events, and the nature of political settings has typically not been associated with these kinds of events. That politics explains *any* part of their occurrence, then, is noteworthy.

It is also worth recalling that the statistical models presented here are meant as rough tests of theories that explain complex social phenomena. The analyses' breadth is their inherent benefit as well as their severest limitation. The greater depth of comparative case studies makes a good companion to statistical analysis and is the focus of much of the larger study of which this analysis is a part (Joyce 1999). Closer studies of several cities and their conflicts also confirms the need for better intercity measures of such phenomena as community organization and intergroup attitudes.

This chapter, and the larger project of which it is a part, has two implications for the more general theme of governing American cities in a time of increasing racial and ethnic diversity. First, political processes and institutions have an impact on social conflict outside the arena of formal politics. The configuration of politics affects the tenor of the larger social discourse in society, or how groups interact with each other, and the configuration of politics differs from place to place, both among nations and within nations. This piece of wisdom has received a great deal of attention in the literature on comparative politics. For example, Donald Horowitz (1985, 1989) and Atul Kohli (1990) have shown how political institutions affect the course of ethnic and other forms of social conflict in developing nations. Work focused on Europe has shown how the structure of political institutions—like corporatism and consociationalism—affects both labor and ethnic relations. It seems likely that more approaches like these to the study of urban politics in the United States could greatly benefit the study of race and ethnic relations here.

Second, scholars have very little understanding of the relationship between violent conflict and nonviolent protest. In social movements, we often see protest degenerating into violence—whether in labor disputes, movements for national independence, or campaigns for freedom and civil rights. But we rarely see adequate explanations for this. At least in some contexts, the answer might lie in the ability of tensions to overwhelm organizational and political resources. If we could develop good measures of the phenomena on both sides of this equation—tensions and organization—we might be able to understand that relationship better.

Notes

1. It should be pointed out that racial motives cannot be assumed in all of these events. Many incidents of violence may be perpetrated with little or no awareness of group identities. But to include only those events obviously motivated by hostility toward the other group (such as those classified by police as "hate crimes") was undesirable for several reasons. First, such motivations are not always clearly reported and in any case are difficult to establish reliably. Second, uncovering of larger patterns in these events across time and space might itself be used to address the question of the existence of racial conflict between the groups. Third, individual incidents of violence not motivated by intergroup hostilities may prompt collective mobilization that does pit groups against each other. I realize that sifting so indiscriminately risks catching too much in the process and overestimating what might in reality be a rather small phenomenon. However, my arguments do not end with descriptions of the frequency with which black-Korean conflicts happen. Moreover, I argue elsewhere that black-Korean conflicts are to a large extent constructed locally, tempering the initial emphasis on what may appear to some as an alarmingly widespread phenomenon. Actually, black-Korean conflicts have been relatively rare. Indeed, if the statistical analysis in this study relies too heavily on similarities among black-Korean conflicts, the case studies I undertake elsewhere, in a larger study, focus more heavily on their differences (Joyce 1999).

2. Events in which an Asian American victim of a different ethnicity was mistaken for Korean were also included.

3. The cities are Mesa, Phoenix, Scottsdale, and Tempe, Arizona; Berkeley, Inglewood, Long Beach, Los Angeles, Oakland, Pasadena, Pomona, and San Francisco, California; Hartford, Connecticut; Washington, D.C.; Hialeah, Miami, and Orlando, Florida; Atlanta, Georgia; Chicago, Illinois; Indianapolis, Indiana; Louisville, Kentucky; New Orleans, Louisiana; Baltimore, Maryland; Boston, Massachusetts; Detroit, Michigan; Minneapolis, Minnesota; St. Louis, Missouri; New York; Cincinnati, Cleveland, and Columbus, Ohio; Philadelphia and Pittsburgh, Pennsylvania; Arlington, Dallas, Fort Worth, and Houston, Texas; Arlington, Virginia; and Seattle, Washington.

4. Some reports of violence include multiple incidents.

5. One boycott was also found in Hawthorne, California, which is not included in the sample of cities due to its small size (population of 75,000). The campaign against the rebuilding of liquor stores in South-Central Los Angeles following the 1992 riots is also not included, even though it consisted of mobilizing community residents, because for a variety of reasons it did not resemble other boycotts. The unique nature of this campaign is discussed in detail elsewhere (Joyce 1999).

6. Violence was also reported in Hawthorne and Compton, California.

7. Min (1996) reports findings from a survey of blacks' attitudes toward Koreans in New York City and argues that his findings support cultural and ideological explanations for conflict between the two groups.

8. In this survey, the U.S. Bureau of the Census (1987) counts firms that are at least one-half owned by members of minority groups; file tax forms for individual proprietorships, partnerships, or subchapter S corporations; have annual receipts of $500 or more; and are not farms, ranches, railroads, postal services, membership organizations, private households, or governments. Data comes from tax records, social security records, a mail survey, and economic censuses.

9. Ideally, an index of intergroup business competition would use data collected at the neighborhood level in order to capture the effects of competition in just those parts of a city where black residents predominate. Unfortunately, the Census Bureau does not count Korean firms even at the city level—it only counts them for Metropolitan Statistical Areas. A ratio of firms at the metro level must suffice, although as a result it can only serve as a rough indicator of competition. The most recent data are from 1987 (the Survey of Minority-Owned Business Enterprises takes place every five years; data on Korean firms were not available in the 1992 edition).

10. Another factor that makes an immigrant group a middleman minority is nonassimilation into the host culture. One measure of this available from the census is the degree to which Korean Americans do not speak English "very well," which is used here to indicate cultural difference.

11. Unpaid family workers are included with self-employed persons.

12. Information on black officeholders comes from Joint Center for Economic and Political Studies (1985–1995).

13. Mayhew (1986, 19–20) assigns states higher TPO scores if they meet five criteria: 1) local party organizations exist autonomously from nonelectoral organizations, 2) these organizations (or patterns of organization) are persistent across time, 3) they have "an important element of hierarchy," 4) they regularly nominate candidates for public office, and 5) they rely on material rather than purposive incentives as a means of enlisting support. Mayhew's scores are based on local political arrangements in the late 1960s. A high TPO score does not necessarily imply that machines in a state control government.

14. Population statistics are taken from the Census of Population (U.S. Bureau of the Census 1980, 1990) and crime statistics are taken from the Federal Bureau of Investigation's Uniform Crime Reports (Federal Bureau of Investigation 1985–1995).

15. The opposite is also possible: that conflict one year makes conflict the next year *less* likely.

16. One-tailed (nondirectional) T-tests were used to determine statistical significance.

17. Using the formula $1/(1 + e^{-[xb]})$.

18. The values for these cities in the mid-1990s were 10.0, 11.1, and 12.5 percent, respectively. Although these cities are representative for this variable, they do not necessarily match the values of other variables used to calculate the probability. The others are set to their mean for the sample.

19. The values for these cities in the mid-1990s were 30.8, 30.0, and 29.41 percent, respectively.

20. The values for these cities in the mid-1990s were 50.0 and 52.38 percent, respectively.

21. Poisson regression models of the frequency of boycotts and violence, represented by the count of incidents between 1990 and 1995 (the only years for which data on the dependent variable was available for all cities in the sample), confirm these findings. The results of these models are not reported here because they essentially repeat those of the logit regression models which I do report, and because they use less of the available data, due to their limited time scope.

22. The measures for black unemployment, the violent crime rate, and the demographic variables, however, used city-level data.

23. Attributing conflict to a clash of ideologies is problematic. For example, the American Dream and black nationalism share a common emphasis on economic self-sufficiency. Moreover, there are different strands of black nationalism, which have different impacts on political mobilization (Joyce 1999).

References

Blalock, Hubert M. 1967. *Toward a Theory of Minority-Group Relations*. New York: Capricorn.

Bobo, Lawrence, Camille L. Zubrinsky, James H. Johnson Jr., and Melvin L. Oliver. 1994. "Public Opinion Before and After a Spring of Discontent." In *The Los Angeles Riots: Lessons for the Urban Future*, edited by M. Baldassare. Boulder, Colo.: Westview Press.

Bonacich, Edna. 1994. "Thoughts on Urban Unrest." In *Race and Ethnic Conflict: Contending Views on Prejudice, Discrimination, and Ethnoviolence*, edited by F. L. Pincus and H. J. Ehrlich. Boulder, Colo.: Westview Press.

Chang, Edward T. 1991. "New Urban Crisis: Intra-Third World Conflict." In *Asian Americans: Comparative and Global Perspectives*, edited by S. Hune, H. C. Kim, S. S. Fugita, and A. Ling. Pullman: Washington State University Press.

Cheng, Lucie, and Yen Espiritu. 1989. "Korean Businesses in Black and Hispanic Neighborhoods: A Study of Intergroup Relations." *Sociological Perspectives* 32: 521–34.

Eisinger, Peter K. 1973. "The Conditions of Protest Behavior in American Cities." *American Political Science Review* 67 (March): 11–28.

Federal Bureau of Investigation. 1985–1995. *Uniform Crime Reports.* Washington: U.S. Government Printing Office.

Freer, Regina. 1994. "Black-Korean Conflict." In *The Los Angeles Riots: Lessons for the Urban Future*, edited by Mark Baldassare. Boulder, Colo.: Westview Press.

Horowitz, Donald L. 1985. *Ethnic Groups in Conflict.* Berkeley: University of California Press.

———. 1989. "Incentives and Behaviour in the Ethnic Politics of Sri Lanka and Malaysia." *Third World Quarterly* 10 (October): 18–35.

Joint Center for Economic and Political Studies. 1985–1995. *Black Elected Officials.* Washington, D.C.: Joint Center for Economic and Political Studies.

Joyce, Patrick D. 1999. *Transforming Tensions: Politics, Protest and Violence in Black-Korean Conflicts.* Ph.D. diss., Harvard University.

Kohli, Atul. 1990. *Democracy and Discontent: India's Growing Crisis of Governability.* Cambridge: Cambridge University Press.

Lee, Heon Cheol. 1993. *Black-Korean Conflict in New York City: A Sociological Analysis.* Ph.D. diss., Columbia University.

Light, Ivan, and Edna Bonacich. 1991. *Immigrant Entrepreneurs: Koreans in Los Angeles, 1965–1982.* Berkeley: University of California Press.

Light, Ivan, Hadas Har-Chvi, and Kenneth Kan. 1994. "Black/Korean Conflict in Los Angeles." In *Managing Divided Cities*, edited by S. Dunn. Keele, Staffordshire, Eng.: Ryburn Publishing.

Mayhew, David R. 1986. *Placing Parties in American Politics: Organization, Electoral Settings, and Government Activity in the Twentieth Century.* Princeton, N.J.: Princeton University Press.

Min, Pyong Gap. 1996. *Caught in the Middle: Korean Merchants in America's Multiethnic Cities.* Berkeley: University of California Press.

Olzak, Susan. 1992. *The Dynamics of Ethnic Competition and Conflict.* Palo Alto, Calif.: Stanford University Press.

Ong, Paul, Kye Young Park, and Yasmin Tong. 1994. "The Korean-Black Conflict and the State." In *The New Asian Immigration in Los Angeles and Global Restructuring*, edited by Paul Ong, Edna Bonacich, and Lucie Cheng. Philadelphia: Temple University Press.

Robinson, Reginald Leamon. 1993. "'The Other Against Itself': Deconstructing the Violent Discourse Between Korean and African Americans." *Southern California Law Review* 67: 17–115.

U.S. Bureau of the Census. 1980. *Census of Population.* Washington: U.S. Government Printing Office.

———. 1987. *Survey of Minority-Owned Business Enterprises.* Washington: U.S. Government Printing Office.

———. 1990. *Census of Population.* Washington: U.S. Government Printing Office.

Wolfinger, Raymond E. 1972. "Why Political Machines Have Not Withered Away and Other Revisionist Thoughts." *The Journal of Politics* 34(May): 377–78.

PART III

COOPERATION AND
COALITION-BUILDING

Chapter 7

Structural Shifts and Institutional Capacity: Possibilities for Ethnic Cooperation and Conflict in Urban Settings

MICHAEL JONES-CORREA

AMERICAN cities experienced four major changes in the 1980s and 1990s: First, immigration transformed urban populations, so that cities' populations at the end of the decade were significantly more ethnically diverse. Second, significant portions of the middle class of all ethnic and racial groups left for the suburbs, leaving urban residents much more polarized along class lines. Third, service industries replaced manufacturing, so that there were fewer secure and well-paying jobs for those with fewer skills. Finally, the federal government scaled back its financial support for urban areas, so that cities had to manage these changes on their own. These structural shifts set the stage for new interethnic tensions that culminated in serious civil disturbances across several cities. This chapter outlines the manner in which urban institutional frameworks mediated and shaped changing interethnic relations over the past two decades. Cities responded differently, and in fact had different capacities to respond, depending on their institutional structure. These institutional structures continue to have important implications for the incorporation of new urban actors and patterns of interethnic coalition building.

Change in Cities:
The New Urban Landscape

In 2000, the Census Bureau announced that more than 10 percent of the American population were immigrants, the highest proportion since the 1940s, and more than double the percentage in 1970 (4.8 percent) (U.S. Bureau of the Census 2001). At the present time, almost half of America's population growth is due to immigration: about a million new immigrants have been arriving yearly, almost equal to the number of babies born in the U.S. each year. Yet though we are living in the midst of swift demographic change, we know very little about how contemporary immigrants are incorporating into the American political system, even though the number of immigrants arriving to the United States since 1965 has surpassed the levels of 1880 to 1920—the last great wave of immigration to this country.

Today's foreign-born population is not distributed evenly throughout the country; they are concentrated both within states and across states. According to the 1990 census, over 93 percent of the foreign-born population resides in metropolitan areas, compared with 73 percent of native-born residents. As a result, major urban areas, and, increasingly, secondary urban and suburban areas as well, have undergone rapid demographic shifts (see figure 7.1). About one half of new immigrants entering the United States in the 1980s live in one of the following eight metropolitan areas: Los Angeles; New York; Miami; Anaheim, Calif.; Chicago; Washington, D.C.; Houston; and San Francisco (Smith and Edmonston 1997, 61).

In addition, three-quarters of immigrants arriving to the United States lived in only six states: California, New York, Florida, Texas, New Jersey, and Illinois. California and New York alone attract over 40 percent of new immigrants (Smith and Edmonston 1997, 59). California is home to 7.7 million foreign-born persons—more than one-third of all immigrants to the U.S. and nearly one-quarter of all California residents. New York ranks second with 2.9 million foreign-born residents and Florida third with 2.1 million. Three other states have over 1 million foreign-born residents: Texas, Illinois, and New Jersey. Selected cities and states, then, have undergone substantial demographic shifts (see figure 7.2).

The fact of dramatic demographic change is not new in the American experience—certainly the previous waves of immigration, the migration of blacks from the South, and the postwar move to the suburbs have all entailed massive change in relatively short periods of time. In one sense, then, the new wave of immigration to urban areas is simply one more in a chain of demographic transformations that have continually made and remade the United States. What is new,

Figure 7.1   Migration from Abroad, 1985 to 1990

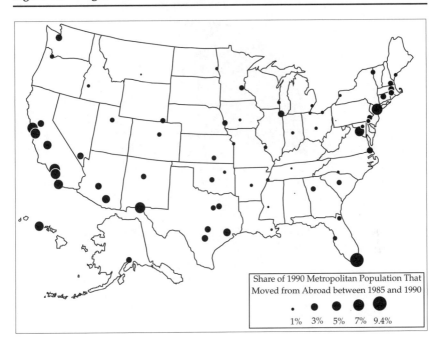

Share of 1990 Metropolitan Population That
Moved from Abroad between 1985 and 1990

1%   3%   5%   7%   9.4%

Source: U.S. Bureau of the Census 1991. *Census of Population. Summary Tape 3*. 1990.
Washington: U.S. Department of Commerce.

however, is the context in which these demographic shifts have been
taking place. Many of these most recent new immigrants arrived into
multiethnic urban areas undergoing fundamental economic transitions with severely constrained public resources. One consequence is
that immigrants from Asia and Latin America were directly or indirectly competing with native-born African Americans for both public
and private resources.

New Actors and Competition over
Resources

The influx of immigrants to cities over the last twenty years over-
shadowed an equally striking movement: the exodus of middle-class
blacks from central cities (Farley 1987; see also Galster 1991; Culver
1982). The suburbanization of African Americans began in the late
1960s, but it accelerated thereafter. Middle-class and working-class
black suburbs appeared, for instance, around predominantly African

Figure 7.2   Foreign-Born U.S. Population by State of Residence

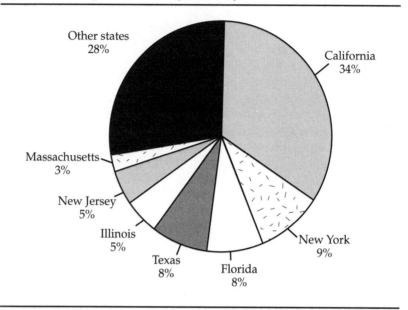

Source: Author's compilation.

American cities such as Detroit; Gary, Indiana; Atlanta, and Washington, D.C., as well as around such other cities as Chicago, Los Angeles, and Miami. The African American population in many cities has remained flat, as middle-class blacks migrated outward either to the suburbs, or in a reversal of patterns earlier in the century, back to the South. The last thirty years, then, were characterized by the suburbanization not only of whites but of other ethnic groups as well (Frey 1995). Without immigration from abroad, many cities, particularly those in the northeastern United States, would have experienced significantly greater population losses. New York City, for example, lost a half million residents in the early 1990s, but these were replaced by at least an equal number of immigrants.

The suburbanization of the black middle class should not obscure the fact that there are significant concentrations of African Americans in central cities (Tobin 1987; Orfield 1986; Massey and Denton 1993).[1] Much of the black population that remains in central cities, though, is substantially cut off from the larger urban economy—unlike the urban black population of the 1950s and 1960s (Wilson 1987, 1997).

Not every city that is home to a substantial poor black population has experienced heavy immigration, but the major cities that have been *most* affected by immigration—Miami, Los Angeles, San Fran-

Table 7.1   U.S. Cities with Populations of 200,000 or More Ranked by Percentage Foreign-Born Residents and Percentage of Residents Speaking Language Other Than English, 1990

	Foreign-Born Persons		Persons Speaking Language Other than English at Home	
	Percentage	Rank	Percentage	Rank
Miami, Florida	59.7	1	73.3	1
Santa Ana, California	50.9	2	69.2	2
Los Angeles, California	38.4	3	49.9	4
San Francisco, California	34.0	4	42.4	6
New York, New York	28.4	5	41.0	9
Anaheim, California	28.4	5	37.4	11
San Jose, California	26.5	7	38.5	10
Jersey City, New Jersey	24.6	8	41.3	8
Long Beach, California	24.3	9	32.8	16
El Paso, Texas	23.4	10	66.7	3
Stockton, California	22.6	11	36.5	13
Honolulu, Hawaii	21.4	12	33.8	14
San Diego, California	20.9	13	29.2	18
Boston, Massachusetts	20.0	14	25.6	22
Oakland, California	19.8	15	27.3	20
Newark, New Jersey	18.7	16	36.8	12
Houston, Texas	17.8	17	30.7	17
Fresno, California	17.1	18	33.1	15
Chicago, Illinois	16.9	19	29.1	19
Riverside, California	15.5	20	25.0	24
Sacramento, California	13.7	21	23.8	25
Seattle, Washington	13.1	22	15.4	32
Dallas, Texas	12.5	23	22.2	27
Tucson, Arizona	10.7	24	27.1	21
Las Vegas, Nevada	10.3	25	15.2	33
Washington, D.C.	9.7	26	12.5	37
San Antonio, Texas	9.4	27	47.3	5
Fort Worth, Texas	9.0	28	19.4	28
Phoenix, Arizona	8.6	29	18.7	29
Austin, Texas	8.5	30	22.4	26

Source: U.S. Bureau of the Census 1996.

cisco, New York, Houston, Chicago, and Washington, D.C.—all have a significant native-born black minority. In these cities, blacks have been joined by sizable contingents of immigrants moving into adjacent, and at times even the same, neighborhoods (see table 7.1). And while many immigrants have moved directly into outlying suburban areas, the central city attracts many others, particularly those with less economic and social capital. Searching for cheap housing and access to transportation and jobs, they may compete with African Americans for the same scarce resources.

Although there seems to be a consensus emerging that immigration is not, as a whole, detrimental to the job prospects of the native-born, this may not hold true for those at the very bottom of the ladder. A National Research Council–sponsored study indicated that workers with lower levels of education are particularly vulnerable to the effects of immigration. Because new immigrants increase the supply of low-skilled labor and compete for the same jobs, immigration accounts for a significant portion of the erosion of wages among native-born high school dropouts (Smith and Edmonston 1997, 236). According to this study, immigration led to a roughly 5 percent wage reduction for this group in the 1980s.[2] High school dropouts account for less than 10 percent of America's total workforce, but make up a significantly larger percentage of the central-city workforce. The wage effects of immigration are concentrated, therefore, in the areas where lower-skilled immigrants and native-born workers are themselves concentrated—in inner cities.

In addition to these wage effects, there may be some job displacement going on as well on the lower rungs of the economic ladder as a result of immigration. Recent research in the New York and Los Angeles metro areas suggests that immigrant social networks serve to reduce the information costs immigrants face in the job market (giving them, for instance, advance notice of job openings), granting immigrants an advantage in the marketplace for lower-skilled jobs and driving out competitors—particularly African Americans (Waldinger 1996). These findings are confirmed by several other studies, which also have found that employers may also strongly prefer to hire immigrants over inner-city blacks (Smith and Edmonston 1997, 394; Kasinitz and Rosenberg 1994; Kirschenman and Neckerman 1991; Neckerman and Kirschenman 1991; Wilson 1987).

Competition, furthermore, does not occur only in the private sphere. Indeed, there is every indication that the more intractable competition takes place in the areas of political representation and public-sector hiring. In the private-sector job market, competition may be detrimental to some, but outcomes are more open ended than elsewhere, meaning that the loss of a job in one area may still allow opportunities in others. This is less likely to be the case, however, in the public sector, which depends on relatively fixed resources. Granting new ethnic groups a share of public jobs, then, means that existing jobs—in city agencies, public schools, and other civil service positions—must be redistributed away from others. This zero-sum situation applies as well to elected representatives too: if representation is seen as descriptive,[3] a gain for one ethnic group entails a loss for another. Public-sector employment has been crucial in the 1970s and 1980s for black mobility into the middle class (Soja 1992, 365); to be asked to open up this avenue to immigrant newcomers when there are few other occupational niches in which blacks have opportunities on par with other ethnic groups is particularly galling for African Americans. Friction among ethnic groups occurs when the actors involved believe they are engaged in a zero-sum game rather than a situation that might have mutually beneficial outcomes. In Los Angeles, for instance, Bobo and Hutchings (1996, 958) found that blacks and Latinos both perceived Asian competition as a zero-sum game, and that "Asian Americans and Latino respondents who are foreign born tend to perceive greater competition with blacks than do their native born co-ethnics." The influx of immigrants thus presents significant challenges for urban institutions. Grievances, both real and perceived, have the potential for triggering conflict.

Economic Restructuring

In a growing economy, cities might have had the resources to address some of the issues underlying ethnic tensions. The 1970s and 1980s, however, were not good decades for American cities. Cities were coping with massive shifts in employment away from manufacturing and toward "corporate, public and non-profit services," while "occupation . . . similarly shifted from manual workers to managers, professionals, secretaries and service workers" (Mollenkopf and Castells 1991, 3). Over a period of twenty-five years, America's cities lost half of their manufacturing base (see table 7.2; see also Kasarda 1988). These jobs moved either elsewhere in the United States or overseas.

As a result, immigrants arriving at cities were no longer swept up into blue-collar jobs in large factories, as they had been in the early decades of the twentieth century. Stable union jobs in the manufacturing sector had largely disappeared by this point. Instead, immigrants became the preferred source of low-skilled labor in the new nonunionized jobs in the service and light-manufacturing sectors of the economy (Waldinger 1989, 221). Nonunionized service-industry and manufacturing jobs, however, were more vulnerable in economic downturns than the unionized jobs they replaced. So, as the economy endured the recessions of 1973 to 1975, 1980 to 1982, and 1987 to 1991, many low-skilled workers lost employment opportunities. This was reflected in the widening gap separating wealthiest and poorest city residents: between 1969 and 1987 the proportion of those earning less than $20,000 to those earning more than $40,000 increased; those with

Table 7.2   **Metropolitan Employment in Manufacturing and Services, Selected Cities, 1970 and 1995 (Percentage)**

	Manufacturing		Services	
	1970	1995	1970	1995
Atlanta	20.7	11.5	14.6	29.3
Baltimore	24.8	8.8	17.0	35.5
Boston	22.1	12.4	24.7	38.3
Chicago	31.8	16.9	16.9	30.0
Dallas	24.6	14.5	15.2	28.5
Denver	17.5	9.5	18.1	30.5
Detroit	38.1	21.6	14.3	30.1
Houston	18.6	10.6	18.2	29.1
Kansas City	25.1	12.5	15.7	28.0
Los Angeles–Long Beach	28.9	16.8	18.7	32.2
Miami	15.8	8.8	15.8	32.0
Minneapolis–St. Paul	27.4	18.0	17.7	28.8
New York City	21.1	8.6	20.1	35.1
Newark	31.5	15.2	17.1	28.8
Pittsburgh	32.3	12.9	18.3	33.9
Portland	22.7	16.4	17.9	27.0
St. Louis	30.9	16.2	17.2	30.8
San Diego	17.9	11.6	14.8	31.8
San Francisco	15.9	8.1	17.6	34.8
Seattle	24.8	15.7	15.8	27.9

Source: Knox 1997, 24, table 1. Reprinted by permission of Sage Publications, Inc. © 1997.

earnings in between decreased proportionally (Soja 1992, 362–63). Poverty in the United States, which had fallen to 11 percent in the 1970s, climbed to 14.7 percent in the late 1980s, and more of this poverty than in previous years was in cities—42 percent in 1992, compared with 30 percent in 1968 (Farrell et al. 1992, 38). Meanwhile, cities in general became poorer relative to their suburbs. According to the National League of Cities, "[in] 1980, per capita incomes in central cities were about 90 percent of suburban per capita incomes. By 1987, per capita incomes of center city residents were only 59 percent of their suburban neighbors" (Farrell et al. 1992, 42). The effects of recession—which were deeper and lasted longer in cities than elsewhere in the United States—were reflected in cities' falling tax receipts, rising debt, and cutbacks in programs. By the end of the 1980s, cities actually had less capacity to address the structural changes underway within their borders than they had at the beginning of the period. This can be seen as well in the erosion of their position within the intergovernmental system—the complex of the federal, state, and local governments.

The Broader Policy Context

The past few decades' changes in urban populations and economies have taken place in the context of broad institutional changes in intergovernmental relations in the United States. Overall, in the postwar period, the federal government has become an increasingly important player in local affairs, particularly in the financing of urban programs. In 1932, for example, only about $10 million in federal grants was given to cities; by 1960 federal aid to state and local governments had reached $7 billion, representing 7.6 percent of total federal budget outlays and 14.5 percent of state and local budgets. By 1980, grants totaled $91 billion, amounting to nearly 16 percent of federal spending and 26 percent of state and local outlays. These figures declined under the Reagan administration, but rebounded under Bush the elder. When Bill Clinton came into office in 1992, grants-in-aid totaled $178 billion and represented 12.9 percent of federal outlays (Ross and Levine 1996, 400–3; see table 7.3).

Yet while urban funding has increasingly depended on federal outlays, there have been clear shifts over the last thirty years from the pattern of direct federalism under President Johnson to the new federalism of Nixon and devolution of responsibilities to states under Reagan and Clinton. Under Johnson, the federal government developed a direct relationship with cities, through a variety of grants programs, that essentially bypassed the states. By the late 1970s, between 25 and 30 percent of all federal intergovernmental aid bypassed states and was negotiated directly with cities (Walker 1995, 111–13). In the Nixon administration, regulations restricting the use of federal grants were loosened, and cities were increasingly given block grants that allowed them considerable freedom in allocating funds. With the arrival of the Reagan administration, federal grants-in-aid to localities and states fell to $88.2 billion in 1982, the first real decline in federal outlays to localities and states. By 1989, grants-in-aid were reduced to less than 11 percent of federal outlays and only 17 percent of state and local budgets (Ross and Levine 1996, 403). But while the declines in the levels of aid were temporary, there was a more permanent shift in the way aid was allocated. Rather than the direct federal-city relationships that had previously characterized postwar intergovernmental relationships, the Reagan administration chose to reemphasize traditional readings of federalism, underlining states' authority over cities. Hence the 1980s saw an increasing reliance on the states as the middlemen for federal funds, a reliance that continued through the Bush and Clinton administrations.

To put it another way, cities in the postwar period have become

Table 7.3   Federal Grants-in-Aid in Relation to State and Local Outlays, Total Federal Outlays, and Gross Domestic Product, 1955 to 1993

Fiscal Year	Amount (Billions)	Percentage Change	As a Percentage of Total State-Local Outlays	Total Federal Outlays (Billions)
1955	3.2	4.9	10.2	4.7
1956	3.6	15.6	10.4	5.0
1957	4.0	8.1	10.5	5.2
1958	4.9	22.5	11.7	6.0
1959	6.5	32.7	14.1	7.0
1960	7.0	7.7	14.5	7.6
1961	7.1	1.4	13.7	7.3
1962	7.9	11.3	14.1	7.4
1963	8.6	8.9	14.2	7.7
1964	10.2	17.4	15.4	8.6
1965	10.9	7.9	15.1	9.2
1966	12.9	19.3	16.1	9.6
1967	15.2	16.9	16.9	9.7
1968	18.6	22.4	18.3	10.4
1969	20.2	9.1	17.8	11.0
1970	24.1	18.2	19.0	12.3
1971	28.1	17.1	19.7	13.4
1972	34.4	22.4	21.7	14.9
1973	41.8	21.5	24.0	17.0
1974	43.4	3.8	22.3	16.1
1975	49.8	14.7	22.6	15.0
1976	59.1	18.7	24.1	15.9
1977	68.4	15.7	25.5	16.7
1978	77.9	13.9	26.5	17.0
1979	82.9	6.4	25.8	16.5
1980	91.5	10.4	25.8	15.5
1981	94.8	3.6	24.7	14.0
1982	88.2	−7.0	21.6	11.8
1983	92.5	4.9	21.3	11.4
1984	97.6	5.5	20.9	11.5
1985	105.9	8.5	20.9	11.2
1986	112.4	6.1	19.9	11.3
1987	108.4	−3.6	18.0	10.8
1988	115.3	6.4	17.7	10.8
1989	122.0	5.7	17.3	10.7
1990	135.4	11.0	19.4	10.8
1991	154.6	14.2	20.5	11.7
1992	178.3	15.3	22.0	12.9
1993	203.7	14.2	n.a.	13.8

Source: Ross and Levine 1996, 404, table 12.4. Reprinted by permission of F. E. Peacock Publishers, Inc. © 1996.

Table 7.4   State Intergovernmental Expenditures to Local Governments, Selected Years, 1954 to 1992

Fiscal Year	Total Dollars (Millions)	Annual Percentage Change
1954	5,679	
1964	12,968	8.6
1965	14,173	9.3
1966	16,928	19.4
1967	19,056	12.6
1968	21,949	15.2
1969	24,779	12.9
1970	28,893	16.6
1971	32,640	13.0
1972	36,759	12.6
1973	40,822	11.1
1974	45,940	12.5
1975	51,978	13.1
1976	57,858	11.3
1977	62,470	8.0
1978	67,287	7.7
1979	75,975	12.9
1980	84,505	11.2
1981	93,180	10.3
1982	98,743	6.0
1983	101,309	2.6
1984	108,373	7.0
1985	121,571	12.2
1986	131,966	8.6
1987	141,426	7.2
1988	151,662	7.2
1989	165,506	9.1
1990	175,096	5.8
1991	186,469	6.5
1992	201,313	8.0

Source: Ross and Levine 1996, 388, table 12.1. Reprinted by permission of F. E. Peacock Publishers, Inc. © 1996.

much more reliant on outside funding, particularly state funding, to pay their bills. Between 1962 and 1967, the percentage of municipal revenue coming from local property taxes, for example, declined from 93.5 percent to 70 percent, and fell still further, by 1986, to 49.3 percent (rising to 52.6 percent in 1992). In part these figures reflect a shift by cities from property taxes to user fees to raise revenue. But these figures also tell the story of the increasing dependence of cities on intergovernmental aid. By 1992, 37.7 percent of local-government revenues derived from intergovernmental aid (U.S. Bureau of the Census

1962, 1967, 1987, 1992). Increasingly this aid was coming through the states. In 1954, state aid to cities stood at slightly less than 42 percent of local own-source revenue. Ten years later, the figure stood essentially unchanged at 43 percent. By 1980, however, states were taking on an increasingly larger role in metropolitan finance, and the figure climbed to nearly 64 percent. Then, even after the Reagan cutbacks took their toll on state spending, state aid to cities still amounted to 55 percent of local own-source revenue (Ross and Levine 1996, 396).

Outside aid has been crucial to cities' ability to maintain infrastructure and provide services, but there is no question that dependence on intergovernmental funding has also made cities more vulnerable to factors outside their control. This may be seen in the 1980s, a decade that well evidences the downside to intergovernmental funding. The Reagan administration cut back its funding to both cities and states, but also shifted urban funding from direct federal aid to aid channeled through the states, and allowed states increasing flexibility on how to spend those funds. As states dealt with the economic downturn of the early 1980s they chose to direct this money away from cities to address their own budget shortfalls (see table 7.4). Cities were thus hit with a double blow: as the federal government cut back on intergovernmental aid, and redirected much of what was left to states, states, in turn, often chose to keep this money from cities.

Cities dealt with the fiscal shortfalls of the 1980s by cutting back on services, neglecting capital improvement, and turning their attention to such cost-cutting measures as the subcontracting and privatization of city functions, ranging from trash pickup to bill collecting (Ross and Levine 1996, 388). Yet even as the immediate crises passed—first in the late 1980s and again in the mid-1990s—and cities turned their attentions once again to basic structural issues, privatization proposals only gained greater currency. This was true at the federal level as well: Clinton's first-term proposals to "reinvent" government, which included giving states greater leeway to experiment with the distribution of federal funds and delivery of services, were a symptom of this trend. In the 1990s and after, government at every level has been reluctant to propose any new spending initiatives to address urban issues. Rather than embark on grand schemes, state and federal governments have instead proposed programs designed to harness private energies without spending public resources.

As a result, the cutting edge of federal urban policy is now on the tax side rather than on the spending side.[4] The best indication of this is that the only major urban proposal to emerge in the 1990s on the federal level was the creation of "enterprise" or "empowerment" zones. The original impetus behind these zones, as advanced in the Bush the elder's administration, was to attempt to "promot[e] local revitalization by *withdrawing* government and thereby creating islands in which free enterprise could flourish" (Ross and Levine 1996, 439). Business would be attracted to areas where taxes were kept low and governmental regulations were relaxed. Still, in spite of a strong endorsement from Housing and Urban Development secretary Jack Kemp, the enterprise-zone proposal was not passed federally under the Bush presidency. Instead, enterprise zones flourished at the state level. By 1993, thirty-five states and the District of Columbia had created over 3,000 enterprise zones, although without any corresponding cuts in federal taxes and regulations. These early zones were rarely targeted for distressed communities, but rather were designed to attract business to the state. Nor were these state zones used on the whole to encourage startups, entrepreneurial ventures, or labor-intensive businesses, but focused instead on bringing in affiliates of established corporations (Ross and Levine 1996, 440).

The enterprise-zone concept was revived by the Clinton administration as a way to direct business investment to distressed areas in the context of a severely constrained federal budget. Combining traditionally Republican free-market principles with Democratic concerns for cities, the idea behind these new "empowerment zones" was to create public-private partnerships aimed at jump-starting economic development in depressed urban areas. Under the program, the federal government would provide the resources and act as a kind of arbitrator: the Department of Housing and Urban Development would award tax breaks and $100 million in federal grant money to each city that put together the best proposals for the zones. Each city was required to work with its private and nonprofit sectors to come up with a plan to aid poorer neighborhoods within its borders. In the first round, urban empowerment zones were awarded to six cities, with two additional cities receiving supplemental zones and four more cities receiving smaller grants as "enhanced enterprise communities" (Ross and Levine 1996, 442–43).

Beginning in the early 1980s, then, the trend in urban financing has been away from directly funding metropolitan areas and toward using states as intermediaries, away from grants toward tax breaks and loans. These shifts—the enhanced role of the states, the emphasis on privatization, the reliance on tax structure rather than spending to shape urban policy—continue to define the philosophy of intergovernmental relations in the United States. In general, these shifts have given cities less financial flexibility and hence fewer degrees of freedom to respond to their own structural changes and the consequent crises arising from those changes. Left to their own devices, cities have had to come up with their own solutions to the structural changes brought about by immigration and a globalizing economy.

The Eruption of Tensions

Given that in the 1980s many of the nation's major cities experienced rapid demographic transformations while government cutbacks left new immigrants and older residents in poorer areas of these cities vulnerable to economic restructuring and openly engaged in competition for scarce resources, it should not have come as a surprise that four of the top immigrant-receiving metropolitan areas were convulsed by serious civil disturbances by the early 1990s (Johnson and Oliver 1989). Together, Los Angeles, New York, Miami, and Washington, D.C., were the destination for almost one in three immigrants settling in the United States in this period; the rapid influx of immigrants to their neighborhoods had an enormous impact, even as these cities' economies shuddered under the strain of adapting to a radically changing economy. Riots occurred in Miami's Liberty City and Overtown neighborhoods in 1980, 1982, 1987, and 1989; in Washington, D.C.'s, Mt. Pleasant and Adams Morgan sections in 1991; and in Crown Heights, New York, and the South-Central area of Los Angeles in 1992. These civil disturbances all involved a mix of recent immigrants and resident minorities, though each displayed its own distinct dynamic and resolution.

In the wake of these disturbances, much of the attention that these cities have received from policy makers and scholars has been, understandably enough, on the riots themselves, which together caused dozens of deaths and billions of dollars' worth of damages. But these disturbances are less interesting for the headlines they produced than for what they indicated about the state of interethnic relations in American cities and the manner in which institutions respond to the structural problems exposed by civil strife. Little attention has been paid to the interethnic renegotiation of access and resources that takes place in the aftermath of these disturbances, or to the institutional context in which these negotiations take place. Unlike the response to the riots in the 1960s, the rebuilding efforts in the aftermath of the 1980s and '90s disturbances have received relatively little attention and scant funding from the federal government. These four riot cities, then, provide examples, albeit extreme ones, of the roles of urban institutions in the context of massive structural changes.

In 1997, five years after the most recent of these riots, I interviewed key actors in each of the four cities that experienced major disturbances. I asked them to look back and reflect on what had been accomplished in the aftermath to address economic and political inequities in these urban areas and to evaluate successes and failures. These efforts yielded 170 interviews across the four cities, including conversations with members of immigrant and ethnic groups, community activists, business leaders, local party officials, and members of city government. The goal of the interviews was to see what could be learned by comparing the experiences of these four cities as they dealt with the fallout from these civil disturbances. The interviews and other data provide examples of how urban institutions address economic dislocation and rapid demographic shifts, how cities respond to these conditions when they themselves are under severe financial pressures, and how communities seek to span ethnic and racial divides.

Problems of Coordination and Coalition Building

Before turning to a more concrete discussion of interethnic relations in a specific context, I would like to pause first to reflect more abstractly on the question of coalitions between new and old actors in institutional settings. How do institutions cope with rapid change? Because institutions and organizations are designed to make environments more predictable—and, hence, stable—they may not be well suited to dealing with change. Institutions are more likely to resist change than to adapt to it, except at their margins (Jones-Correa 1998; North 1990). So the question of what happens when the context in which institutions operate shifts dramatically, as it has in many American metropolitan areas with the arrival of immigrants, is not simply interesting but is important from a theoretical standpoint.

If institutions and organizations resist change then, ceteris paribus, we would expect that there would be an increasing "institutional mismatch," as I hypothesized previously, between the personnel, goals, and services of established urban institutions and their potential clientele, even in the face of overwhelming demographic shifts. As neighborhoods change, the services provided by community-based organizations would increasingly diverge from the needs of the growing immigrant population. But what happens when things are no longer held constant? In the post-disturbance city, we would expect a renegotiation of institutional access, position, and resources among ethnic groups. What affects these negotiations, and what outcomes might we expect?

For negotiation to actually take place, the parties involved must believe that a negotiated outcome will be worth their while and that a negotiated agreement can be enforced. The first condition requires that negotiation be a better alternative than other alternatives (the most basic one being not negotiating). The second condition requires that there be an institutional or organizational constraint that holds the parties to their promises. These conditions give us some idea of what might influence the outcome of negotiations. Immigrant and ethnic groups in an urban area are unlikely to get involved in serious negotiations over resources, access, and positions if they are able to retain what they have without negotiating and believe they are likely to be worse off after the negotiations than they were before. Negotiations are also less likely to succeed if they concern zero-sum goods (such as elected positions, budget items, municipal civil service jobs).

So what are the implications of these points? Cities in which some groups are dominant (in terms of population or power) are unlikely to enter into negotiations with weaker groups (such as immigrants) because these dominant groups have nothing to gain, and everything to lose, through such negotiations. This is particularly the case because most of the things that new urban constituents want are zero-sum goods—making a gain for them a loss for someone else.

Sometimes these zero-sum contests can be avoided if there are additional resources coming from some other source, perhaps a growing tax base or federal funds. Through the late 1980s and into the early 1990s, however, this was not the case in American urban areas: the four cities having serious ethnic disturbances at this time all had serious budgetary constraints and were unable to draw on the resources of the federal government, which was in the midst of its own budgetary crisis.

In the two cities that had dominant ethnic groups (Miami and Washington, D.C.) it was unlikely that either of these dominant groups—Cubans and African Americans, respectively—would enter into serious bargaining with the marginalized rioters (African Americans and Central Americans, respectively). Bargaining was more likely in cities where there was no clear dominant group, or where ethnic bargaining positions were in flux (as in Los Angeles and New York City).

But even where ethnic negotiations did take place, they tended to involve actors who were able to enforce the negotiated outcomes. This happened in one of two ways. In the first, new groups (immigrants), represented by their elites, were coopted as junior partners in governing coalitions composed of elected officials and business elites. This happened only when *symbolic* goods rather than any redistribution of material resources were discussed. Negotiations were possible, therefore, when dominant parties were able to regard the costs of participation as minimal and thus could easily be persuaded to bring new actors to the table. In the second scenario, new groups were brought into existing coalitions in which the established players had long-standing relationships with one another and expected to continue in these relationships. Such a relationship existed in two situations: among ideologically similar civil rights organizations in Los Angeles, and in the context of "machine politics" in New York (inasmuch as they still exist). In these instances, coalition partners were held to cooperative behavior by the costs they would incur from their peer organizations (Los Angeles) or at the hands of a political broker (New York) should they back out. In other words, negotiated outcomes are achieved only when the costs are low or when there are means of enforcing cooperative behavior. Because the overall institutional context of cities goes a long way toward determining what enforcement structures exist, the institutional context of cities matters very much in determining what the incorporation and accommodation of new actors (immigrants, for instance) looks like.

At least two variables, then, seem to matter in determining if ethnic negotiations occur and the shape they take. The first is the relative strength of ethnic groups in the urban area: the existence of a dominant ethnic group, as opposed to a number of groups vying for power, makes a difference. The second factor is the institutional context of the urban area, and in particular, whether cities have tight or loose networks of organizations mediating between elected officials and residents (which might be called "vertical" versus "horizontal" cities). Plotting outcomes for these variables yields the two-by-two table in figure 7.3.

The Los Angeles Case:
The Privatizing Impulse

A detailed discussion of Los Angeles, the city that experienced the largest interethnic disturbance, can help to put some flesh on the bones of this abstract discussion. As the foregoing discussion suggests, we should expect that responses to the 1992 disturbances and attempts to mediate the city's fluid ethnic demographics would be shaped by the city's institutional structure, particularly the "horizontal" character of its politics.

If New York City's politics are organized vertically with private organizations and city service agencies acting as intermediaries between residents and local government, Los Angeles is horizontally stratified. Los Angeles doesn't have one politics, but many, existing in various layers that often have little to do with one another. The city's executive branch, its administration, and the city's community-based organizations (CBOs)[5] all have minimal contact with one another. In part this reflects the city's history as a reform city—with reform's characteristic nonpartisan, managerial-style politics—a city characterized by an antigovernment political style. Political authority is dispersed and if possible rendered impotent. The city seems to have

Figure 7.3   Determinants of Ethnic Negotiation

Relative strength of ethnic groups

		In flux	Dominant
Institutional context	Traditional	New York City	Washington, D.C.
	Reform	Los Angeles	Miami

Source: Author's compilation.

taken to heart the philosophy of "every tub on its own bottom"—a call for the city's branches and departments to exercise fiscal and organizational self-sufficiency. Interestingly, the city's reformist history is reflected as much in its *non*-governmental institutions as in its governing structures: the city's political design encourages minimal government and the privatization of communal efforts over channeling these efforts through public systems. As a result, CBOs orient themselves, on the whole, away from city politics and toward an alternative political vision of their own.

This was particularly evident in the city's response to the disturbances in April 1992, when each sector (the three primary ones being the city's administration, business community, and nonprofit organizations) had independent—and divergent—reactions. These distinct responses were not simply a matter of each sector playing to its own strengths and working to maximize its comparative advantage—but of fundamentally different visions of the city. The response of the city's administration—the mayor's office and the city's administrative agencies—emphasized an economic vision of the city, while the nonprofit sector focused on racial and ethnic tension. These visions are not mutually exclusive, by any means; many progressive CBOs had an economic program of their own. But again, the key point here is that both the city's and the CBOs' reaction to the disturbances was to call for largely private-sector rather than public-sector responses, eschewing appeals for government intervention.

The city's official response to the April 1992 riots was to form a private organization, Rebuild Los Angeles (RLA), and pass responsibility for the aftermath of the crisis to this entity. If one were cynical, an easy conclusion to draw would be that this step constituted an attempt by the city's administration to foist responsibility for dealing with the crisis on someone else, and let the city, and particularly the mayor's office, walk away free and clear. And while there may be some truth to this, it is also true that relying on the private sector to deal with a civic emergency very much accorded with the city's style of governance.

Community-Based Organizations

It was no surprise that Richard Riordan, the former businessman who governed Los Angeles as a Republican mayor through much of the 1990s, was a backer of privatization. In an interview with *Los Angeles Times* reporters Tim Rutten and Peter Hong during his reelection campaign in 1997, he spoke, for instance, about the formation of neighborhood groups under his administration. "For two years," he said, "I've been speaking with them and saying damn near the same thing: 'If you want to solve problems in the community, you have to organize and take responsibilities.' At our meetings, somebody will ask me a question about 'what are you, as mayor, going to do about the tree that's overhanging my driveway.' I'll say, 'Organize, get something going. Then you go to the council office or come to me as an organization, or better yet, do what I would do. Cut the tree down without asking anybody'" (Rutten and Hong 1997). What is interesting is that CBOs in Los Angeles seem to share Riordan's beliefs: the city's nonprofits are not generally oriented toward altering city policy, but rather see themselves as an *alternative* to government, and perhaps at times as a kind of substitute for government, stepping in to do what government can't or won't do. Possibly this comes of working in a system where government is difficult to access and generally unresponsive when access is gained. Whatever the reason, in many ways, CBOs share the city's ethos of private endeavor.

The CBOs' perspective is also likely in part the result, or at the very least made possible, by their fiscal independence. The city plays a minor role in financing community organizations and other CBOs in the city. Unlike such other cities as New York, where city council members have a significant pool of funds at their disposal to use as they wish to fund projects in their communities, the Los Angeles city council has a proportionately much smaller fund to contribute to community groups. These funds, usually disbursed $500 at a time, serve mostly as a symbolic token of a council member's support—again, unlike New York City, where funds from a councilman can sustain nascent community organizations. In addition, service organizations in New York receive much of their funding through state-service contracts that are disbursed through the city's borough party organizations. This has the effect of tying New York's CBOs directly to patronage politics, so organizations are beholden to elected officials. In Los Angeles, state funds are allocated through the county's board of supervisors, so that CBOs are largely independent of the city's institutional politics.[6]

On the plus side, this has the effect of weaning nonprofits from any dependence on city funding and giving them significant leeway in their actions. CBOs in Los Angeles, in direct contrast to their New York City counterparts, often operate largely independent of local political considerations. On the negative side of the ledger, though, the nonprofit universe in Los Angeles is considerably more fragile than New York's, as it lacks the option to draw on the public resources that can make the difference between viability and insignificance. For nonprofits that can find alternative sources of funding—either from federal or county government, foundations, or the private sector—this absence of institutional ties can seem liberating. It can mean having a distinct power base from which to play a role in local affairs, a chance to play the role of mediator among the city's feuding factions. An example of this latter is the role that MALDEF, the Mexican American Legal Defense and Education fund, played in the redistricting dispute of 1992 when it brought city and state politicians to the table to construct a coordinated strategy. No elected official had the status or perceived impartiality to bring together the city's various feuding Latino political factions. On the negative side, the distance of CBOs from formal politics results in the CBOs' relative marginality in city politics—seen in little leverage over elected officials and a weak bargaining position when it comes to lobbying city government. With the exception of some very clearly defined cases—the intervention, for instance, of the Coalition Against Substance Abuse against the rebuilding of liquor stores in riot-damaged areas—CBOs have stayed clear of Los Angeles city politics. In short, the lack of institutional linkages between the city's formal and informal political sectors is very much a double-edged sword.

Coalition Building

Los Angeles's political style and that style's impact on different political players in the city, has an effect on the mechanics of coalition building in the city. The discussion of coalitions here is based on Raphael Sonenshein's (1993) discussion of the prerequisites for coalition in *Politics in Black and White,* his book on Los Angeles. He points to three key ingredients to successful coalition building—common interests, similar ideologies, and strong personal ties among leadership.

All three of these factors are important in facilitating coalition building, but I would point out as well that political actors face a different calculus of *costs* to coalition building. It is these costs that I would emphasize in any attempt at understanding the behavior of three kinds of actors—the city council, neighborhood service providers, and civil rights organizations.

The City Council   The council is a prime example of the way that the costs of coalition building impede ethnic cooperation. Even though there are ideological commonalities among some, maybe even a majority, of the council members, a number of factors work against long-term coalition building among members of the city council. First, the downturn in the local economy from the late 1980s through the early 1990s and the general resistance in California to increased local taxes meant that the council had to allocate shrinking resources among an expanding population base. The effect of shrinking resources is exacerbated in turn by the institutional design of the council, which reinforces territorial and ethnic protectiveness. Council members are encouraged to think of their council districts exclusively—several of my respondents referred to "fiefdoms." Within these fiefdoms, council members are elected in nonpartisan elections, which means that in the absence of party politics, ethnic politics is often the path of least resistance, for constituents if not the council members themselves. Further, because council members are elected by only about 30 percent or less of the electorate (and in many districts a much smaller proportion of the total population), they pay much more attention to active voters than apathetic voters. In the city of Los Angeles, this means that they have to follow the racial politics that energizes activists, rather than thinking about the longer-range benefits of ethnic cooperation in the city or the importance of introducing new players into city politics. This short-term perspective will only be aggravated by term limits. While the impact of term limits is not yet clear, the logic of term limits would seem to reinforce the short-term political thinking of council members. Term limits encourage council members to tailor their plans to stay within the boundaries not only of their districts, but also of their time in office as well.

For elected officials, the costs of coalition building are high and the benefits small. Elected officials are well aware of the changing demographics of the areas they serve. But as individuals they can wait the changes out. Potential challengers from other ethnic groups who might conceivably threaten incumbents are also content to wait the changes out. Mexican-American politicians, for example, have been reluctant to challenge African American incumbents in Central and South Los Angeles, even though it might be justified simply by looking at the population figures. It seems more politic to continue to focus on the day-to-day decisions and compromises of policy making than to strive to institute a new governing coalition at the city level. Elected officials, as individuals, have little to gain from entering into risky ethnic coalitions or introducing new political players to the table.

Neighborhood Service Providers Ethnic incorporation and coalition building have not gone any more easily among Los Angeles's service providers and community organizations. The city's demographic shifts are felt most deeply at the neighborhood level, where transitions in population happen much more quickly than institutions can keep up with. In South-Central Los Angeles, for instance, community organizations and service providers in the community which were designed to address the needs of the city's African American population in the aftermath of the 1965 Watts civil disturbances, now find themselves in radically different neighborhoods than those of even fifteen years ago, serving a primarily Latino clientele. A number of these older, mature institutions have found it difficult to meet these demographic changes, and many have resisted adjusting their personnel or their boards to reflect the new neighborhood population.

For these established community organizations, any change involves a net loss for a hard-won African American institutional presence and job opportunities in the area. The situation seems truly zero-sum. Any gain in Latino organizational presence is perceived as a corresponding black loss. Given this situation, coalition or inclusion efforts come at a high cost. This is not because black-led organizations are *actually* being replaced by Latino organizations or personnel. This is not happening in most cases. A few examples of displacement received disproportionate amounts of publicity, like the situation in Martin Luther King Hospital, where Latinos and blacks were at odds over hiring, and similar disputes over staffing in the public school system. But the situation in Watts is more typical. Although Latinos make up more than fifty percent of the population in Watts, Latino organizational presence in the area is so weak as to be almost nonexistent. While there are roughly sixty African American CBOs in the area, apart from church-related organizations there is only one Latino CBO: the Century/Watts Latino organization. Nevertheless black community organizations regard themselves as under siege.

While African American institutions are not immediately threatened, African American activists view the longer-term situation as a zero-sum game. Like black politicians in the city, African American community organizations and service providers calculate that any shift in the current balance of resources is almost certain to leave them with less, not more. On the basis of this analysis, politics at the grassroots level is often extremely conservative. The tragedy of the situation is that there are any number of common issues affecting both older and newer residents, and these common issues could potentially, and have in practice led to coalition efforts. Again, the Coalition Against Substance Abuse, which mobilized neighborhood residents of all ethnicities against the rebuilding of liquor stores in the aftermath of the 1992 disturbances, is one example. Common efforts around other quality of life issues, schools, crime, drugs, and so on, have the potential to lead to greater cooperation. However, the logic of organizational maintenance which drives many older established community groups is unlikely to make them partners in these efforts.

The Civil Rights Community   Most of the ethnic coalition-building attempts in Los Angeles have originated in the city's civil rights community. A number of factors facilitate the incorporation of new players and the opportunities for coalition building in this sector. For one, as Sonenshein points out, there is significant ideological congruence, particularly among similar types of institutions (Sonenshein 1993). Often this shared ideology includes a commitment to cross-ethnic bridge-building efforts, hence bridge-building efforts among churches and synagogues, for instance, or among dispute-resolution groups. Second, there are few material interests at stake in the civil rights community, and the nonmaterial interests at issue are negotiable, given the common ideological starting points. These are not resource-intensive coalitions: what these civil rights and dispute-resolution organizations bring to the table are their services, not funding (except in the rarest of cases). Finally, Sonenshein's third key category in coalition building—leadership—is often closely knit in the civil rights sector. Many of the key players in these coalitions have worked together for years, and sometimes decades, in different incarnations of coalition-building efforts. The individuals involved in coalition-building efforts are, as many respondents pointed out, the "usual suspects."

These factors, taken together, significantly lower the costs associated with including new players and constructing coalitions in the civil rights community. Coalition building here is a relatively low-cost, low-risk enterprise. Resources are not seen as zero-sum, as there are few material resources at stake. Inclusiveness is seen as a strength, rather than a disadvantage. And as noted earlier, community-based organizations in Los Angeles operate relatively independent of the city's formal political structure, which is also an advantage when it comes to coalition building, because as a result these organizations have few obligations to others, and therefore few toes to be stepped on. Of course, the relative independence of coalition organizations means that they are relatively weak as well. Ironically, the strongest coalition building in the city occurs among organizations on the periphery of the political process as a whole—but this may be the only way that these kinds of coalitions can actually form and succeed.

Conclusions

Los Angeles's political culture, shaped by the legacy of the city's reform history,[7] profoundly affects the nongovernmental sector as well as the city's formal political structure. This was clearly evident in the aftermath of the 1992 civil disturbances: the strategy chosen by nongovernmental organizations—to build coalitions as an alternative to looking to the city government for action—and that of the city government itself—to rely on efforts by the city's private sector—reflected the city's privatizing ethos. However, if the 1992 civil disturbances had the effect of mobilizing new coalitions, the effects of these coalitions have nevertheless been at the margins. Their efforts had negligible results, and if there were results they were far removed from the political arena. Unfortunately, the marginality of these efforts and the low costs of the coalition building go hand in hand.

More generally, theories of urban interethnic partnerships require a better understanding of cities' structural and institutional contexts—of the kinds of economic and demographic shifts underway in metropolitan areas and the difference that urban institutions make in shaping these structural changes. Institutional and structural contexts vary across cities, and blanket generalizations about urban problems and solutions are rarely applicable. Rather, we need to think systematically about how institutions and structures interact, how they give actors different roles in different cities, and how they shape the opportunities and limitations of coalition building.

Notes

1. The Census Bureau divides metropolitan areas into "central cities" and their urbanized surroundings. Los Angeles, for example, qualifies as a central city, while Pasadena, part of the Los Angeles metropolitan area, does not.

2. According to *Business Week*, "Low-skilled white men in their twenties saw their annual income fall by 14% after adjusting for inflation, from 1973 to 1989. The annual earnings of white male dropouts in their twenties fell by 33%. But black men in their twenties . . . suffered the most. Their earnings over the same time period fell by 24% and by . . . 50% for high school dropouts" (Farrell et al. 1992, 40).

3. Hanna Pitkin (1969) outlines the distinction between descriptive and sub-
    stantive representation. Representation is descriptive if the representative
    shares ascribed characteristics with their constituents: race, ethnicity, gen-
    der, or religion. Substantive representation implies that the representative
    and constituents share similar views of issues, ideology or principles,
    which may supersede ascribed characteristics. The two modes of repre-
    sentation may vary independently.

4. Except in the area of crime prevention. Budgets for policing and incarcer-
    ation both increased substantially in the 1980s and 1990s.

5. CBOs are community development organizations, mutual housing organi-
    zations, land trusts, reinvestment corporations, and the myriad of other
    civic, neighborhood, and citizen volunteer organizations found in urban
    areas.

6. Though state funding is distributed through the county board of super-
    visors, the board, being more remote and politically insulated than even
    the Los Angeles City Council, has not developed a politicized relationship
    with urban organizations similar to New York City borough governments.

7. Progressive-era reforms had five main elements: the introduction of the
    merit system and civil service appointments in city government; detailed
    accounting procedures; independently elected boards and commissions;
    the elimination of single-member districts; and the replacement of an elec-
    ted executive, the mayor, with an appointed executive, the city manager.
    (See Banfield and Wilson 1963.)

Sources

Advisory Commission on Intergovernmental Relations. 1986. *Significant Features of Fiscal Federalism 1985–1986*. Washington, D.C.: Advisory Commission on Intergovernmental Relations.

———. 1989. *Significant Features of Fiscal Federalism 1989*. Washington, D.C.:
Advisory Commission on Intergovernmental Relations.

Banfield, Edward, and James Q. Wilson. 1963. *City Politics*. New York: Vintage.

Beck, Roy. 1994. "The Ordeal of Immigration in Wausau." *The Atlantic Monthly*
273(4): 84–97.

Bobo, Larry, and Victor Hutchings. 1996. "Perceptions of Racial Group Competition: Extending Blumer's Theory of Group Position to a Multiracial Social Context." *American Sociological Review* 61(6): 951–73.

Culver, Lowell W. 1982. "Changing Settlement Patterns of Black Americans,
1970–1980" *Journal of Urban Affairs* 4(4): 29–48.

Farley, John. 1987. "Segregation in 1980: How Segregated Are America's Met-
ropolitan Areas?" In *Urban Affairs Annual Review 32: Divided Neighborhoods:
Changing Patterns of Racial Segregation*, edited by Gary A. Tobin. Newbury
Park, Calif.: Sage Publications.

Farrell, Christopher, Michael Mandel, Michael Schroeder, Joseph Weber, Michele Galen, and Gary McWilliams. 1992. "The Economic Crisis of Urban America." *Business Week.* May 18, 1992: 38–44.

Frey, William. 1995. "The New Geography of Population Shifts: Trends Toward Balkanization." In *State of the Union: America in the 1990s, Volume Two: Social Trends,* edited by Reynolds Farley. New York: Russell Sage Foundation.

Galster, George C. 1991. "Black Suburbanization: Has It Changed the Relative Location of Races?" *Urban Affairs Quarterly* 26(4): 621–28.

Jaret, Charles. 1991. "Recent Structural Changes and U.S. Urban Ethnic Minorities." *Journal of Urban Affairs* 13(3): 307–36.

Johnson, James H., and Melvin Oliver. 1989. "Interethnic Minority Conflict in Urban America: The Effects of Economic and Social Dislocations." *Urban Geography* 10(5): 449–63.

Jones-Correa, Michael. 1998. "Cities as Institutions and the Incorporation of Immigrants as New Urban Actors." Paper presented to the American Political Science Association. Boston (September 2–6, 1998).

Kasarda, John D. 1988. "Jobs, Migration and Emerging Urban Mismatches." In *Urban Change and Poverty,* edited by Michael G. H. McGeary and Laurence E. Lynn Jr. Washington, D.C.: National Academy Press.

Kasinitz, Philip, and Jan Rosenberg. 1994. "Missing the Connection? Social Isolation and Employment on the Brooklyn Waterfront." Working paper. New York: Michael Harrington Institute, Queens College.

Kirschenman, Jaleen, and Kathryn Neckerman. 1991. "'We'd Love to Hire Them, But . . .' The Meaning of Race for Employers." In *The Urban Underclass,* edited by Christopher Jencks and Paul Peterson. Washington, D.C.: Brookings Institute.

Knox, Paul L. 1997. "Globalization and Urban Economic Change." *Annals of the American Academy of Political and Social Science* 551 (May): 17–27.

Massey, Douglas, and Nancy Denton. 1993. *American Apartheid: Segregation and the Making of the Underclass.* Cambridge, Mass.: Harvard University Press.

Mollenkopf, John, and Manuel Castells. 1991. "Introduction." In *Dual City: Restructuring New York,* edited by John Mollenkopf and Manuel Castells. New York: Russell Sage Foundation.

Neckerman, Kathryn, and Jaleen Kirschenman. 1991. "Hiring Strategies, Racial Bias, and Inner City Workers." *Social Problems* 38(4): 433–47.

North, Douglass. 1990. *Institutions, Institutional Change, and Economic Performance.* New York: Cambridge University Press.

Orfield, Gary. 1986. "Minorities and Suburbanization." In *Critical Perspectives on Housing,* edited by Rachel G. Bratt, Chester Harman, and Ann Myerson. Philadelphia: Temple University Press.

Pitkin, Hanna. 1969. *The Concept of Representation.* Berkeley: University of California Press.

Portes, Alejandro, and Rubén Rumbaut. 1990. *Immigrant America: A Portrait.* Berkeley: University of California Press.

Ross, Bernard H., and Myron A. Levine. 1996. *Urban Politics: Power in Metropolitan America.* Ithaca, Ill.: F. E. Peacock.

Rutten, Tim, and Peter Y. Hong. 1997. "Candidates' Complex Views on Race Issues." *Los Angeles Times*, March 30, 1997, p. A1.

Smith, James P., and Barry Edmonston, editors. 1997. *The New Americans: Economic, Demographic, and Fiscal Effects of Immigration*. Washington, D.C.: National Academy Press.

Soja, Edward W. 1992. "Poles Apart: Economic Restructuring in New York and Los Angeles." In *Dual City: Restructuring New York*, edited by John Hull Mollenkopf and Manuel Castells. New York: Russell Sage Foundation.

Sonenshein, Raphael. 1993. *Politics in Black and White: Race and Power in Los Angeles*. Princeton, N.J.: Princeton University Press.

Tobin, Gary A., editor. 1987. "Divided Neighborhoods: Changing Patterns of Racial Segregation." *Urban Affairs Annual Review* 32. Newbury Park, Calif.: Sage Publications.

U.S. Bureau of the Census. 1962. *Census of Governments, v. 4 Governmental Finances*. Washington: U.S. Government Printing Office.

———. 1967. *Census of Governments, v. 4 Governmental Finances*. Washington: U.S. Government Printing Office.

———. 1987. *Census of Governments, v. 4 Governmental Finances*. Washington: U.S. Government Printing Office.

———. 1992. *Census of Governments, v. 4 Governmental Finances*. Washington: U.S. Government Printing Office.

———. 1996. *County and City Databook 1994*. Washington: U.S. Government Printing Office.

———. 2001. *Current Population Reports: Foreign Born Population of the United States, March 2000*. Washington: U.S. Government Printing Office.

Waldinger, Roger. 1989. "Immigration and Urban Change." *Annual Review of Sociology* 15: 211–32.

———. 1996. *Still the Promised City: African-Americans and New Immigrants in Post-Industrial New York*. Cambridge, Mass.: Harvard University Press.

Walker, David. 1995. *The Rebirth of Federalism*. Chatham, N.J.: Chatham House.

Wilson, William Julius. 1987. *The Truly Disadvantaged: The Inner City, the Underclass, and Public Policy*. Chicago: University of Chicago Press.

———. 1997. *When Work Disappears: The World of the New Urban Poor*. New York: Vintage.

Chapter 8

When Ideologies Agree and Interests Collide, What's a Leader to Do? The Prospects for Latino-Jewish Coalition in Los Angeles

Raphael J. Sonenshein

"Jews live like Episcopalians and vote like Puerto Ricans."
—Milton Himmelfarb

T O GAIN a foothold in American society and secure their rights and interests, minority groups historically have had to choose from several paths of political action. Should they go it alone, join forces with other minorities against the dominant majority, or forge alliances with elements within the majority group? And on what basis should any alliances be forged?

For Latinos and Jews, two pivotal groups in contemporary urban America, these questions have special currency and arise within a paradoxical sociological framework: it would be difficult, if not impossible, to find two other groups whose current political behavior so resemble each other's, but whose social circumstances differ so enormously. What is more relevant to coalition: how people believe and act politically, or how they live?

Some believe that common beliefs or ideologies are the best grounds for coalition. Others see self-interest as the glue and view coalitions as, at best, short-lived arrangements between or among self-interested groups. My research on coalitions suggests that shared political beliefs are the firmest foundation for interethnic and interracial coalitions. At the same time, however, each group's perceptions of what constitutes its most immediate interests can enhance or destroy these coalitions and, even when groups share beliefs, leaders have the capacity to push interests toward alliance or conflict.

Jews and Latinos in Urban Coalitions

The dynamics of coalition hold particular importance for Jews and Latinos in California, and especially in the City of Los Angeles. The 2000 Census revealed that nearly 47 percent of the city's residents were Latino, 30 percent were white, 11 percent were African American, and nearly 10 percent were Asian American (Los Angeles Department of City Planning 2001). While not counted as a separate group in the Census, Jews are estimated to represent about 6 percent of the city's population (Los Angeles Department of City Planning 2001)—though with their high voter turnout, Jews may represent as much as three times that share of the city electorate.

Among the electorate, the Latino "sleeping giant" began to stir in response to Republican governor Pete Wilson's anti-immigrant politics, which reached their high-water mark in 1994 with the passage of Proposition 187.[1] In 1993, Latinos cast 10 percent of the votes in the Los Angeles mayoral election. Four years later, in 1997, Latino voters constituted 15 percent of the total, and 22 percent in 2001. Through the late 1990s, the resurgence of the Democratic Party to dominance in California politics has been reinforced by a tide of Latino office holding and voting.

With the decline of the African American community as the primary driving force of progressive urban politics, with the rise of Latinos, and with cities becoming more diverse, new options appear open to Latinos. Restive with their secondary role in the black-white coalitions that dominated progressive urban politics in recent decades, Latinos in the 2000s may play a different role than ever before. How they do so will have a major impact on urban governance.

Some in the Latino community believe that pursuing the formation of a coalition of nonwhite minorities is the best path to follow. They note that demographic change in American cities is turning whites into minorities and that, collectively, nonwhite minorities are on the road to majority status. Conservatives, white and Latino, believe that Latinos are on the road to assimilation along the classic lines of earlier immigrants, and that to favor coalitions with "people of color" is to segregate Latinos from the mainstream, an act that would be both sociologically incorrect and strategically foolish. Still others are drawn to a more nationalistic politics of identity that envisions Latinos mobilizing their numbers simply to take over municipal power on their own, in a modern version of the "ethnic succession" exercised by immigrant groups many decades ago. There is also the possibility that Latinos could forge ties with those liberal whites (including Jews) who had been previously drawn into alliances with African Americans. Finally, Latinos might ally with moderate or conservative whites.

Jews, for their part, represent a significant constituency in urban politics. Particularly in New York City and Los Angeles, and to a lesser degree in other cities, Jews participate heavily in political life, whether as voters, as campaign donors, or as candidates. In Los Angeles, Jews represent an estimated 6 percent of the total population, but participate at a much higher rate: according to a *Los Angeles Times* exit poll, Jews cast 19 percent of the votes in the 1993 general election for mayor; of the nine white members of the city council on the eve of the 2001 city elections, six were Jewish (*Los Angeles Times*, 9 June 1993). Jews have been crucial participants in the history of Los Angeles coalitions as well, playing, for example, a central role in the development and stability of the twenty-year Tom Bradley coalition between 1973 and 1993 (Sonenshein 1993).

Theoretical Perspectives

While the debate over interracial coalitions is highly political and pragmatic, it is also very much an argument over a *theory* of biracial coalitions. In fact, the relationship between Latinos and Jews can be understood using the same approaches with which interracial alliances in general have been analyzed.

The debate over the viability of interracial coalition politics has been an enduring and intensely argued one. Minority groups have had to choose among several paths. Should racial minorities go it alone, join forces with other minorities against the majority, or form alliances with elements of the majority group? These practical decisions in turn lead to a more theoretical question: What is the most solid basis on which to build coalitions? Some analysts focus on the role of ideology, emphasizing the enduring and solid character of interracial coalitions based on common beliefs. Others see pragmatic self-interest as the glue holding coalitions together and view biracial coalitions as at best short-lived compromises between self-centered groups.

Carmichael and Hamilton (1967, 75) in their book *Black Power* described the self-interest explanation of coalition behavior succinctly: "[P]olitical relations are based on self-interest: benefits to be gained and losses to be avoided. For the most part, man's politics is determined by his evaluation of material good and evil. Politics results from a conflict of interests, not of consciences."

This view has been reinforced by theories of realistic group conflict, which argue that members of groups have a clear and accurate view of the threat that other groups represent. Their coalition actions are likely, therefore, to be influenced by their perception of self-interest in the face of group threats (Bobo 1983; Giles and Evans 1986).

Meanwhile, a different stream of thought has emphasized the importance of belief systems, attitudes, and ideologies in explaining how people and groups of different races and ethnicities interact. In this view, racial attitudes help shape the perception that members of groups have about their group's self-interest (Kinder and Sears 1981). Browning, Marshall, and Tabb's (1984) study of the political incorporation of minorities in ten northern California cities found that coalitions pursuing minority power involved mobilization and unity among African Americans combined with the support of liberal whites and, often, Latinos. Their research strongly supported the role of ideology in the development of minority power: "Liberals on race issues are very different from conservatives, and ideology has an important influence on the nature and outcome of the minority struggle for access to local government" (248).

My application of the Browning, Marshall, and Tabb model in Los Angeles found that the same pattern defined Los Angeles politics in the modern era (Sonenshein 1993). Whether the issues were taxes, school board races, voting for partisan offices, or ballot measures to ensure police accountability, the pattern was the same: African Americans were the most liberal voters, and they formed coalitions with liberal whites, especially Jews, and Latinos in opposition to conservative whites.

The experience of New York City, however, challenged the model. In that city, where white liberalism has been historically strong, minority incorporation in multiracial and multiethnic coalitions was weak and precarious, creating what John Mollenkopf (1997) called "the great anomaly": despite the presence of a large base of white liberals, minority incorporation failed to win a stronghold in New York City. Just as Carmichael and Hamilton (1967) had predicted, conflict of interest between minorities and white liberals appears to have greatly weakened the possibilities for interracial coalition in New York City (Sonenshein 1993). In New York, white liberals were strongly represented in the civic institutions, particularly the schools, which came under attack from minority activists in the 1960s. By contrast, the minority surge in Los Angeles was tied to the struggle of white liberals, principally Jews, for representation in Los Angeles civic life. The coalition of Los Angeles outsiders thus represented a

fundamental alliance of interest joined to a shared set of political beliefs (Sonenshein 1993).

However, neither ideology nor interest fully explain coalition outcomes. Group relations are not simply the result of objective interests
or poll-measured attitudes. Political actions are taken by human beings and are therefore affected by the actions of leaders who seek out
trusting relationships with other political actors. As Barbara Hinckley
(1981, 66) put it, "Real political games occur in time. They occur as
one of an experienced or expected series, where players know each
other and expect to meet and play again. . . . Bargaining is shaped by
historical alliances. Deception is constrained by the risk of retaliation."

In keeping with this approach, I have contended that the outcomes
of interracial coalitions are profoundly shaped and influenced by
leadership and the extent to which trusting relationships are built at
the leadership level. Leaders and organizers have an impact on how
group interests are perceived. Interracial coalitions' prospects for success depend heavily on the willingness and ability of leaders to create
and sustain such coalitions. In matters of race and ethnicity, leaders
may find it easier to overcome interest conflicts among ideological
allies than to create an interest alliance among ideological foes.

Urban Coalitions in the Postincorporation Era

The development of interracial urban coalitions has had a major impact in shaping not only electoral politics, but also the governance of
cities. In many cities, a movement for minority incorporation led by
African Americans enjoyed unprecedented success over a period
from the 1960s through the 1980s, highlighted by the election and
reelection of African American mayors. These coalitions not only created the conditions for minority incorporation in the political process
(Browning, Marshall, and Tabb 1984, 1997); they also fostered new
ruling regimes (Stone 1989). Despite the success of these movements,
however, their victories were not to be permanent.

Between 1987 and 1993, African American mayors were succeeded
by white mayors in all four of the nation's largest cities. The shift was
by no means uniform or unidirectional; in Houston and in Philadelphia, African Americans succeeded white mayors. But the shift raised
questions about the strength and durability of the liberal interracial
coalitions that helped to bring about the accession of black mayors.

As immigrants continued to flood into American cities, the black-
white paradigm that had long defined urban politics became more
complex, perhaps even confused. From this point, then, the old

models no longer apply. As Mollenkopf (1997, 111) states, in the future, "the course of urban politics will depend on who can construct broader and more complex coalitions than the relatively simple biracial coalitions discussed by Browning, Marshall, and Tabb."

One aspect of today's broader and more complex coalitions is a changed agenda; no longer are urban interracial and interethnic coalitions virtually by definition "progressive" or "liberal." Some researchers, for instance, have found in both Jews and immigrant populations the roots of a pro-entrepreneurial coalition far different from the pro-government orientation of the coalitions that had linked minority aspirations with white liberals in the past. As Jim Sleeper (1993) wrote, "The more genuinely multicultural and racially diverse a city becomes, the less 'liberal' it is." Indeed, some observers of urban politics discern an emerging Latino-Jewish coalition—with a moderate political orientation (Beinart 1997).

As Latinos increase their demographic presence in urban areas, the question of coalition becomes increasingly important. In particular, what is the alignment of ideology, interest, and leadership between two key urban groups, Latinos and Jews?

Ideology: ". . . and Vote Like Puerto Ricans"

According to Peter Beinart (1997), "At the ballot box, if not yet in the minds of politicians and community activists, Latinos and Jews are in political alliance. In city after city, state after state, the two groups vote the same way. What they do not do—to the great surprise of leaders in both communities—is vote like African Americans."

In Los Angeles as well as in other cities, a discernible pattern has emerged. Despite predictions to the contrary, Latinos and Jews vote Democratic in great majorities in state and national elections. To a greater extent than non-Jewish whites, Jews continue to oppose measures to roll back civil rights gains. Yet while Jews support broad civil rights measures, they have been ambivalent about sensitive local issues.

In both New York City and Los Angeles, Latinos and Jews voted for mayoral candidates less liberal than their predicted choice. Despite their continuing loyalty to the Democratic Party, many Jews and Latinos broke ranks with African Americans, voting to reelect Richard Riordan in Los Angeles and Rudolph Giuliani in New York City in 1997. Roughly two-thirds of Latinos and Jews voted to reelect Riordan; comparable percentages of Jews and Latinos voted to reelect Giuliani.

When Nicholas Valentino of the University of Michigan and I examined the 1993 Los Angeles mayoral election, however, we found

Table 8.1   Descriptive Differences Between Jews and Non-Jewish Whites in Los Angeles, 1993

	Jews	Non-Jewish Whites
Education		
High school or less	14%	20%
Some college	24	29
College graduate	63	50
Family income		
Less than 20K	11	12
20K to 60K	40	48
More than 60K	49	40
Issues important in respondent's vote*		
Jobs and the economy	51	53
Taxes	2	4
Age		
Eighteen to twenty-nine years old	6	10
Thirty to forty-nine years old	36	42
Fifty years old or older	58	48
Union membership		
One or more members of house in union	23	28
No member of house in union	77	72
Retrospective financial trend		
Worse off than four years ago	39	41
Same as four years ago	41	40
Better off than four years ago	20	20
Mayoral vote		
Woo	51	28
Riordan	49	72
Party registration		
Democrat	82	48
Independent	4	8
Republican	14	44
Ideology		
Liberal	45	25
Moderate	44	43
Conservative	11	33
Problems of urban minorities caused by		
Racism	37	21
Personal responsibility	26	40
Both or neither	37	39
Total N =	540	1606

Source: Sonenshein and Valentino 2000.
Note: Percentages for each variable may not add to 100 due to rounding.
*Respondents were asked "Which issues—if any—were most important to you in deciding how you would vote today? (Check up to two issues)." Entries are percentages of respondents who chose economic issues in either the first or second position. The list also included education, the environment, homelessness, race relations, rebuilding Los Angeles, crime, illegal immigration, and improving the police department.

evidence of persistently distinctive Jewish voting behavior (Sonenshein and Valentino 2000). Our analysis of exit polls conducted by the *Los Angeles Times*, which included an unusually large sample of Jewish voters, found that despite significant Jewish support for Riordan's candidacy, Jewish distinctiveness from non-Jewish whites on ideology, racial attitudes, and partisanship remained very strong (see table 8.1).

Compared to non-Jewish whites, Jews were nearly twice as likely to call themselves Democrats. Even though 49 percent of Jews supported Riordan, this backing was dwarfed by the 72 percent of non-Jewish whites who voted for him. A commonly used measure of racial attitudes is whether one believes that the problems of racial minorities result from racism or are attributed to personal responsibility. Jews were twice as likely to select the liberal position on race and to describe themselves as liberal.

There appeared to be no significant difference among the generations with regard to these beliefs; younger Jews were no less likely than their elders to be Democrats with shared liberal attitudes on race. There was no discernible connection between income and Republican identification or ideological conservatism among Jews, while among non-Jewish whites, class strongly predicted both (Sonenshein and Valentino 2000).

Somewhat similarly, a strong minority of Latinos supported Riordan, though the community remained overwhelmingly Democratic. Latinos were less liberal than Jews with regard to issues of race, but for the most part shared with Jews the belief that the problems of urban minorities largely result from racism rather than personal responsibility.

My research on the behavior of California Jews (Sonenshein 1997) found that Jewish voting behavior combines broad liberalism with selective conservatism. In partisan elections, Jews constitute a distinctively progressive bloc of whites. But with regard to such threatening issues as crime, Jews are prepared to break ranks with classic liberal doctrine. As Earl Raab (1996) noted, "Scratch a Jewish voter and you will find a Democrat; but the complicating news today is that you will not always find a liberal."

Latinos exhibit a similar sort of ambivalence. They resemble Jews in that with the exception of certain issues, they are frequently on the same side as African Americans. Those who hope that Latinos and Jews are becoming an illiberal constituency are unlikely to be vindicated, at least in the near future. In their attitudes toward crime and welfare, Latinos again resemble Jewish voters; they are prepared to exercise selective conservatism within a hearty, broad liberalism and Democratic loyalty. For example, polling in Los Angeles has consistently shown that Latinos are significantly more likely than African Americans to believe that police treat their community fairly, which is closer to the conservative position on police reform.

The political behavior of the two groups, then, is remarkably similar. That does not mean, though, that the two groups reach that common point by the same path. In fact, broader analysis of the attitudes of Jews and Latinos reveal vast differences, almost chasms, on some underlying attitudes. In just one case, Jews are highly secular and strongly supportive of a woman's right to choose. Latinos, by contrast, are far more traditional and oriented toward religious values in public life, and are thus much less likely to support abortion rights. What is striking, then, is that two groups with different social standing and different philosophical underpinnings—some of them divisive and diametrically opposed to one another—end up in the same general area politically. Part of the oddity may be explained by the enduring appeal of the Democratic Party to once and future disadvantaged groups, as well as by the failure of Republicans to expand their ranks to include those who have experienced racial and ethnic discrimination.

Interest: ". . . Live Like Episcopalians"

Despite the similar political behavior of Jews and Latinos in Los Angeles (even in the face of obvious differences in the underlying approaches and philosophies of each group), there is little evidence of Latino-Jewish coalition in Los Angeles politics. In fact, the indications are that intergroup conflict is at least an equal—if not more likely—possibility. Still, if the two groups are in a de facto voting coalition already, what is keeping a strong alliance from forming? Part of the answer to this question lies in the area of group interest.

Milton Himmelfarb's aphorism about Jewish lifestyle versus voting behavior is often cited for its second part—the similar voting patterns of Jews and Puerto Ricans—but what is crucial to understand is the neglected first part, which highlights the differences in how people live. Los Angeles provides a case in point, for while Jews and Latinos there vote alike, they could not lead more different lives. This fact has important implications for prospective coalition building.

The socioeconomic divide between Jews and Latinos in today's Los Angeles is greater than that which prevailed between Jews and African Americans during the formative years of the biracial Bradley coalition. Examining the Bradley era, I found that middle-class African Americans active in progressive politics tended to live in general proximity to their Jewish allies, who were also middle-class liberal activists (Sonenshein 1993). In the multiracial Tenth Council District in midcity Los Angeles, for example, upwardly mobile, home-owning African Americans lived near politically active, liberal Jews in the 1950s and 1960s. They shared participation in civil rights activities and such political organizations as the California Democratic Clubs (CDC).

Today, according to Waldinger and Lichter's (1996) examination of ethnic groups in Los Angeles, Jews and Latinos represent the top and bottom of the Los Angeles economic pyramid. Moreover, my analysis (conducted with Nicholas Valentino) of *Los Angeles Times* exit polls found Jewish voters ranking ahead of white non-Jews on such key socioeconomic factors as education and income (Sonenshein and Valentino 2000). Latinos lagged far behind—a fact that is even more telling of the socioeconomic disparities between Jews and Latinos when one considers that Latino voters themselves are likely to be at the higher end of the Latino social pyramid. In the *Times* poll, nearly half of Latino *voters* lacked any college education, compared to only 15 percent of Jews and 31 percent of African Americans. And while 62 percent of both Jews and Asian Americans were college graduates, only 30 percent of Latino voters were. Income differences were also marked: only a quarter of Latino voters had family incomes in excess of $60,000, compared to half of Jews and Asian Americans.

As middle-class or wealthy residents of Los Angeles, Jews share in the complex bargain of immigration by providing employment for large numbers of immigrants. Latinos represent a significant proportion of a massive service class that attends to the daily needs of middle-class Los Angeles. In affluent areas of Westside and the San Fernando Valley, Latinos care for the children, clean the houses, staff the restaurants, and mow the lawns.

Thus, not only are Jews and Latinos poles apart on the socioeconomic scale, but they frequently encounter each other in the context of direct, personal relationship of paid service. These circumstances reflect a bifurcated Los Angeles economy in which the most dynamic job markets exist for well-educated middle-class people and for those who provide personal services to them (Waldinger and Bozorgmehr, 1996).

The Latino community, meanwhile, is split into two groups: one an insecure cadre of recent immigrants holding low-paying jobs, and the other a more established group of native-born people with professional, middle-class, or working-class jobs. Thus, whereas the Bradley coalition was built around the upward mobility of home-owning African Americans involved in peer relationships with liberal Jews, there are relatively few opportunities for similar interaction between the growing vital Latino middle class and Jews.

Latinos and Jews in Los Angeles are at different points in their political evolution: one is moving up; the other, already an established force in the city, is likely facing a long-term decline in influence. Unlike the African Americans and Jews of 1950s Los Angeles, they are not two excluded, insurgent groups with an equal stake in reshuffling the urban deck.

Furthermore, each group has options in addition to alliance with the other, options that grow out of their differing positions in the city's civic life. The paramount political priority of Los Angeles Latinos for some time to come will remain the mobilization of a cohesive Latino community comprising Mexican-born immigrants, American-born people of Mexican origin, and the large block of Central Americans relatively recently arrived in Los Angeles. While preoccupied with building this internal cohesion, many Latinos are likely to have mixed feelings about calls to build coalitions with whites, specifically Jews. In fact, rejecting such coalitions may be politically expedient in the short term, as Latino leaders may attempt to build internal unity through treating outsiders as impediments to Latino advancement. Latinos may decide to push toward the day when their political impact is commensurate with their population, or to seek alliance with African Americans in a coalition of minorities on the one side, and whites on the other, with Jews included among whites. Of course, none of these options is mutually exclusive, but an emphasis on one will profoundly shape the viability of the others.

Jewish leaders may face a parallel situation. For the foreseeable future, it may be enough to unify whites around a middle-class agenda that emphasizes order, stability, and government reform. A majority of Los Angeles's registered voters are white (just over 50 percent in 2001). Representing a reliable 15 to 18 percent of the electorate, Jews will continue to be crucial participants in building winning citywide coalitions. Hence, Jews and other middle-class whites can rely on their existing political strengths for a while longer.

Simple disparity in participation in the political process is another factor impeding coalition building between Jews and Latinos. Levels of political mobilization in two city council districts with roughly equal population underscore the gap in participation between the two constituencies. The First Council District, comprising Latinos and low-income non-Latinos, had 41,895 registered voters in 1997. Meanwhile, the affluent Fifth Council District, with the largest Jewish population in Los Angeles, had 137,471 registered voters. By contrast, in the formation of the Bradley coalition, the Jewish and African American communities were already highly mobilized and ready to compete for citywide power, and the gap in participation was not nearly as great.

What's a Leader to Do?

Leadership calls upon the human dimension in coalition development. As Barbara Hinckley (1981) has indicated, coalitions are built by human beings who have memories, and who can make choices based upon trust and experience. Coalitions are not built by computers calculating rational gains and losses. Uncertainty is a significant factor in any political actor's decision-making process. Would going it alone offer any advantages that would be foreclosed by coalition, and vice versa?

On a political level, opportunities exist for Jews and Latinos to interact as equals, but there are also possibilities for intense political competition. Members of the two groups challenged for the mayoralty after the completion of Richard Riordan's second term in 2001, for example; among the main potential contenders were city council member Joel Wachs and businessman Steven Soboroff, both Jewish, and two major Latino candidates, assembly speaker Antonio Villaraigosa and Congressman Xavier Beccerra. All were seeking to challenge the front-runner, City Attorney James K. Hahn, whose support base lay in the African American community. There was no assurance that either Latinos or Jews would cross over to vote for candidates of the other group.

During a special state senate election in 1998 in which Richard Alarcon narrowly defeated Richard Katz, the potential bitterness of Latino-Jewish political competition became visible. Both sides used very harsh campaign materials, with fallout extending into both Latino and Jewish communities. Latinos bitterly resented Katz for using print materials with a photograph of dirty hands to suggest that Alarcon was allied with dirty politics. To some Latinos, the underlying message was that they are a dirty, working-class community that is ill-suited to leadership. Likewise, many Jews were alienated when Alarcon used campaign materials that falsely connected Katz to intimidation of Latino voters. In a very close race decided by a tiny margin of votes, Alarcon defeated Katz. The considerable damage from the campaign clearly showed the pitfalls of allowing political candidates and their ambitions speak for two very sensitive communities just getting to know each other. Whether the lessons have been learned from this experience remains to be seen.

There are few settings within which Jewish and Latino leaders can meet as peers and develop the mutual trust necessary for long-term coalition behavior. Unions may provide a productive meeting place for the two groups. With its vastly increased emphasis on Latino workers, and its deep ties to the Democratic Party, the union movement may play the role that Democratic reform organizations played in the Los Angeles of the 1950s in forging ongoing joint activity involving Jews and African Americans. Unions were a key element of the Bradley coalition (Regalado 1991). Today, the ability of Los Angeles labor unions to reach out to immigrant workers has generated a massive increase in membership and extensive political influence. The historic ties of Los Angeles Jews to the labor movement means that workplace organizing may yet bring activists from the Latino and Jewish communities into peer relationships.

Some Key Elections

The spring 1997 primary ballot featured the reelection of Mayor Richard Riordan, who won a sizable majority of both Jews and Latinos on his way to winning a majority in the nonpartisan primary. The same ballot contained Proposition BB, a bond issue to provide air-conditioning and other physical repairs in the city's schools. In a previous election, the measure had failed to garner the required two-thirds majority of the vote needed for passage.

The schools are a potential civic meeting point for the two vastly separated communities of Latinos and Jews. Jews have always had a high degree of commitment to public education, even when their children no longer attend the public schools in great numbers. And as it has nationally for generations, the education system represents the opportunity for upward mobility for the children of working-class immigrants. The current population of the Los Angeles Unified School District is 70 percent Latino.

Strikingly, the coalition that propelled Proposition BB to victory— with well over a two-thirds majority—was composed of Latinos and Jews, with strong support from African Americans as well. Latino and Jewish women represented the two most favorable voting blocks for the measure, according to the *Los Angeles Times* exit poll. The BB coalition, which also received the endorsement of Mayor Riordan, was one of the most hopeful signs of potential coalition behavior in recent years, in an area critical to the success of the Latino population.

Another case of Latino-Jewish voting coalition was the June 1999 election on charter reform. When a vast rewrite of the Los Angeles City Charter was placed before the voters, prospects for its passage were unclear. While Mayor Riordan strongly supported the rewrite, a majority of the city council and most of the municipal unions opposed it on the grounds that the reform would concentrate too much power in the mayor's office. A number of leading Latino elected officials joined the opposition, including city council members Mike Hernandez and Richard Alatorre.

The proposed charter contained an array of innovations to expand local democracy, symbolized by a system of advisory neighborhood councils. It also included a strengthened system of civilian oversight over the Los Angeles Police Department and a living-wage requirement for firms doing business with the City. If passed by the voters, it would be the first comprehensive revision of the city charter since its implementation in 1925. As voters went to the polls, it was widely assumed that the opposition of leading Latino politicians would doom the Charter among working-class Latino voters.

In June 1999, the new charter was approved with a 60 percent city-wide majority. It drew heaviest support in the Westside and San Fernando Valley, areas of the city with large Jewish populations. But it also did extremely well in the low-income east-side districts where Latinos predominate. The revised charter was endorsed by three-quarters of the voters in the Jewish Fifth District—and two-thirds of the voters in the Latino First District, which was represented by a leading opponent of the charter. Charter reform lost only in the African American community, where Mayor Riordan had been extraordinarily unpopular, and where there was a high concentration of city employees.

In 2001, a direct test of the possibilities of a Latino-Jewish alliance emerged in the tightly contested election to succeed Richard Riordan as mayor. While many observers had believed that Latinos were at least one mayoral election away from having a chance to win the mayor's office, events moved much more swiftly than expected. Under the surface, the mobilization of Latino voters that had started with the reaction to Proposition 187 in 1994 had continued. Latinos were expected to represent as much as 20 percent of the voters who went to the polls, up from 10 percent in 1993. But there were two Latino candidates—former speaker of the state assembly Antonio Villaraigosa and Congressman Xavier Baccerra—and there were strong white candidates who seemed certain to make the nonpartisan runoff between the top two finishers. City attorney James K. Hahn, heir to the one of the few political dynasties in Los Angeles, was the clear front-runner.

The chemistry of the race was dramatically changed by Villaraigosa's ability to create a new coalition model that bore a strong resemblance to the Tom Bradley coalition. With strong support from the state Democratic party organization and the Democratic governor, Gray Davis, as well as the County AFL-CIO, Villaraigosa went directly after the support of the Jewish voters he had been cultivating for years. He was clearly the most liberal candidate in the race, and the most oriented to multiracial coalition building.

Villaraigosa's effort to reach out to Jewish voters highlighted the human element of leadership in coalition development. He had already established himself as one of the most likely Latino politicians to avoid inter-ethnic warfare when he resisted pressure to demand the retention of embattled school superintendent Ruben Zacarias several years before.

In a major surprise, Villaraigosa finished first in the April primary with 30 percent of the vote, to Hahn's 25 percent. The *Los Angeles Times* exit poll reported that Villlaraigosa had made a better showing than Hahn among whites and among Jews. The two Jewish moderate candidates, Steven Soboroff, a Republican, and Joel Wachs, an independent, also did better than Hahn with these groups. Among Jewish voters, Soboroff had 27 percent; Villaraigosa 26 percent, Wachs, 22 percent, and Hahn only 16 percent (*Los Angeles Times* Poll, 2001a).

Hahn made it into the runoff because of his overwhelming support from African Americans. If Villaraigosa could retain and expand his support among whites, particularly Jews, he would win the election.

Although the Jewish population was only 6 percent of the city, Jews cast 16 percent of all votes in the primary election and 18 percent of runoff votes (*Los Angeles Times* Poll 2001a, b). White non-Jews were leaving the city, but Jews were staying. In 1993, Jews cast one-fourth of all white votes; in 2001, they cast one-third. As Latinos replaced non-Jewish whites in the electorate, Jews were holding their steady role.

With Jews more liberal than white non-Jews, Villaraigosa's hopes rested largely with Jewish voters. Among liberal Jews, he developed strong support. Columnist Marlene Adler Marks (2001) wrote in the *Jewish Journal*: "A good case could be made, and many in the Jewish community are making it, that Villaraigosa is the 'Jewish candidate.'" Villaraigosa won the support of liberal rabbis and other community leaders. County Supervisor Zev Yaroslavksy, the most popular Jewish politician in Los Angeles, endorsed Villaraigosa. Yaroslavsky was thereby able to mend some fences with the Latino community, after his advocacy of a successful ballot measure in 1998 to block subway expansion into the Eastside and Pasadena.

The unknown was the preference of those Jews who supported Soboroff or Wachs, who were more likely to be moderate voters. As they had in 1993, Jewish voters provided strong support for Jewish moderate candidates in the primary, and were given a choice between moderate and liberal non-Jewish candidates in the runoff. One worrisome sign for Villaraigosa was that his support among Jews had dropped before the primary after a series of mysterious calls to Jewish voters that purported to attack Soboroff's Jewish connections.

The campaign ultimately turned on Hahn's ability to portray Villaraigosa as too liberal on crime issues, as he contrasted his own efforts as city attorney to fight gangs with the former speaker's call for preventive programs to stop gang violence. Hahn hurt Villaraigosa badly with his law-and-order campaign. The final blow was a Hahn ad that used Villaraigosa's letter to President Clinton on behalf of the pardon request of a convicted drug dealer to argue that Villaraigosa could not be trusted. Like Sam Yorty against Tom Bradley in 1969, and like Richard Riordan against Michael Woo in 1993, Hahn was able to counter-balance the liberal leanings of Jewish voters with their instinct for security and self-preservation. And as a Democrat tied to

African Americans and city labor unions, Hahn was a comfortable choice even for liberal or moderate Jews.

When the final votes were counted, Hahn had defeated Villaraigosa 54 to 46 percent. According to the *Los Angeles Times* exit poll, white voters went heavily for Hahn. Jewish voters were split, with 54 percent for Hahn, and 46 percent for Villaraigosa. Westside Jews, historically the most liberal, went for the Latino candidate. Valley Jews, historically more moderate or conservative, went for Hahn. Jews as a whole were more likely to vote for Villaraigosa than were non-Jewish whites, but a majority were clearly not ready to take the step of electing a liberal Latino to the mayoralty. As in 1993, liberal ideology brought Jewish voters close to the liberal choice, but was not strong or intense enough to overcome threats to self-interest or community interest.

The Villaraigosa campaign showed both the potential for Latino-Jewish alliance and the obstacles than stand before it. Had Villaraigosa been better-known locally, and were he less vulnerable on the crime issue, he might well have won enough Jewish votes to defeat Hahn. Tom Bradley, after all, was a well-known city councilman and former police officer who found a way to blunt the crime issue, and won huge Jewish support.

The 2001 election also shows that Latinos and Jews, both Democratic constituencies that are not always predictably liberal, will often be attuned to their own interests. It will be difficult to construct the sort of liberal biracial alliance that Jews had with African Americans.

The battle for city attorney between a liberal Jewish city councilman, Michael Feuer, and a moderate Latino mayor's staffer, Rocky Delgadillo, adds evidence to this conclusion. Like the liberal Villaraigosa, the moderate Delgadillo won a heavy majority of Latino votes. Feuer won the support of 75 percent of Jews, a constituency that in the mayor's race had chosen the moderate candidate over the liberal one (*Los Angeles Times* 2001b). In other words, both Latinos and Jews not only voted their ideologies, but also their ethnic loyalties.

Los Angeles politics are changing as the aspirations of Latinos are becoming incorporated into city politics, and as Jewish voters continue to represent key white swing voters. The Bradley coalition is one of the competing models for Latinos and Jews, in which shared liberal and Democratic values join with ethnic identification to create a liberal bi-ethnic alliance. But the liberal bi-ethnic model competes with moderate coalitions or ethnic-centered alliances. In both contested citywide races in 2001, the moderate candidate beat the liberal. In the mix-and-match world of Los Angeles coalition politics (Sonenshein 2001), Latinos and Jews are likely to still find that with their combination of Democratic identification and ideological moderation, they are the pivot points of Los Angeles politics if not always on the same side of the political fence. When political interests conflict, it will not be easy for leaders to draw upon shared ideology to form a durable coalition. In other cases, political interests will coincide, and then leaders will have an easier time forging coalitions.

Conclusions

The prism through which interracial coalitions have been explored in this study is the interplay among ideology, interest, and leadership. These dimensions present a contradictory picture of the Latinos and Jews of Los Angeles. By most measures of political behavior, the two groups are not only similar to each other, but occupy pivotal ground in the shifting politics of Los Angeles. From this similar political behavior it is not yet clear that there is a permanent ideological affinity, but certainly at the ballot box, the two groups are more often on the same side than in opposition.

On the other hand, the vastly different circumstances of the two groups, in terms of socioeconomic status and role in the civic culture of Los Angeles, present numerous obstacles to coalition. Rather than the two out-groups fighting to get in that provided the context for the historic black-Jewish alliance in Los Angeles, Latinos are instead an outsider group pushing in and Jews an insider group fearing being pushed out. Rather than the simple "black and white" question of who is in and who is out, there is a more complex question of whether complementary methods can be devised to achieve different goals.

Finally, there are few opportunities for Jewish and Latino leaders to meet as equals and to participate in activities that forge the long-term trust essential to coalition behavior. In fact, quite the opposite is true: there is no shortage of opportunities for serious competition and conflict among individual leaders.

Jews and Latinos alike are seeking to protect their group interests and advance their beliefs, and it will be very difficult for either to achieve their goals without friendly relations with the other. Jews continue to play a major civic role in Los Angeles, hard-won after a half century of exclusion between 1900 and the 1950s. But Jews are an older demographic group, and they will not always represent a disproportionate share of the electorate. Alliance with Latinos could help lessen a siege mentality that could easily become the mindset of a vital community that feels it is losing its place, and a positive tie to Latinos could continue to keep the Jewish community at the center of the city's life.

Conversely, Latino leaders are wrestling with the gap between the Latino population's demographic strength and relatively paltry political empowerment. The day will come when Los Angeles will be a Latino-dominated city, but that moment has not yet arrived. Even after a great surge of political interest among Latinos, they still represent only about 20 to 22 percent of the electorate. Once drawn to the notion that they could make it alone in Los Angeles, Latino candidates are quickly realizing that no group can succeed independently in a city so diverse.

Were Jews to withdraw from the civic culture and retreat into a defensive mode and were Latinos to forswear the politics of coalition, Los Angeles would be a far less productive and progressive city than one in which the two groups worked together for the common good. But at the dawn of the 2000s, Latino Los Angeles and the Los Angeles of middle-class whites are further apart than the Los Angeleses of African Americans and their allies in the Jewish community decades before. For new immigrants and old residents to reach the situation where they find coalition useful and morally right, they must find a way past the mutual isolation within which they live. The issues that preoccupy middle-class whites often seem worlds away from the worries of the city's large and growing Latino population. For the city to make real progress, for genuine coalitions to form, the potential of political affinity must be harnessed to a common purpose that can open up and improve Los Angeles.

Implications

Los Angeles provides a test case from which lessons may be drawn for a theory of interracial coalition in the multiracial setting of modern American cities. First, theories of interracial coalition devised for the relationship between blacks and whites can be useful for the exploration of new relationships between and among other groups. Second, political behavior is not simply the outgrowth of social status and political conflict. Third, the human element can never be overlooked in coalition analysis. If there are more settings for individual leaders to compete with leaders from other groups than there are settings to cooperate, the odds of coalition will decline. Fourth, the experience of multiracial coalition building is likely to be more complicated than the liberal biracial coalitions of an earlier day.

Intergroup relations between Jews and Latinos can be confusing: rarely can one find such a clear gap between political behavior and the interests shaped by daily life. This presents a singular challenge for leaders who must decide whether the ideological affinities and mutual needs of these groups will blossom into full-blown coalition, or whether the social gap and political competition will lead in the opposite direction. In any case, building interracial coalitions will always be difficult, and will depend on the construction of peer relationships.

Standing amidst the decline of traditional interracial coalitions in urban politics, it is easy to forget how difficult it was to forge those coalitions. For many years, conflicts of interests prevented alliances between groups sharing ideological affinities. Sometimes the process of developing group consciousness was blocked; sometimes demagogic leaders alienated coalition allies. Sometimes clever politicians split potential allies through offers of material benefits or through effective threats.

The reason why coalitions emerged at all, despite the odds against them in a racially and ethnically polarized society, is that they came to be seen as pragmatically useful, ideologically consistent, and even morally right. They seemed to become vehicles for reaching solutions to long-festering problems in the community. They became vehicles for the entry of long-excluded groups into the governance of cities and provided openings for equity and opportunity.

While coalition politics across racial and ethnic lines still faces significant barriers, the benefits of mutual effort are still significant. In diverse metropolitan areas, where alliances have moved beyond black and white, and where the incorporation of immigrant groups has become a central issue in city life, interethnic coalition building is still an activity that can be productively and persistently pursued if leaders choose to shape interests in the context of shared beliefs.

Note

1. Proposition 187 would have denied public services, including education, to undocumented residents, and was bitterly resented by Latino voters.

References

Beinart, Peter. 1997. "New Bedfellows: The New Latino-Jewish Alliance." *The New Republic* 217(6–7): 22.

Bobo, Lawrence. 1983. "Whites' Opposition to School Busing: Symbolic Racism or Realistic Group Conflict?" *Journal of Personality and Social Psychology.* 45: 1196–210.

Browning, Rufus P., Dale Rogers Marshall, and David H. Tabb, editors. 1984. *Protest Is Not Enough: The Struggle of Blacks and Hispanics for Equality in Urban Politics.* Berkeley: University of California Press.

———. 1997. *Racial Politics in American Cities*, 2d ed. New York: Longman.

Carmichael, Stokely, and Charles V. Hamilton. 1967. *Black Power: The Politics of Liberation in America.* New York: Random House.

Giles, Michael W., and Arthur Evans. 1986. "The Power Approach to Inter-group Hostility." *Journal of Conflict Resolution* 30: 469–86.

Hinckley, Barbara. 1981. *Coalitions and Politics.* New York: Harcourt Brace Jovanovich.

Kinder, Donald R., and D. O. Sears. 1981. "Prejudice and Politics: Symbolic Racism versus Racial Threats to the Good Life." *Journal of Personality and Social Psychology.* 40: 414–31.

Los Angeles Department of City Planning. Demographic Research Unit. 2001. *City of Los Angeles—Population Statistics from the 2000 Census.* Available at www.ci.la.ca.us.

Los Angeles Times Poll. 2001a. *How They Voted.* April 12, Study #457.

———. 2001b. *Voter Demographics: The L.A. Mayoral & City Attorney's Races.* June 7, Study #460.

Marks, Marlene Adler. 2001. "Mayors R Us." *Jewish Journal of Greater Los Angeles.* 16 March.

Mollenkopf, John. 1994. "Politics Beyond Black and White." *Dissent* 41(21): 282–84.

———. 1997. "New York: The Great Anomaly." In *Racial Politics in American Cities,* edited by Rufus P. Browning, Dale Rogers Marshall, and David H. Tabb. New York: Longman.

Raab, Earl. 1996. "Are American Jews Still Liberal?" *Commentary* 101(2): 43–5.

Regalado, Jaime. 1991. "Organized Labor and Los Angeles City Politics: An Assessment in the Bradley Years, 1973–1989." *Urban Affairs Quarterly* 27(September): 87–108.

Sleeper, Jim. 1993. "The End of the Rainbow? America's Changing Urban Politics." *The New Republic* 209(18): 20–25.

Sonenshein, Raphael. 1993. *Politics in Black and White: Race and Power in Los Angeles.* Princeton, N.J.: Princeton University Press.

———. 1997. "Jewish Participation in California Politics: A Revisit in the 1990s." In *Racial and Ethnic Politics in California,* vol. 2, edited by Michael B. Preston, Bruce E. Cain, and Sandra Bass. Berkeley, Calif.: Institute for Governmental Studies.

———. 2001. "Coalition Politics in Los Angeles Takes on a Mix-and-Match Style." *Los Angeles Times,* opinion column. 7 June.

Sonenshein, Raphael J., and Nicholas Valentino. 2000. "The Distinctiveness of Jewish Voting: A Thing of the Past?" *Urban Affairs Review* 35(3): 358–89.

Stone, Clarence. 1989. *Regime Politics: Governing Atlanta, 1946–1988.* Lawrence: University of Kansas Press.

Waldinger, Roger, and Mehdi Bozorgmehr, editors. 1996. *Ethnic Los Angeles.* New York: Russell Sage Foundation.

Waldinger, Roger, and Michael Lichter. 1996. "Anglos: Beyond Ethnicity?" In *Ethnic Los Angeles,* edited by Roger Waldinger and Mehdi Bozorgmehr. New York: Russell Sage Foundation.

Chapter 9

Interethnic Politics in the Consensus City

MATTHEW MCKEEVER

I N MOST major American cities, it is increasingly difficult for politicians to run as the representatives of any single ethnic or racial
community. While social science research has been charting the
rise of African Americans in urban politics over the past twenty-five
years, American cities have been undergoing great demographic
changes that have forced both politicians and analysts to abandon the
not-so-old model of biracial urban politics. The influx of large numbers of immigrants from Asia and Latin America, as well as the increased urbanization of Mexican Americans throughout the Southwest, has greatly changed the racial balance of most major cities. In
many cities, particularly those in the West and Southwest, African
Americans often find that they are no longer even the largest minority
group, just as whites increasingly find that they no longer constitute
the majority of residents or voters. Thus, the study of urban politics
must now focus on a multiethnic model in which three or four major
racial or ethnic political-interest groups compete for influence.

The political changes resulting from increasing diversity are unclear, as demographic and political changes are not perfectly correlated. For one thing, citizenship and age differences mean that the
demographic and electoral compositions of a city are rarely the same.
In practice, this often results in the underrepresentation of Hispanics
among registered voters. This disparity between Hispanic demographic numbers and political strength is evident as well in the political process as a whole. The ability to translate demographic or electoral power into political power is variable and depends greatly on a

city's political traditions, the strength of its minority communities, and individual politicians and their campaigns.

In this chapter, I explore these issues in the context of the 1997 Houston mayoral election. In that election, Houston elected Lee Brown to be mayor, making him the first African American to hold that post. I argue that this election was not simply a sign of the success of an African American–led political coalition in this city, as has been true for many cities that have elected black mayors. Rather, Brown's victory reflected the ability of a politician to reach out to an increasingly diverse city. The first section of the chapter lays out a brief description of the ethnic history and political traditions of Houston. Specifically, I focus on Houston's reputation as a "consensus" city in which interethnic relations have been managed by elites and relatively free of high tension or violence. The chapter then describes the election in more detail and offers an analysis of the electorate's voting behavior. Finally, I discuss the implications of Houston's mayoral election for interethnic political relations in a changing urban environment.

Houston: Ethnic History and Political Traditions

Houston is both large and diverse, but it has come by these attributes relatively recently. Although its 1.8. million residents make it currently the fourth largest city in the United States, in 1900 Houston boasted a population of but 44,000. Today, the city population is 38 percent non-Hispanic white (or "Anglo"), 32 percent Hispanic, 26 percent African American, and nearly 4 percent Asian American, but for most of its history Houston was a biracial city. Even as late as 1960, Houston's residents were three-quarters white and one-fifth black, with just 5 percent of Hispanic origin. The harsh local climate had discouraged the establishment of any permanent settlement by the Spanish and Mexican governments (Beeth 1992; McComb 1981). Consequently, early residents were predominantly Anglos and African Americans who moved to the region following the U.S.-Mexican War. The demise of the rural plantation economy in East Texas following the Civil War and active recruitment of black workers has led to Houston's having the largest African American population of any city in the South (Bullard 1987). The city's African American population, nearly 500,000 in 1996, even outnumbers the entire populaces of most American cities.

Since 1960, Houston has seen a number of major changes in its ethnic composition. By 1970 Hispanics had nearly doubled their population share (Thomas and Murray 1991), and today there are more than a million Hispanics living in the metropolitan region. A large majority of these people are of Mexican origin, but there is a significant, and growing, population of Central Americans. Since 1980 the Asian American population has also expanded rapidly in Houston. The Census Bureau's estimated Asian-origin population for the metropolitan area in 1996 was 210,000, with those of Vietnamese origin forming the largest group (U.S. Bureau of the Census 1997). Houston thus typifies the major demographic changes undergone by the United States as a whole (Farley 1996).

This new diversity has, of course, in part reflected the high volume of international immigration to the region. In 1990, Houston had the seventh-largest foreign-born population among American metropolitan areas, and since 1990 it is estimated that net immigration has increased the region's population by 150,000. What makes Houston unusual among the major immigrant-receiving regions is that, except during the region's sharp recession in the 1980s, international migration to Houston has been accompanied by net internal in-migration as well. In fact, Houston is one of only four metropolitan areas—along with Dallas, Atlanta, and Seattle—with both estimated net international migration in excess of 50,000 and positive internal migration balances in the 1990s (Frey 1996). Among this handful of cities, Houston has experienced the largest immigration flows.

Migration to Houston has come from a variety of places around the United States and is of diverse composition; it includes people from throughout the country and both middle-class professionals and blue-collar workers. Much has come from inside Texas itself: one reason for the rapid growth of the region's Mexican-American population has been the large-scale in-migration of native Tejanos (Texas residents of Mexican ancestry) from rural areas in south Texas. Thus, while international migration has helped reshape Houston's population in recent years, it has not become as dominant a factor in the region as it has in other major immigrant ports of entry. In 1990, the foreign-born constituted just 12 percent of the region's population, and since then immigrants have accounted for only an estimated 30 percent of Houston's population growth. This is in direct contrast to immigration's role in other major cities; in the 1990s, immigration accounted for *all* of the population growth in such cities as New York, Los Angeles, and San Francisco.

Houston's dramatic demographic change has occurred in a city with political and social traditions of consensual interethnic relations and a pro-growth, business-oriented political elite. At times, the city has been labeled the "consensus city" because of its history of consensual, rather than conflictual, interethnic and interracial relations.

This is not a recent moniker; for most of its history Houston has been described as having comparatively cordial interracial relations (SoRelle 1992). The city has not experienced a major race-related riot since 1917.[1] This tradition of consensus is an important consideration in an examination of the way in which Houston's politics and political campaigns are viewed and conducted. For many residents, city hall is seen as something that can be worked with, no matter who is in the office, so competition is not necessarily seen as a winner-take-all proposition (National Immigration Forum 1997). This carries over to how mayoral races are conducted and how candidates portray themselves to the public.

Researchers cite many reasons for the apparent lack of racial tensions in Houston. On the one hand, researchers have pointed to the relative affluence of the local black community (Bullard 1987; Bullock 1957). For example, throughout the 1970s, black unemployment in Houston was about half the national average for blacks, and blacks' income and occupational status was also comparatively higher than that of blacks nationwide (Beeth and Wintz 1992). Blacks lag far behind whites within the city on all measures of economic performance, but they have remained affluent in comparison to blacks living in many other cities, particularly in the South (Bullard 1987; Cole 1997). Another reason cited for the low level of tensions is that the size of the black community, coupled with extreme residential segregation, meant that people of both races rarely intermingled and thus had few opportunities to come into conflict (SoRelle 1992). Finally, there have always been well-defined local political and economic elites, both black and white, who have regularly dealt with each other to diffuse potentially violent situations.

The best example of this last type of interracial relations was the quiet dismantling of public-facility segregation laws in the 1950s and '60s (Cole 1997). The original push for desegregation was initiated by court challenges brought by organizations such as the NAACP, as well as sit-ins and other demonstrations, many of them organized by students at Texas Southern University (Cole 1997). These events were similar to those that occurred in other urban areas of the South, but unlike in those other cities, Houston city officials did not resort to violent methods to stop the protests. Instead, they negotiated with leaders in both the African American and business communities concerning the course of action to take. In the end, desegregation of public businesses and facilities was accomplished primarily in the back offices of major city businessmen. Officials of major downtown businesses were eager to avoid the negative publicity surrounding segregation and protests seen in other cities, and so cooperated with black organizations to quickly and quietly desegregate public facilities (Beeth and Wintz 1992). In addition, these changes were instituted without a lot of fanfare, due to a voluntarily agreed-upon press blackout surrounding them (Cole 1997). For this reason, the period of sit-ins and other demonstrations associated with the civil rights movement was relatively short in Houston.

This is not to say, however, that all social change over the past few decades in Houston has taken place this smoothly. The desegregation of schools in the Houston Independent School District, for example, was much more prolonged and controversial (De Leon 1989). Overall, though, the image that Houston sought to project was that of a city where community leaders worked together to quickly and quietly enact social change, and it has for the most part succeeded at that.

The tradition of cordial relations has to a certain extent been carried over to new ethnic communities and established Houstonians as well (National Immigration Forum 1997). One recent example of this occurred in the early 1990s, during a tense period in relations between Asians and African Americans. Tensions began when the son of an Asian American convenience-store owner killed an African American youth he accused of stealing, and was subsequently not convicted of murder. Initially, members of the African American community responded by picketing the store, forcing the owners to sell it. In addition to this action, however, leaders from both communities held community meetings to address and diffuse the problem (Rodriguez 1996). These meetings were intended both to lower the potential for uncontrolled public outbursts and to prevent future problems between store owners of Asian heritage and their African American customers.

Public-opinion data from the Houston Area Survey backs up claims of cordial relations (Klineberg 1998). In early 1998, soon after the mayoral election, 41 percent of those surveyed felt that relations among Houston-area ethnic groups were either excellent or good, another 40 percent claimed they were fair, and just 14 percent termed them poor. Since 1992, in fact, no more than 30 percent have ever answered that relations were poor. And though these numbers are somewhat less rosy for blacks and Hispanics, they are still positive overall: just 24 percent of blacks and 45 percent of Hispanics rated relations among ethnic groups in the city as excellent or good, but at the same time, only 19 percent of blacks and 23 percent of Hispanics rated relations as poor. By comparison, in April 1997, two-thirds of respondents to a *Los Angeles Times* poll rated ethnic relations in that city as poor (Merl 1997).

A second important institutional feature in Houston is the traditional domination of local politics by an Anglo business elite whose main aim has been to enhance local economic growth. In the political science literature, Houston has been portrayed as a city exemplifying the "growth machine" theory of urban politics (Feagin 1988; Fleischmann and Feagin 1988; Schaffer 1989; Thomas and Murray 1991). Until the 1970s, a tight-knit economic elite (known as the "8-F crowd" in reference to a downtown hotel suite where they would meet) dominated local politics (Lin 1995; Murray 1980). Policies promoted by this group focused on keeping the city and its economy growing, held local taxes down, and controlled dissenting voices among political leaders. This aspect of Houston resembles the "informal partnership between city hall and the downtown business elite" that Stone (1989, 3) and Hunter (1980) describe in modern Atlanta's urban "regime."

The old economic elite growth coalition lost much of its influence in the early 1980s, when the collapse of worldwide oil prices caused a severe local recession. Still, Houston's politics remain influenced by the distinct tradition instituted by the tight-knit economic elite (Schaffer 1989). Even today Houston has no zoning laws and a very small planning department, and the city continues to take advantage of Texas's quite liberal annexation laws to constantly expand the size of the city. The changes associated with the globalization of the U.S. economy have had little effect on Houston's political structure because the city has been an international trading center for decades, particularly in areas such as oil processing and transportation.

Houston Politics and Mayoral Elections

With national changes in demographics and voting rights over the past forty years, minority voters have become important actors in Houston politics—as they have in most major urban areas. Although blacks in Houston have always constituted a large percentage of the overall city population, racially based voting restrictions meant that the black vote was not an important factor in city politics until the late 1960s and early 1970s (Davidson 1972; Thomas and Murray 1991). Even after court rulings repealed restrictions limiting the black vote, the annexation of surrounding white suburbs served to dilute the minority vote in a city council system of at-large seats (Murray 1980). It was not until action in the 1970s by the Department of Justice, under provisions of the Voting Rights Act, that Houston switched from a local council system of eight at-large seats to one with nine district and five at-large seats. Under the new system, minority representation on the city council immediately increased, and mayoral candidates realized the importance of a growing and politically active African American population. Fred Hofheinz, elected mayor in 1973, actively courted black votes, and when he won he hired more blacks into city positions and brought in a new police chief in response to concerns over racial discrimination by Houston police (Thomas and Murray 1991). This change in campaign strategies, to actively appeal to African American voters, continued with the next two mayors; Kathy Whitmire reached out further to the black community when she became the first Houston mayor to name an African American chief of police, Lee Brown, in 1982.

Further demographic change has increased the importance of Hispanic voters as well. As of 1997, Hispanics outnumbered blacks on the city council four to three. Overall, though, while there is no demographic majority of any one ethnic or racial group in the city's population, Anglos do represent a majority of the voters. There are some 800,000 registered voters in the city of Houston, with African Americans comprising 25 percent, Hispanics 10 percent, and Asians 3 percent; the rest are white. Even without a majority, though, minority voters constitute a large block of potential voters, and candidates in mayoral elections cannot afford to ignore them.

In Houston, the mayoral election is generally a two-stage process. The general election traditionally involves multiple candidates, as there are no party primaries to winnow down the field. Candidates are not formally labeled as Democrat or Republican, though often those labels are informally attached to candidates due to their political history, positions on major issues, or links to supporters. If no candidate garners a majority of the vote, a runoff between the two with the highest proportion of the general election vote is held roughly four to six weeks after the first election. This general pattern was followed in Houston's 1997 mayoral election. In addition, the mayoral election that year was openly contested. Houston's elections are held every two years, and in 1991 term limits were instituted that allowed a mayor to serve a maximum of three two-year terms. The incumbent mayor had been elected in 1991, and was thus prohibited from running again. In the following sections, I describe how the general election and the runoff unfolded in 1997. Before doing so, however, it is useful to examine how the issues of race and ethnicity played out in 1991, when Houston's mayor was chosen in an openly contested runoff election.

The 1991 Elections

In Houston's 1991 mayoral race, there were three major candidates: incumbent mayor Kathy Whitmire and two challengers, Bob Lanier, a white real estate developer, and Sylvester Turner, a black state representative. Whitmire was knocked off the ballot in the first round, and the runoff proved to be very close, with both Turner and Lanier exchanging the lead in opinion polls throughout the race. There was a great deal of negative campaigning, particularly from Lanier's camp, and the general perception was that these tactics helped Lanier achieve a come-from-behind victory in the final two weeks. Specifically, a television news report that linked Turner to a life-insurance scam was considered to be important in discrediting his campaign. (Turner later won a libel verdict against the reporter and the TV station, but it was overturned on appeal.)

In addition to negative campaigning, though, Lanier spent a great deal of time courting the Hispanic vote, spending a great deal of money on both Spanish and English campaign advertising aimed at these voters. In the end, Hispanic voters were crucial in deciding the election. Lanier received about 70 percent of the Hispanic vote, which roughly translated into his margin of victory in the overall total, and also won 78 percent of the Anglo vote, while Turner got 97 percent of the black vote. This election in part fit a common pattern of racially polarized voting—but Hispanics did not vote for the minority candidate, instead opting to vote with Anglos, and Turner was not able to win. Although he won the election only narrowly, Lanier went on to become an extremely popular mayor. Initially, his approval rating in the black community was damaged because of his campaign tactics, but following his election his approval rating among these constituents rose to rates comparable to those he enjoyed among whites. In the end, most political observers agreed that he would have had no problem winning the 1997 election, had he been allowed to run.

The 1997 Elections

Houston's 1997 mayoral election approached amid several other unfolding events in the region. First, an economic recovery was pushing the city toward its highest level of growth since the end of the oil boom in 1982. Traditionally, Houston's economy has done quite well, and except for the 1980s, the city had experienced continuous economic growth (Thomas and Murray 1991). Even during the Great Depression, the region added jobs. Second, the crime rate in the city, as in most other urban areas nationwide, was falling. In fact, in public-opinion polls leading up to the election, voters did not even mention crime as a major area of concern, instead citing issues such as traffic and keeping the economic recovery going. Consequently, crime was mentioned only infrequently by the candidates. In the absence of crime, two major themes in the elections were the development of regional business ties to Latin America and planning for some new form of mass transit.[2]

A third important factor in the election was a general-election ballot proposal to scrap the city's affirmative action policies. These policies set guidelines concerning the race and gender of owners of companies awarded city contracts for construction and other services. The referendum was placed on the ballot by private organizations; the current mayor, Lanier, led the fight against it. This proposition focused a great deal of attention on the importance of voting in the general election, particularly concerning minority voters. Because overall turnout for the two previous mayoral elections had been quite sparse, there was some concern voiced in the media that few would show up to vote on the affirmative action measure, which would be seen nationally as a defining moment for the city.

Four major candidates emerged from a large field in the race. The front-runner, from almost the beginning, was Lee Brown. He had headed the Houston police department from 1982 to 1989, in which capacity he had been charged with improving the way the department treated minorities and how minorities viewed it. Since leaving the police post in Houston, he had served as national drug czar and chief of police in Atlanta and New York. He opposed the proposition to end the city's affirmative action policy and was the only major African American candidate. In addition, although he was commonly thought of as the "Democratic" candidate due to his platform and publicized connections to the Clinton administration, Brown was a friend of the current mayor, who was considered a Republican, and was able to utilize some of the same campaign managers who had gotten Lanier elected in 1991.

The candidate closest to Brown in the opinion polls leading up to the election was Bob Mosbacher, a wealthy white businessman whose father, Rob Mosbacher, had founded Mosbacher Energy and had been secretary of commerce under George Bush. As was commonly reported, he had spent a great deal of his own money on failed U.S. Senate and lieutenant governor races in 1984 and 1990, respectively. Throughout the campaign he cited his experience in international business and argued that he would run the city as a business—such as by outsourcing many city departments to both save money and streamline local government. While in many cities this might not be a great campaign slogan, it fit in quite well with Houston's business-friendly political traditions. Mosbacher claimed that he was against the referendum that would abolish the affirmative action policy of the city, but he also indicated that he would remove the policy if elected. The reason behind this contradiction, he claimed, is that he thought the referendum unnecessarily divisive, but at the same time he wanted to use public contracts to reward all small businesses, not just those owned by minorities and women.

The next two major candidates, Gracie Saenz and George Greanias, placed far lower in the polls from the beginning of the campaigning. Saenz was only the second established Hispanic politician in Houston history to seek the mayor's office. The last one, Leonel Castillo, had run in 1979, before the boom in the local Hispanic population in the 1980s. Saenz had been elected to an at-large seat on the city council in 1991, the first Mexican American to accomplish this. However, she was approaching her term limit and could not run again. From the very beginning of the election she came out in favor of affirmative action and argued for the importance of rebuilding Houston's communities through planned growth. The fourth major candidate, Greanias, was the city controller, an Anglo often seen as Lanier's major political antagonist. He claimed to support affirmative action, but thought that the specific program in place guiding city contracts needed to be overhauled because there was no need for specific quotas.

During the campaign, minority issues arose quite frequently. For example, Brown constantly mentioned how as police chief he worked toward creating a climate of mutual respect between the department and the community. He claimed that neighborhood-oriented police patrols, a program instituted under his watch, had benefited all neighborhoods, and he promised to establish "neighborhood-oriented" government that would be equally responsive to the needs of those communities whose members felt ignored by city hall. Brown's appeals resonated most among minority communities because they felt the least respected by the police and city politicians. Brown also advocated better police training and swifter, more decisive action concerning hate crimes.

The candidates also discussed the development of downtown and inner city neighborhoods. This too was predominantly a minority issue, because minorities compose the greatest proportion of those who live in areas that had been neglected. As someone who had represented these constituencies for many years, Saenz often claimed that this was "her" issue, pointing out that the two front-runners, Brown and Mosbacher, were living outside of the city. Saenz also discussed the need for extensive urban planning to improve the quality of life for city residents. Finally, all candidates talked about developing international trade, particularly with Latin America. Brown claimed that his experience in Washington, D.C., would help, Mosbacher that his experience in international business would be of use, and Saenz that her knowledge of the Hispanic community would be critical.

Voter turnout for the election was relatively high, around 41 percent. This was 20 percent higher than 1995's turnout, 12 percent higher than 1993, and comparable to the 1991 election that put Lanier

Table 9.1   Mayoral Vote by Racial-Ethnic Group, 1997 (General Election)

Candidate	White (n = 247)	African American (n = 165)	Hispanic (n = 58)	Other (n = 27)	Total (n = 497)
Mosbacher	51	1	3	33	28
Brown	14	97	16	56	44
Saenz	4	1	69	4	11
Greanias	30	1	12	7	17

Source: Exit Poll data.
Note: Numbers are column percentages.

into office. The ethnic-racial makeup of the voters was 53 percent white, 35 percent African American, 9 percent Hispanic, and 3 percent Asian American or other. Thus African American turnout was about 10 percent higher in terms of actual votes compared to voter registration, a factor in all likelihood owing to the presence of both a front-running black candidate and a proposition on abolishing the city affirmative action policy. The total vote for each of the four major candidates was 42 percent for Brown, 29 percent for Mosbacher, 17 percent for Greanias, and only 7 percent for Saenz.

In looking at exit-poll data, it is clear that there was some racial polarization of the vote. As shown in table 9.1, 97 percent of African American voters voted for Brown, 69 percent of Hispanic voters for Saenz, and 81 percent of white voters for Mosbacher or Greanias. Furthermore, as shown in table 9.2, most candidates' support came from members of their own racial or ethnic group. This was most true for the two white candidates, with 91 percent of those voting for Mosbacher, and 81 percent of those voting for Greanias, being Anglo. In

Table 9.2   Racial-Ethnic Group by Mayoral Vote, 1997 (General Election)

Candidate	White	African American	Hispanic	Other
Mosbacher (n = 139)	91	1	1	6
Brown (n = 218)	16	73	4	7
Saenz (n = 54)	20	4	74	2
Greanias (n = 86)	87	2	8	2
Total (n = 497)	50	33	12	5

Source: Exit Poll data.
Note: Numbers are row percentages.

Table 9.3   Mayoral Vote by Affirmative Action Vote, 1997 (General
            Election)

Candidate	Against Affirmative Action	For Affirmative Action
Mosbacher (n = 138)	88	12
Brown (n = 199)	17	93
Saenz (n = 44)	39	61
Greanias (n = 83)	58	42
Total (n = 464)	48	52

Source: Exit Poll data.
Note: Numbers are row percentages.

contrast, only three-quarters of those voting for Brown and Saenz were African American or Hispanic, respectively.

The proposal to end affirmative action practices was defeated, with most of those from minority precincts voting against abolition and the majority of those voting in Anglo precincts favoring the initiative. In addition, to the extent that this issue mobilized minority voters, it probably helped the two minority candidates: as shown in table 9.3, the majority of those voting for either these two candidates—93 percent of those who voted for Brown and 61 percent of those who voted for Saenz—also voted against ending affirmative action.

These two variables—voters' race and their position on affirmative action—were important even when controlling for political orientation. Table 9.4 shows the results of a multinomial logistic regression that predicts the odds that the vote of anyone who cast a ballot for one of the top four went to a candidate other than Brown. The first column, model A, shows that African Americans were more likely to vote for Brown than other candidates, and Hispanics were more likely to vote for Saenz, even after controlling for voters' political orientation.[3] The second column, model B, shows that even after controlling for race and political orientation, voters' position on the affirmative action issue was still significantly related to whom they wanted to be mayor.

The 1997 Runoff Election

With no candidate receiving the majority of the vote in the general election, the mayor scheduled a runoff election between the top two vote getters, Mosbacher and Brown, for the first week of December 1997. It didn't take long for the runoff campaign to turn to negative campaigning, with the first negative advertisements coming from the

Table 9.4   Models of Candidate Choice, 1997 (General Election)

Variable	Model A	Model B
For Mosbacher		
African American	−6.01**	−4.88**
Hispanic	−2.31**	−1.67
Female	−0.13	−0.05
Moderate	0.99*	0.17
Conservative	2.41**	1.25*
Income		0.00
For affirmative action		−2.42**
For Saenz		
African American	−2.96**	−2.88**
Hispanic	2.91**	2.77**
Female	−0.26	−0.21
Moderate	0.10	−0.067
Conservative	−0.06	−0.29
Income		−0.00
For affirmative action		−0.58
For Greanias		
African American	−4.81**	−4.50**
Hispanic	−0.66	−0.56
Female	−0.15	−0.29
Moderate	0.15	−0.41
Conservative	0.45	−0.33
Income		0.00
For affirmative action		−0.90*

Source: Exit Poll data.
Note: Numbers are coefficients from a multinomial logistic regression.
*$p < .05$. **$p < .01$.

Mosbacher campaign a couple of days after the election. The general perception from the previous contested election, in 1991, was that negative campaigning had helped Lanier win, but this time those in charge of the Lanier campaign were working for Brown. Campaign tactics aside, the issues did not change from general election to runoff, and neither candidate came out with strong new policy proposals.

Soon after the general election, Saenz came out in support of Mosbacher. She had gained only 7 percent of the total vote, but, as shown in table 9.1, received the majority of Hispanic votes. In giving her endorsement, Saenz argued that she was supporting Mosbacher because of his business experience, which she thought would best help the city and the Hispanic community. Most of her supporters from local businesses also switched to Mosbacher. This action appeared to perhaps indicate that, as in 1991, the Hispanic community would help elect another Anglo mayor. At the same time, however, Brown was endorsed by other local Hispanic leaders, such as state senator Mario Gallegos, who had supported Saenz in the first round of the election. These leaders felt that Brown best represented their interests as a minority group.

About one week later, Greanias, who had gained 17 percent of the general-election vote, came out in support of Brown. He cited Brown's experience in bringing diverse groups together as the reason his supporters should consider Brown. This endorsement helped Brown because Greanias had attracted more support among both Hispanics and liberal whites than Brown had in the general election, and both of these groups were now seen as more likely to support Brown than Mosbacher.

As the runoff campaign continued, each candidate received additional endorsements. Brown got the support of Vice President Al Gore and President Bill Clinton; the two previous mayors, Lanier and Whitmire; and Asian American community leaders. Brown also continued to primarily focus on minority social issues, maintaining his campaign theme that deemed him "mayor for all of Houston." Mosbacher, meanwhile, got the endorsement of former president George H. W. Bush and his wife, Barbara, and he often portrayed himself as the conservative, business-oriented candidate who would best help the city by keeping the economic boom going. He also got support from Rudolph Giuliani, then mayor of New York, who criticized Brown's performance as New York police chief.

In the end, Brown won the election with 156,307 votes, or 53 percent, compared to 140,448, or 47 percent, for Mosbacher. As shown in table 9.5, once more there was a major difference in voting among members of different ethnic and racial groups. Brown again received 97 percent of the black vote, while Mosbacher received the majority of the white vote, 77 percent. The voting patterns of Hispanics and

Table 9.5   Mayoral Vote by Racial-Ethnic Group, 1997 (Runoff Election)

Candidate	White (n = 259)	African American (n = 160)	Hispanic (n = 65)	Other (n = 27)	Total (n = 511)
Mosbacher	77	3	34	37	46
Brown	23	97	66	63	54

Source: Exit Poll data.
Note: Numbers are column percentages.

Table 9.6   Racial-Ethnic Group by Mayoral Vote, 1997 (Runoff Election)

Candidate	White	African American	Hispanic	Other
Mosbacher (n = 237)	84	2	9	4
Brown (n = 274)	22	57	16	6
Total (n = 511)	51	31	13	5

Source: Exit Poll data.
Note: Numbers are row percentages.

others was more evenly split, with Brown gaining two-thirds of the vote from members of these two groups. Brown's victory thus hinged not only in attracting some of the white vote, but also in gaining a strong majority among Hispanic and Asian voters. As shown in table 9.6, only 57 percent of the total support for Brown in the run-off came from African American voters, compared to 73 percent of his total support in the first round of the election. Merely maintaining his previous votes from this constituency would not have been sufficient for Brown to win the mayoral race.

The endorsements from candidates who had been eliminated in the general election appear to have had little effect in the runoff. As shown in table 9.7, a majority of those who supported Saenz in the general election, 69 percent, voted for Brown. Thus, most sided with Hispanic politicians and community leaders who had supported Brown, over the advice of Saenz. Among those who had voted for Greanias in the general election, 54 percent voted for Brown in the runoff. While perhaps fewer would have done so had it not been for Greanias endorsing Brown, this still does not represent an overwhelming show of support from these voters. In order to control for factors such as political affiliation, gender, and income, I again ran a logistic regression on the final vote in the runoff election. As shown in table 9.8, overall race and political affiliation does appear to have affected whom voters selected. African American, Hispanic, and liberal voters

Table 9.7   Mayoral Vote by Previous Mayoral Vote, 1997 (Runoff Election)

Candidate	General Election					Total
	Mosbacher	Brown	Saenz	Greanias	Other	
Mosbacher	97	1	31	46	47	46
Brown	3	99	69	54	53	54
N	164	172	35	61	79	511

Source: Exit Poll data.
Note: Numbers are column percentages.

Table 9.8   Models of Candidate Choice, 1997 (Runoff Election)

Variable	
For Mosbacher	
African American	−4.44**
Hispanic	−1.37**
Female	−0.02
Moderate	1.13**
Conservative	2.30**
Income	0.00

Source: Exit Poll data.
Note: Numbers are coefficients from a logistic regression.
*$p < .05$. **$p < .01$.

all went for Brown, while white, moderate, and conservative voters sided with Mosbacher.

Conclusions

With the decline of African Americans as the largest block of minority voters, some have argued that African American political candidates must downplay racial themes in order to attract both white support and that of other minorities to their campaigns (Perry 1991). In Houston, one would expect that local conditions would make such a political strategy crucial. Blacks not only do not constitute a majority, but they also represent a slowly declining sector of both the population and registered voters. As one local newspaper writer put it, Brown won in 1997 because "[l]ike Mayor Ron Kirk of Dallas, Detroit's Dennis Archer and other successful black candidates, Brown relied on a non-racist, non-threatening appeal" (Rodriguez 1997).

Such a view, however, is oversimplified. It inadequately captures the new reality of cities, such as Houston, that are undergoing a transition to a majority-minority distribution of voters. In such an environment, the deemphasis on race that makes an African American politician more appealing to Anglo voters will not be sufficient to gain the candidate the necessary majority to win. Instead, candidates of all races must attempt to appeal to voters of all ethnic groups. For this reason, throughout the Houston mayoral campaign both Brown and Mosbacher constantly touched on themes that were considered important to Hispanics and Asians. Brown consistently referred to himself as the champion of minority interests and spoke of his service to the community in creating a multiracial police force, the introduction of a hate-crime task force, and the importance of business ties to

Latin America. His campaign slogan, "mayor for all of Houston," emphasized the multiethnic and racial appeal of his platform. On the other side, it could be argued that Mosbacher, by courting Hispanic votes and gaining the support of the only Hispanic candidate in the general election, also tried to broaden his appeal across ethnic and racial groups.

The Houston mayoral election of 1997 was not "deracialized" but instead reflected the importance of minority politics in urban elections. The mayoral candidates structured their campaign themes around the common interests of minorities, rather than setting the specific interests of one group over against another. What this multiethnic strategy means in practice, though, is quite variable, for many reasons. First, it is important to remember that the impact of ethnic diversity on a city will reflect not only the people who are increasingly changing the ethnic makeup of cities, but also the political traditions of the cities they live in. In Houston, there are few interethnic political institutions; however, there *is* a tradition of leaders of distinct ethnic and racial communities working with city officials and business leaders to solve social problems. Cities lacking both traditions of cooperation or institutional frameworks will have quite different experiences from Houston and will have greater difficulty in negotiating politics within the context of a changing racial and ethnic population.

Second, the elections made it very clear that Hispanics as a political community may display greater internal heterogeneity than do African Americans. Hispanics in Houston come from many diverse points of origin: some have been in Texas for many generations, others are recent immigrants; some come from Mexico and others from a number of Central American countries. These different population groups have different experiences and expectations, and will consequently exert different political forces and constraints on political actors (Rodriguez 1993).

Finally, how a political campaign is translated into specific city policies is a complex matter. Newly elected officials who are expected to further the interests of members of one minority group over another might find their tenure short-lived. While candidates might find that members of the ethnic or racial group to which they belong expect special treatment, or at least a privileged airing of their concerns, they must walk a fine line in addressing the concerns of the diverse communities whose support they sought in their election. (At the same time, constituencies must temper their expectations with reality as well: an editorial in the *Houston Chronicle* soon after the 1997 election, for example, cautioned against the African American community seeing Brown as a "black messiah" who could deliver African American communities from years of neglect by the city [Williams 1997].) This, of course, is the province of a good politician: They must appear to be specifically and authentically concerned with the issues of all racial and ethnic groups, even those whose support they did not fully gain in the election. This done, reelection should not prove difficult.

The Exit Poll data used in this article were provided by Robert Stein. This chapter also benefited from comments on previous drafts from Chandler Davidson, Karl Eschbach, and participants of the Governing American Cities conference.

Notes

1. Although there were major race-related violent incidents in the late 1960s—for example, an incident between police and Texas Southern University students in 1967 in which one policeman died and five hundred students were arrested following a protest over previous arrests of student activists (Davidson 1972)—these were nowhere near the scale of the riots occurring in other major American cities during the same period.

2. Houston remains the largest city in the United States, by far, that does not have any rail-based public transportation system.

3. Unfortunately, the data do not contain a measure of respondents' education, so it is not possible to control for this factor in these models predicting voting behavior.

Sources

Beeth, Howard. 1992. "Historians, Houston, and History." In *Black Dixie: Afro-Texan History and Culture in Houston*, edited by Howard Beeth and Cary D. Wintz. College Station: Texas A&M University Press.

Beeth, Howard, and Cary D. Wintz. 1992. *Black Dixie: Afro-Texan History and Culture in Houston*. College Station: Texas A&M University Press.

Bullard, Robert D. 1987. *Invisible Houston: The Black Experience in Boom and Bust*. College Station: Texas A&M University Press.

Bullock, Henry Allen. 1957. *Pathways to the Houston Negro Market*. Ann Arbor, Mich.: J. W. Edwards.

Cole, Thomas R. 1997. *No Color Is My Kind: The Life of Eldrewey Stearns and the Integration of Houston*. Austin: University of Texas Press.

Davidson, Chandler. 1972. *Biracial Politics: Conflict and Coalition in the Metropolitan South*. Baton Rouge: Louisiana State University Press.

De Leon, Arnoldo. 1989. *Ethnicity in the Sunbelt: A History of Mexican Americans in Houston*. Houston: University of Houston Mexican American Studies Program.

Farley, Reynolds. 1996. *The New American Reality: Who We Are, How We Got There, Where We Are Going*. New York: Russell Sage Foundation.

Feagin, Joe R. 1988. *Free Enterprise City: Houston in Political and Economic Perspective*. New Brunswick, N.J.: Rutgers University Press.

Fleischmann, Arnold, and Joe R. Feagin. 1988. "The Politics of Growth-Oriented Urban Alliances: Comparing Old Industrial and New Sunbelt Cities." *Urban Affairs Quarterly* 23(2): 207–32.

Frey, William. 1996. "Immigration, Domestic Migration, and Demographic Balkanization in America: New Evidence for the 1990s." *Population and Development Review* 22(4): 741–63.

Hunter, Floyd. 1980. *Community Power Succession: Atlanta's Policy-Makers Revisited.* Chapel Hill: University of North Carolina Press.

Klineberg, Stephen. 1998. *The Houston Area Survey.* Electronic data file available from author.

Lin, Jan. 1995. "Ethnic Places, Postmodernism, and Urban Change in Houston." *Sociological Quarterly* 36(4): 629–47.

McComb, David G. 1981. *Houston: A History.* Austin: University of Texas Press.

Merl, Jean. 1997. "City Still Viewed as Racially Split." *Los Angeles Times,* April 29, 1997.

Murray, Richard. 1980. "Houston: Politics of a Boomtown." *Dissent* 27, no. 4(121): 500–4.

National Immigration Forum. 1997. *The New Americans: A Look at America's Gateway Cities. Houston: Diversity Works.* Washington, D.C.: National Immigration Forum.

Perry, Huey L. 1991. "Deracialization as an Analytical Construct in American Urban Politics." *Urban Affairs Quarterly* 27(2): 181–91.

Rodriguez, Lori. 1997. "Mayoral Win Sends Message About Houston." *Houston Chronicle,* December 6, 1997.

Rodriguez, Nestor. 1993. "Undocumented Central Americans in Houston: Diverse Populations." *International Migration Review* 21(1): 4–26.

———. 1996. "U.S. Immigration and Intergroup Relations in the Late 20th Century: African Americans and Latinos." *Social Justice* 23(3): 111–24.

Schaffer, Albert. 1989. "The Houston Growth Coalition in 'Boom' and 'Bust.'" *Journal of Urban Affairs* 11(1): 21–38.

Shelton, Beth Anne, Nestor P. Rodriguez, Joe R. Feagin, Robert D. Bullard, and Robert D. Thomas. 1989. *Houston: Growth and Decline in a Sunbelt Boomtown.* Philadelphia: Temple University Press.

SoRelle, James M. 1992. "Race Relations in 'Heavenly Houston,' 1919–1945." In *Black Dixie: Afro-Texan History and Culture in Houston,* edited by Howard Beeth and Cary D. Wintz. College Station: Texas A&M University Press.

Stone, Clarence N. 1989. *Regime Politics: Governing Atlanta 1946–1988.* Lawrence: University of Kansas Press.

Thomas, Robert D., and Richard W. Murray. 1991. *Progrowth Politic: Change and Governance in Houston.* Berkeley: Institute for Government Studies, University of California.

U.S. Bureau of the Census. 1997. *Statistical Abstract of the United States: 1997.* 117th edition. Washington: U.S. Government Printing Office.

Williams, Michael P. 1997. "New Mayor Will Fail if He Plays Favorites." *Houston Chronicle,* December 13, 1997.

Index

Numbers in **boldface** refer to figures or tables.

Europe, immigration from, **6**, 24, **25**, 28, **29**

federal financial restructuring of urban programs, 183, 189–95, **192**
Feuer, Michael, 225
FirstSearch Abstracts, 159
Florida, immigrants in, 3, **4**, 19, 23. *See also* Miami, FL
foreign-born persons. *See specific immigrant information*
"foreigners" in Chinatown, 79–83
Franklin, John Hope, 111, 112

Gallegos, Mario, 243
garment workers in Chinatown, 76, 80–83, 87–89
Garza v. Los Angeles County, 44
ghettos, African American, vs. ethnic enclaves, 75
Gifford, Kathie Lee, 82
Giuliani, Rudolph, 42, 52, 103, 215, 243
Glover, Danny, 131–32
Golden Exiles, 139–40, 154
Gonzalez, Elian, 146–47
Gore, Al, 243
governance, urban. *See specific topics and cities*
government, federal, financial restructuring of urban programs, 183, 189–95, **192**
Greanias, George, 239–44
Grenier, Guillermo J., 10
group relations, minority. *See* multiracial society, minority group relations in
"growth machine" theory of urban politics, 235

Hahn, James K., 43, 64, 223–25
Halle, David, 65
Hall of Common Virtue (Tang Dak Tong), 86
Hamilton, Charles V., 113, 212, 213
Harvard University, Center for American Political Studies, 7
Hastings, Alcee, 152

Hayden, Tom, 43
Hernandez, Humberto, 153
Hernandez, Mike, 95, 222
Hialeah, FL, 10. *See also* Miami, FL, Cuban-black relations in
Himmelfarb, Milton, 210, 218
Hinckley, Barbara, 214, 220
Hispanews, 151
Hispanics. *See* Latino immigrants and Latino heritage
Hofheinz, Fred, 235–36
Holden, Nate, 95
Hong, Peter, 201
Horowitz, Donald, 175
Housing and Urban Development, U. S. Department of (HUD), 195
Houston, TX: immigrant impact on, 24; immigrants in population, 3, 184, **187**, 231–32
Houston, TX, interethnic politics in, 230–48; about, 12, 230–31, 245–47; the 1991 elections, 236–37; the 1997 elections, 237–45; ethnic history and political traditions, 231–35; mayoral elections and city politics, 235–45
Houston Chronicle, 246
HUD (Department of Housing and Urban Development), 195
Hunter, Floyd, 235
Hutchings, Victor, 189
Hynes, Charles, 82

ideological explanation for Korean-black conflicts, 163
ILGWU (International Ladies Garment Workers Union), 81, 87, 88
Illinois, immigrants in, 3, **4**, 184
immigrant generation by race, 31, **32–33**, 34
immigrants. *See specific topics*
Immigration Act (1965), 5, 19, 72, 73
Immigration and Naturalization Service (INS), 40, 42
Immigration Coalition, New York, 42
income and wages: multiracial socioeconomic and political out-